REPORT

OF THE

COMMISSION OF ENGINEERS

APPOINTED TO

INVESTIGATE AND REPORT A PERMANENT PLAN

FOR THE

RECLAMATION OF THE ALLUVIAL BASIN

OF THE

MISSISSIPPI RIVER

SUBJECT TO INUNDATION.

WASHINGTON:
GOVERNMENT PRINTING OFFICE.
1875.

43D CONGRESS, 2d Session. } HOUSE OF REPRESENTATIVES. { Ex. Doc. No. 127.

ALLUVIAL BASIN OF THE MISSISSIPPI RIVER.

MESSAGE

FROM THE

PRESIDENT OF THE UNITED STATES,

TRANSMITTING

A report of the Commission of Engineers appointed to investigate and report a permanent plan for the reclamation of the alluvial basin of the Mississippi River subject to inundation.

JANUARY 25, 1875.—Referred to the Select Committee on Mississippi Levees and ordered to be printed.

To the Senate and House of Representatives:

I have the honor to transmit herewith the report of the Commission of Engineers appointed, in compliance with the act of Congress approved June 22, 1874, to investigate and report a permanent plan for the reclamation of the alluvial basin of the Mississippi River subject to inundation.

U. S. GRANT.

EXECUTIVE MANSION, *January* 25, 1875.

WAR DEPARTMENT,
Washington City, January 23, 1875.

SIR: I have the honor to transmit copy of the report of the Board of Commissioners appointed, under the act approved June 22, 1874, "to investigate and report a permanent plan for the reclamation of the alluvial basin of the Mississippi River subject to inundation."

I inclose a copy of the order appointing the board, (General Orders No. 73, of 1874.)

Very respectfully, your obedient servant,

WM. W. BELKNAP,
Secretary of War.

The PRESIDENT OF THE UNITED STATES.

General Orders No. 73.

WAR DEPARTMENT,
ADJUTANT-GENERAL'S OFFICE,
Washington, July 2, 1874.

By direction of the President, Major G. K. Warren, Major H. L. Abbot, and Captain W. H. H. Benyaurd, Corps of Engineers United States Army, are hereby assigned, and Jackson E. Sickles and Paul O. Hébert appointed, to serve as a board of commissioners under the act approved June —, 1874, "to provide for the appointment of a commission of engineers to investigate and report a permanent plan for the reclamation of the alluvial basin of the Mississippi River subject to inundation."

Major Warren is designated as president of the board.

Captain Benyaurd is designated as disbursing officer for the appropriation provided by section 3 of the act.

The board will assemble at Newport, Rhode Island, on the 20th instant, or as soon thereafter as practicable, for the purpose of organizing and entering upon the performance of their duties.

The following is the act of Congress above referred to:

AN ACT to provide for the appointment of a commission of engineers to investigate and report a permanent plan for the reclamation of the alluvial basin of the Mississippi River subject to inundation

Be it enacted by the Senate and House of Representatives of the United States of America in Congress assembled, That the President be, and he is hereby, authorized and directed to assign three officers of the Corps of Engineers United States Army, and to appoint two civil engineers eminent in their profession, and who are acquainted with the alluvial basin of the Mississippi River, to serve as a board of commissioners; the president of said board to be designated by the President of the United States. It shall be the duty of said commission to make a full report to the President of the best system for the permanent reclamation and redemption of said alluvial basin from inundation, which report the President shall transmit to Congress at its next session, with such recommendations as he shall think proper.

SEC. 2. That the members of the commission who may be appointed from civil life shall receive compensation at the rate of five thousand dollars per annum. The commission may employ a secretary, at a rate of compensation not exceeding two hundred dollars per month for the time he is employed; and the necessary traveling expenses of the members of the commission not officers of the Army, and of the secretary, shall be paid, upon the approval of bills for the same, by the Secretary of War.

SEC. 3. That the sum of twenty-five thousand dollars, or so much thereof as may be necessary to carry into effect the foregoing provisions, is hereby appropriated, and shall be subject to disbursement by the Secretary of War in accordance with the provisions of this act.

Approved June 22, 1874.

By order of the Secretary of War.

THOMAS M. VINCENT,
Assistant Adjutant-General.

OFFICE OF THE CHIEF OF ENGINEERS,
Washington, D. C., January 22, 1875.

SIR: I transmit herewith the report to His Excellency the President of the United States of the board of commissioners appointed to examine into the question of protecting the alluvial lands of the Mississippi River against inundation.

I beg leave to say that the views, plan, and recommendations of this board meet with my full concurrence. The surveys proposed by the board are equally necessary, whatever system of administration may be adopted for executing the plan of protection proposed.

Compared to the magnitude of the work, the estimated cost of these surveys is small. They are essential to determine the exact location, dimensions, and cost of the levees, and may proceed simultaneously with the execution of the plan of protection. They should be begun at once, and the sum of $160,000 is their estimated cost for the first year, the appropriation of which is recommended. Their total cost, extending over a period of three years, is estimated to be $300,000.

A wide distribution of this report is very desirable, both in the alluvial region and to the engineering profession; and as its cost will be comparatively small, (the report making about 125 printed octavo pages,) the printing of 10,000 copies is respectfully recommended.

I have the honor to be, very respectfully, your obedient servant,

A. A. HUMPHREYS,

Brigadier General and Chief of Engineers.

Hon. WILLIAM W. BELKNAP,

Secretary of War.

WASHINGTON, D. C., *January* 18, 1875.

GENERAL: As the president of the commission, I have the honor to transmit through you the report made in accordance with "An act to provide for the appointment of a commission of engineers to investigate and report a permanent plan for the reclamation of the alluvial basin of the Mississippi River subject to inundation," approved June, 1874.

This act authorized the President of the United States "to assign three officers of the Corps of Engineers, United States Army, and to appoint two civil engineers, eminent in their profession, and who are acquainted with the alluvial basin, to serve as a board of commissioners." The assignments and appointments were made by General Orders No. 73, War Department, Adjutant General's Office, Washington, July 2, 1874. The act itself is printed in this order.

The officers of the Engineer Corps United States Army thus empowered were the undersigned, Maj. Henry L. Abbot and Capt. W. H. H. Benyaurd; the civil engineers were Mr. Jackson E. Sickles and Mr. Paul O. Hébert. The act authorized the appointment of a secretary to the commission, and Mr. Charles M. Fauntleroy was appointed.

The wording of the act of Congress makes it "the duty of said commission to make a full report to the President," and we have therefore addressed the report to him, but it is transmitted through your Office, which has been the channel of all the official communications of the commission.

The foundation of the report of the commission rests upon your invaluable surveys and investigations, which, begun in 1850 and continued till 1861, are published in the great work "The Physics and Hydraulics of the Mississippi River, and upon the protection of the alluvial region against overflow," &c., and upon the further contributions to these subjects contained in your published official reports in 1866 and 1869. The commission has obtained the additional data upon subsequent floods, and the results of the more recent experience in building and rebuilding levees, as far as they are attainable, so that their report is in a great measure exhaustive of the subject, and the conclusions reached may be considered entitled to confidence.

The only want of information that now exists, is in regard to the exact configuration of the land and water, which is as yet too indefinite to enable exact and proper location of levees to be made. The commission estimates that the necessary hydrographical and topographical surveys will occupy three years, and cost about $300,000. These surveys should be begun at once, and $160,000 is desired for the first year. The results of the surveys can be almost immediately made applicable to levee location, and construction.

The report is divided into a general report, and four special reports, forming chapters to the general report, the whole accompanied by seven appendices and five diagrams.

The plan recommended for a permanent system of reclamation of the alluvial lands subject to inundation will be found at the end of the general report. Special attention is called to its position in the general report, as it cannot be given in more condensed form than as it there appears. A table of contents enables any part of the report to be readily referred to.

The commission regard it as important that a large edition of the whole report should be published for general distribution among the residents of the alluvial regions, in order that a general comprehension of the whole subject be made to reach every locality.

It is very necessary that the five diagrams should accompany the printed report. To facilitate doing this, the diagram relative to the heights of recent floods has been already engraved, and can be furnished, as rapidly as needed, at the mere cost of printing and paper. The other four diagrams are the monthly rain-charts of the United States Signal Corps, for the months of February, March, April, and May, 1874. These can probably be obtained also, as fast as needed, at the cost of printing and paper.

There have been considerable valuable data, contained in records, maps, and diagrams, obtained by the commission, which are not attached to their report. These will be sent to engineer headquarters, with a special communication respectfully requesting that they be placed on file for preservation and future consultation.

The commission is indebted for valuable assistance, such as records of observations, from officers of the Engineer Corps, United States Army, in charge of western river improvements; from General Albert J. Myer, Chief Signal-Officer United States Army; and from numerous gentlemen in various State or local offices, or in private life. A more extended notice of all these contributions will be found in the different special reports to which they relate.

Very respectfully, your obedient servant,

G. K. WARREN,
Major Engineers and Brevet Major-General, U. S. A.,
President of Commission.

Brig. Gen. A. A. HUMPHREYS,
Chief of Engineers United States Army.

REPORT AND PLAN

FOR THE

RECLAMATION OF THE ALLUVIAL BASIN OF THE MISSISSIPPI RIVER SUBJECT TO INUNDATION,

BY

THE BOARD OF COMMISSIONERS APPOINTED UNDER ACT OF CONGRESS APPROVED JUNE, 22, 1874.

TABLE OF CONTENTS.

	Page.
GENERAL REPORT:	
Introductory	7
Cut-offs	7
Diversion of tributaries	8
Reservoirs	8
Outlets	8
LEVEES:	
1. Theoretical considerations	16
2. Organization	18
3. Height	19
4. Cross-section	21
5. Inspection and guarding	23
6. Location	25
Surveys needed	27
Levee estimates	29
Plan recommended	31
CHAPTER I. Analysis of recent floods	33
" II. State of the levees in Missouri and Arkansas	56
" III. State of the levees in Mississippi	65
" IV. State of the levees in Louisiana	69
APPENDIX A. Mr. C. M. Fauntleroy's report upon application of reservoir system to valley of Red River	86
" B. Prof. C. G. Forshey's report of borings at site of proposed outlet at Lake Borgne	95
" C. Statistics of cotton, sugar, and corn crops in the alluvial basin of the Mississippi River since 1840, by Mr. A. D. Banks	105
" D. Flood-notes upon tributary rivers	111
" E. Gauge records of 1874	116
" F. Tables of relative heights of high waters, levees, and ground from Commerce, Missouri, to Louisiana line	142
" G. Minutes of the proceedings of the commission	160
DIAGRAMS AND CHARTS:	
Diagram showing comparative heights of recent floods in the Mississippi River.	
Precipitation charts of signal-service United States Army for February, March, April, and May, 1874.	

REPORT AND PLAN FOR THE RECLAMATION OF THE ALLUVIAL BASIN OF THE MISSISSIPPI RIVER SUBJECT TO INUNDATION.

WASHINGTON, D. C., *January* 16, 1875.

To His Excellency the President of the United States:

SIR: The board of commissioners appointed by you, in accordance with the provisions of an act of Congress approved in June, 1874, "to investigate and report a permanent plan for the reclamation of the alluvial basin of the Mississippi River subject to inundation," have the honor to submit the following report and plan:

INTRODUCTORY.

The commission first met on July 20, 1874, at Newport, R. I., and remained in session for four days. This session was devoted to a general comparison of views, and to dividing up the work of collecting information and discussing results among the several members. The minutes of proceedings, appended and marked G, give all requisite information respecting the details of these and of the subsequent meetings.

The commission re-assembled on December 7, 1874, at Washington, D. C., for final discussion and for the preparation of the report. The notes of the several members upon the special investigations intrusted to them were first read; they constitute the chapters following this report.

After carefully considering the subject in all its bearings, with the aid of all available records and information, the commission have agreed upon the following views and recommendations. A brief notice of such of the plans proposed for protecting the alluvial region against overflow as are worthy of mention, will first be given.

CUT-OFFS.

Exact observations upon the Po, the Mississippi, and other rivers have established that the effect of a cut-off is to raise the water-level just below its site by an amount equal to half the fall in a straight portion of the river of equal length, and to depress its height just above by an equal amount, plus the head requisite to overcome the resistance due to the curvature of the bend. If it were possible to extend the system from the foot of the alluvial region to its head, the result would be to greatly raise the flood-level in the region below and to depress it in the region above the middle point. Hence, even if no other injury than this of submerging the lower half of the valley would result, the plan would be utterly inadmissible either in an engineering or a political point of view. But this is not all. The local increase of velocity and change of direction of currents resulting from a cut-off, increases the caving in the bends both above and below its site. Indeed it is largely due to the frequent occurrence of these interruptions to the normal conditions of an unvarying river-bed, that the excessive caving in the upper part of the alluvial region is to be attributed. Five of them have occurred during the past quarter of a century, all with disastrous results to the river. So far from artificially aiding in their recurrence, it is therefore the emphatic opinion of this commission that in every case they should be prevented, or at least retarded, if this can be done at any reasonable cost.

DIVERSION OF TRIBUTARIES.

Various wild projects have from time to time been proposed looking to the reduction of the flood-volume of the Mississippi by diverting some of its tributaries. It is sufficient to state that no such works are practicable except at enormous expense; and that the injury to navigation which would be sure to result, would in any event forbid their execution.

RESERVOIRS.

This plan consists in arresting, by reservoirs, that part of the sudden drainage from the valleys of the tributaries which, if allowed to escape freely, would combine to cause floods in the lower channels. When the rainy season has passed, the gates of the artificial dams would be opened and the extreme low stages, so injurious to navigation, would thus be prevented. In theory this system is very attractive; but in practice it promises no relief to the lowlands of the Mississippi, simply because there are no available sites for reservoirs sufficiently large to produce the desired effect.

The floods of Red River are so peculiarly disastrous on the Mississippi, below its mouth, that the secretary of the commission was instructed to visit the lake region, near Shreveport, to ascertain whether any artificial increase in their capacity sufficient to materially reduce the flood-level of the Mississippi is practicable. His report, which is appended and marked A, shows that such works must submerge large areas of land now under cultivation, and be too costly for serious consideration. The question of absolute practicability could only be decided by a series of extensive and elaborate surveys, for which neither funds nor time were available, nor in the opinion of this commission are they needed. Here, as elsewhere in the valley, this plan, as an efficient means of restraining the floods of the Mississippi, is, in every sense of the word, chimerical.

OUTLETS.

This plan consists in abstracting from the river, and conducting by separate channels to the Gulf, such a volume of the flood-discharge as shall be sufficient to bring down the flood-level to a height easily under control by levees. It merits, and has received, the careful consideration of the commission. This plan has been stoutly opposed by certain writers of ability, upon the ground that reducing the flood-volume will produce deposits in the channel below the outlet, and will thus ultimately raise instead of lowering the height of the floods.

This argument, theoretically, is only tenable upon the assumption that the river-water is always charged with sedimentary matter to its maximum-supporting capacity, an assumption which has been shown, by three years of accurate daily observations at Carrollton and Columbus, to be utterly unfounded. Indeed, it often happened that the amount of sedimentary matter per cubic foot of water was greater in low than in high stages of the river, and never was there any fixed relation between these quantities. In other words, Mississippi River water is undercharged with earthy matter, and therefore no reasonable reduction of its flood-velocity by an outlet will produce a deposit in the bed below.

But, it is alleged, actual measurement has established that great crevasses do create bars in the river below them, and the several breaks at Bonnet Carré bend are cited in support of the statement. This is an error of fact; no such evidence really exists. The mistake has been caused by the discovery from soundings made *after the crevasses have ceased to flow*, that the channel below is smaller than that above; and it has been *assumed* that the difference is due to the crevasses. The truth is, there is a natural contraction in the channel at this point, which has remained unchanged for at least a quarter of a century; and it is highly probable that this contraction, combined with the sharp change in direction of the river, and the excessive height and sandy nature of the levees, is the cause of the many breaks at this locality. To put this matter beyond cavil, a re-sounding of the old lines, as nearly as the want of exact bench-marks would permit, was made for the commission by Mr. G. W. R. Bayley, of Louisiana, in September, 1874. He made a map, and five sections of the river, which were carefully compared with the original plots now on file in the bureau of the Engineer Department of the Army, at Washington. The results are presented in the following table, which, considering the fact that the high waters of different floods are used as the datum, shows a surprising accordance, and puts this vexed question forever at rest. Mr. Bayley found considerable accretions of sand upon the point naturally forming opposite the fundus of the bend in which the break in the levee was situated; as indeed might have been anticipated from the change of direction of the current produced by this immense crevasse; but the channel bar has been a permanent feature for at least twenty-four years, and consequently has not been formed by any escape of water from the river.

Comparison of soundings near Bonnet Carré crevasse of 1850.

Grouping of sections.	Authority.	When made.	High-water dimensions.		
			Year.	Width.	Area.
				Feet.	*Sq. ft.*
Above crevasse, (Bayley section between other two which were 1,000 feet apart.)	H. and A. No. 37	June, 1851	1851	3, 500	263, 000
	Bayley No. 1	Sept., 1874	1874	3, 120	247, 710
	H. and A. No. 38	June, 1851	1851	3, 500	237, 000
Upper end of crevasse of 1850	Forshey	July, 1850	1849	3, 500	216, 300
	Ellet	Feb., 1851	1849	....	200, 000
	H. and A. No. 39	June, 1851	1851	3, 480	208, 100
	H. and A. No. 40	Feb., 1859	1858	3, 480	207, 822
	Bayley No. 2	Sept., 1874	1874	3, 210	223, 295
Near middle of crevasse of 1850	H. and A. No. 41	June, 1851	1851	3, 380	168, 000
	Bayley No. 3	Sept., 1874	1874	3, 700	172, 300
Lower end of crevasse of 1850	Forshey	July, 1850	1849	....	147, 500
	Ellet	Feb., 1851	1849	....	154, 000
	H. and A. No. 42	Feb., 1859	1858	3, 200	154, 084
	H. and A. No. 43	June, 1851	1851	3, 145	163, 500
	Bayley No. 4	Sept., 1874	1874	3, 300	151, 797
	Bayley No. 5	Sept., 1874	1874	3, 430	162, 029

Dismissing, then, as utterly groundless, the fear that an outlet of dimensions likely to be desirable will produce any effect upon the bed of the river below, we will proceed to consider the other features of this method of protection.

Since it is an essential part of the plan that the water taken from the river shall be conducted to the Gulf without injury to the back country, it is evident that the question whether there is danger that the efflux from the river shall enlarge itself so as to draw off more water than can be safely disposed of, is of primary importance.

Authentic records establish that, during the historic period, the Po, the Rhine, the Vistula, and the Rhone, have all permanently changed their beds from natural or artificial works of this kind. Let us consider whether there is any evidence of a like tendency in the Mississippi—remembering that it is not necessary that there shall be danger of an outlet actually becoming the main channel, but only of its passing beyond the limit of control at the point where it debouches from the river.

The Jump, or Wilder's Bayou, leaves the Mississippi on the right bank at a point about ten miles above the head of the passes. In 1840 it did not exist, the site being occupied by a fisherman's canal, connected with the river by a lock, large enough to admit small vessels. In 1841 or 1842 the river broke into this canal, which was very short and conducted to a net-work of bayous winding among shell-reefs and sand-islands. The break rapidly enlarged and soon carried off an immense volume of water, creating a current in the river during its high stages sufficient to endanger passing tows. Indeed, it is reported that a steamer was once drawn into the new outlet. The deposits soon began to form mud islands and willow battures, with ramifying channels; and now a dense forest of large trees covers the land thus made.

The Jump was gauged by Lieutenant Davis, Corps of Engineers, on July 27, 1874, when the Carrollton gauge indicated 2.78 feet, or nearly extreme low water of the Mississippi. Two parallel sections of the Jump, 200 feet apart, were made near the river; and were found to be regular in form and nearly equal in size. The width was 560 feet, the maximum depth 55 feet, the sectional area 18,452 square feet, and the discharge 11,875 cubic feet per second, or about equal to the flood volume of Bayou La Fourche. At this stage of the Mississippi the difference in level between the river-surface and the Gulf did not probably exceed six inches; while in flood the same quantity is about 4 feet. The discharge at that stand must probably equal 100,000 cubic feet, or nearly that of the Atchafalaya in flood. Here, then, is a permanent and important high-water outlet formed more than thirty years ago by a crevasse.

Cubitt's Gap is situated on the left bank of the Mississippi, about 4 miles above the head of the passes. It occurred during the late war from a cut made by the Navy through the bulk-head of a fisherman's canal to provide a boat passage to the oyster-beds. It was gauged by Lieutenant Davis, Corps of Engineers, on the same day and in a similar manner as the Jump. It consists of four distinct but connected channels, two very small and two of immense size. One of the latter is 900 feet wide, with 100 feet maximum depth on one of the sections, and 50 feet on the other; the mean sectional area being 30,590 square feet. The other large channel is 1,420 feet wide, with maximum depths on the two sections (200 feet apart) of 126 feet and 108 feet respectively; its mean sectional area is 58,206 square feet. The eddies in the former prevented the use of floats, but the extreme low water discharge of the latter was found to be 33,000 cubic feet per second, or about that of Bayou Plaquemine in flood. The high-water discharge through the whole gap must be enormous, as there is then a difference of level of about 3.2 feet between the river-surface and the Gulf. This outlet rapidly shoals as the distance from the river increases, but the surveys do not give a profile.

A survey of the site of the great Bonnet Carré crevasse of 1874, which was situated just below that of 1871, and was identical with the lower part of that of 1850, was made for the commission by Mr. G. W. R. Bayley; it shows that a hole 530 feet wide, and from 35 to 40 feet deep, was excavated near the immediate bank of the river, and that it extended with diminishing depth to the rear for a distance of about 2,000 feet. If the channel at the date of high water had been enlarged to the full extent shown at the date of the survey, the area of discharge would have been about 35,000 square feet; the total length of the break being 1,370 feet.

The history of Bayou Plaquemine, also, has a bearing upon this question of the probable enlargement of an outlet. The old records show conclusively that, a century ago, it was a mere overflow coulé choked with growing timber. To secure water communication with the Attakapas country, this timber was removed; and ultimately an outlet having a cross-section of 6,000 square feet, and carrying 35,000 cubic feet per second, was formed. The high-water fall from the Mississippi to Indian Village, a distance of 8.3 miles, was 20 feet; and the corresponding velocity was about 6 feet per second. The bed of the bayou was formed in hard blue clay, which resisted abrasion so well that exact measurements made in 1851 and 1859 by the Mississippi Delta Survey showed no enlargement near the point of efflux. In 1865 the bayou was closed by a levee, upon the ground that this clay showed signs of yielding, and that there was danger of its rapid enlargement, which would endanger the back country. The truth of these statements has never been verified by accurate survey.

In fine, then, we must conclude that no outlet should be attempted until extensive borings have established the fact that its bed will consist of the hard blue clay which forms the true bed of the Mississippi, and effectively resist abrasion. Unless such a deposit be found, there will be danger that the outlet will ultimately have to be closed to prevent its efflux from enlarging beyond control, and thus deluging the country.

Having thus decided that, under certain conditions, a high-water outlet is admissible, it remains to fix upon its locality; and here lies the practical difficulty, which renders this plan of protection of little avail.

The highest point suggested is at Lake Providence, where the difficulty of protecting the country will soon be shown to be greatest. Such an outlet would only relieve the river locally, for the volume abstracted (and about 100,000 cubic feet per second could probably be carried off by the swamp-drains without material injury to the back country) would all return at the mouth of Red River. Actual measurement in the flood of 1851 showed that the sudden addition of such an amount to a river already beginning to fall, would raise its height, anomalously, at least a couple of feet above what it would have attained had the water remained in the river bed. This fact, added to the cost, and danger to the back country, renders the plan, in the judgment of this commission, inexpedient.

We now reach Atchafalaya River, a large natural outlet carrying to the Gulf 120,000 cubic feet per second in times of flood. This outlet it has been proposed to close; and we desire to place on record our decided disapproval of any such scheme. On the contrary, the rafts and obstructions in its bed near its point of entrance into the lakes should be removed, and its capacity to discharge its waters without overflowing its banks in that vicinity be thus improved.

Bayou Plaquemine is the next point where an outlet is practicable without overflowing the back country. We recommend that a careful survey, including many borings, be made, to decide whether the statements respecting its tendency to dangerous enlargement are well founded. If they should prove erroneous, this bayou should be reopened, its levees being first repaired so as to protect the neighboring plantations from overflow. Its closure has raised the flood-level at New Orleans several inches.

Bayou La Fourche is the only other natural outlet of value to the river. It discharges 12,000 cubic feet per second in times of flood, and we are of the opinion that, in justice to the plantations bordering the Mississippi below, it should be left open. Its closure was recently recommended by a majority in a board of State engineers, in our judgment unadvisedly.

No other outlet is practicable on this bank of the river, for the reason that there is no natural channel capable of conducting the water to the Gulf without overflowing the back country, and no artificial channel could be made at any reasonable cost. We have, therefore, only to consider the left bank below Baton Rouge; showing that outlets, as a plan of protection, are of so restricted application that at best they can only be regarded as an auxiliary to the levee system.

The proposition to reopen old Bayou Manchac is inexpedient, for the reason that its capacity is too insignificant to sensibly relieve the Mississippi. This has been satisfactorily established by surveys made by the State of Louisiana.

It only remains to consider two proposed artificial outlets—one opening from Bonnet Carré bend into Lake Pontchartrain, and the other from the English Turn to Lake Borgne. At the former the difference of level between the high-water surface of the river and the lake is 20 feet, the distance being 6 miles. At the latter these quantities are 13.0 feet and 5.3 miles respectively.

The Bonnet Carré outlet, so far as the river itself is concerned, would be much the more useful of the two. If a waste-weir capable of discharging 250,000 cubic feet per second in great floods, should here be made, it would render the country below secure with the existing levees, and would have a sensible influence upon the high-water mark in the region above, at least as far as Baton Rouge. The objections to the project, however, are weighty. First, it would raise the level of Lake Pontchartrain at least 4 feet, thus exacting a continuous levee on its borders, to secure the plantations and New Orleans itself against overflow from the rear. As the lake is already subject to sudden oscillations, amounting to 3 or 4 feet, from the effect of strong southeasterly gales, this levee would be costly, both from its height and from its difficult location. Second, the outlet would certainly destroy the easy navigation of the lake, which is of too much importance to New Orleans to be lightly surrendered. Third, it would increase the difficulty of railroad communication between the city and the North, and would entail considerable expense on this account. Fourth, it would require the expenditure of a large sum for the purchase of the site; for opening the outlet, including the removal of a dense forest from its bed; and for the lateral levees requisite to prevent the water from spreading to the right and left over the plantations. Add to these solid grounds of objection the uncertainty that, after the work was executed, its speedy closure might be demanded to prevent the point of efflux at the river from enlarging beyond the limit of safety, and the project assumes a very questionable shape.

Turning to the Lake Borgne outlet, we find, although its beneficial influence would be much less—hardly extending above New Orleans—

several of the objections to the construction disappear. The very important question, however, whether the outlet might not so enlarge its bed as to become dangerous, can only be intelligently considered after the substrata have been determined by boring. Accordingly, Professor C. G. Forshey was employed to make a detailed survey. His report is appended, and marked B; but it is proper to add that the commission does not indorse all the opinions and inferences therein expressed.

The survey lay between bayous Bienvenue and Duprez. The river front was 8,000 feet, and the lake front (5.3 miles distant) 16,000 feet long. The total area examined was about 12.5 square miles. Of this, 1.2 square miles consisted of lands under cultivation; 4.74 square miles of cypress swamps, and 6.50 square miles of marsh prairie. Both swamp and prairie are but little elevated above the lake, and are exposed to daily tidal overflow. The total difference of level between the high-water surface of the Mississippi and the lake is 13 feet, of which 11.5 feet are gained in the first mile, and nearly all of this in the first 3,000 feet from the river bank. The lake has a depth of 10 feet 1,500 feet from the shore-line, and its bottom is of hard black or blue clay.

Fourteen borings were made; Nos. 1, 2, 3, and 4 were on the immediate bank of the river; Nos. 5, 6, 7, and 8 were distant about 1.5 miles from this line; Nos. 12, 13, and 14 were on the lake shore, and Nos. 9, 10, and 11 were intermediate between the last two lines, No. 9 being in the swamp, and Nos. 10 and 11 in the prairie. The following table indicates the character of the successive strata with sufficient exactness for the practical purposes of this report. To make the specimens obtained from the borings subserve, as far as they may, the scientific investigation of the substrata of the delta, they have been submitted to experienced investigators of this subject.

Outlet at Lake Borgne.

Character of strata.	Thickness of strata.	Top of strata below surface.
BORING NO. 1.		
	Feet.	*Feet.*
1. Surface, dark soil; immediately under surface, stiff mud	5	0
2. Blue clay	5	5
3. Blue clay with plain sand indications	10	10
4. Blue clay with plain sand indications and with chips of wood	23	20
5. Blue clay with very slight sand indications	10	43
6. Blue clay	20	53
7. Quicksand and fine shells	22	73
8. Blue clay	5	95
Total depth	100	......
BORING NO. 2.		
1. Surface—black soil, changes to clay of yellowish brown with sand	5	0
2. Yellow brown clay and sand	12	5
3. Blue clay with slight sand. At 45 feet below surface inflammable gas was discovered; it threw the water up 5 feet from the mouth of pipe, and burned very freely, with a flame 2 feet high	51	17
4. Quicksand and fine shells slightly intermixed	14	68
Total depth	82	......
BORING NO. 3.		
1. Surface—light sandy soil	5	0
2. Light brown stiff mud or clay, and sand	6	5
3. Yellow clay and sand	12	11
4. Blue clay	5	23
5. Blue clay, with plain sand indications and with chips of wood	5	28
6. Sand and a little clay	5	33

Outlet at Lake Borgne—Continued.

Character of strata.	Thickness of strata.	Top of strata below surface.
	Feet.	*Feet.*
7. Blue clay with slight sand. At 45 feet below surface inflammable gas was discovered, and burned freely	18	38
8. Blue clay	13	56
9. Blue clay and sand	3	69
10. Blue quicksand	25	72
11. Blue clay	3	97
Total depth	100	......
BORING NO. 4.		
1. Surface-soil stiff and dark	5	0
2. Brown mud, sticky	11	5
3. Blue clay with slight sand	6	16
4. Blue clay	10	22
5. Blue clay very sandy, with water indications at 42 feet below surface	24	32
6. Blue clay with slight sand	8	56
7. Bluish gray quicksand	28	64
8. Blue clay mixed with fine shells	8	92
Total depth	100	......
BORING NO. 5.		
1. Light brown mud	10	0
2. Blue mud, sand, and wood chips	10	10
3. Blue clay and sand	10	20
4. Quicksand mixed with chips	15	30
5. Blue clay and sand	8	45
6. Blue clay	4	53
7. Quicksand and fine shells	15	57
8. White soap-stone clay mixed with white sand	6	72
9. White and red sand	22	78
Total depth	100	......
BORING NO. 6.		
1. Brown mud mixed with chips	10	0
2. Brown mud and sand mixed with chips	10	10
3. Gray and black quicksand	20	20
4. Gray and black quicksand mixed with clay	10	40
5. Blue clay	9	50
6. Fine quicksand and shells	22	59
7. Blue clay and shells	2	81
Total depth	83	......
BORING NO. 7.		
1. Surface-soil, black swamp-mud	0.3	0
2. Blue clay	14.7	0.3
3. Blue clay and sand	20	15
4. Coarse dark-gray sand	37	35
5. Fine shells, sand, and clay mixed	15	72
6. Blue clay	1	87
7. White sand, a slight mixture of clay, and fine shells	12	88
Total depth	100	.....
BORING NO. 8.		
1. Surface-soil, black, stiff mud	5	0
2. Dark clay, with slight sand	12	5
3. Blue clay, with slight sand	24	17
4. Blue clay	17	41
5. Blue clay and sand	5	58
6. Quicksand and fine shells	14	63
7. Blue clay and fine shells	2	77
Total depth	79	......
BORING NO. 9.		
1. Surface-soil, soft mud	5	0
2. Dark-brown mud	6	5
3. Blue clay	4	11

Outlet at Lake Borgne—Continued.

Character of strata.	Thickness of strata.	Top of strata below surface.
	Feet.	*Feet.*
4. Blue clay, very sandy	9	15
5. Coarse gray sand	16	24
6. Blue clay and sand	10	40
7. Blue clay	14	50
8. Sand mixed with fine shells	9	64
9. Blue clay and shells	7	73
10. Blue clay mixed with sand	11	80
11. Blue clay	9	91
Total depth	100	......
BORING NO. 10.		
1. Blue swamp-mud	5	0
2. Mud mixed with blue clay	10	5
3. Blue mud	45	15
4. Gray sand, shells, and slight mixture of blue clay	10	60
Total depth	70	......
BORING NO. 11.		
1. Swamp brown mud	30	0
2. Blue mud	10	30
3. Blue clay	12	40
4. Dark gray sand mixed with shells; at 70 feet below surface, was discovered inflammable gas; it burned freely, throwing up blue mud, shells, and sand	18	52
Total depth	70	......
BORING NO. 12.		
1. Swamp brown mud	30	0
2. Blue clay and mud	10	30
3. Blue clay	15	40
4. Sand, shells, and clay, mixed	16	55
Total depth	71	......
BORING NO. 13.		
1. Swamp mud	30	0
2. Blue clay mixed mud	10	30
3. Blue clay	16	40
4. Sand mixed slightly with blue clay; and, also, inflammable gas was discovered; it burned freely	13	56
Total depth	69	......
BORING NO. 14.		
1. Swamp mud	25	0
2. Blue mud with slight mixture of sand	5	25
3. Blue clay	19	30
4. Blue clay of soapstone color	7	49
5. Bluish-gray sand	14	56
Total depth	70	......

These borings, which are not unlike in character to those of the artesian well at New Orleans and to the borings recently made near the site of the proposed Fort Saint Philip Canal, establish the fact that there is no deep and unyielding stratum of hard clay in which to place permanently the bottom of an outlet. The gradual oscillation and limited range of the Mississippi in this vicinity would insure a long-continued discharge through the weir; the steep pitch in the first mile would induce a rapid rush of water in that vicinity; and, unless protected at a great cost, there would be danger of the efflux enlarging beyond the contemplated size, and thus gradually passing beyond control. Drift-logs would be likely to lodge near the lake, and, perhaps, might so obstruct the channel there as to give much trouble in providing a free way for the abstracted water. The original cost of making the outlet, including the payment of damages to private property, would hardly fall below $1,500,000. Lastly, the experience of Prussia, which has expended $2,000,000 in regulating the discharge through the artificial channel between the Nogat and Vistula, admonishes us that an outlet under circumstances like the above is not lightly to be undertaken.

In fine, then, this commission is forced unwillingly to the conclusion, that no assistance in reclaiming the alluvial region from overflow can judiciously be anticipated from artificial outlets. They are correct in theory, but no advantageous sites for their construction exist.

LEVEES.

There are certain theoretical views concerning the effects of the levee system which are raised again and again in discussing the subject, and which, therefore, it may be well to consider here.

Theoretical considerations.—It is claimed, since the effect of embanking a river is to confine its sedementary matter to the channel, that the deposit formerly made on the banks must settle on the bottom, and thus ultimately raise the bed, and with it the high-water mark. This idea, utterly without any good foundation either in theory or experience, is usually defended by appealing to the example of the Po, which is asserted to have thus raised its bed several feet. In point of fact, such is not the case. The error was first promulgated by De Prony, who made a hasty visit to that river in the early part of this century. His statements have been refuted in the most conclusive manner by the great Italian hydraulic engineer, Lombardini, who has proved that there is no ground whatever to believe that levees have produced the slightest elevation of the bed of the Po. Observations upon the Rhine, extended over a period of eighty years, demonstrate the same truth for that river. The most careful measurements upon the Mississippi have failed to detect any indication of a filling of its channel by levees. No change of the kind attributable to levees can be shown to have occurred on any river, and the theory is, therefore, without any foundation in fact.

Diametrically opposed to this theory is another, which, for the Mississippi, is equally erroneous. It is asserted in the most confident manner that the river is flowing in a bed composed of its own deposit, with dimensions regulated in accordance with its own needs; and hence that the increased velocity resulting from the confinement of its flood-volume between levees will rapidly excavate its bed to a correspondingly greater depth, thus avoiding any permanent increase in the high-water mark.

This reasoning, if true, would establish conditions singularly fortunate for the levee system; but, unluckily, the wish has been father to the thought. Uncompromising facts show that the premises and conclusion are both erroneous for the Lower Mississippi. Very numerous soundings, with leads adapted to bringing up samples of the bottom, were made by the Mississippi Delta Survey throughout the whole region between Cairo and the Gulf. They showed conclusively that the *real bed*, upon which rest the shifting sand-bars and mud-banks made by local causes, is always found in a stratum of hard blue clay, quite unlike the present deposits of the river. It is similar to that forming the bed of the Atchafalaya at its efflux, and, as is well known, resists the action of the strong current almost like marble. Clearly, then, the bed of the

Mississippi cannot yield, and if the velocity be increased sufficiently to compel an enlargement of the channel, it must be made by an increased caving of the banks, an effect which it is not quite so agreeable to contemplate.

In truth, no marked effect of the kind is to be anticipated, owing to the comparatively short duration of the increased discharge; for, evidently, the levees can produce no effect upon the regimen of the river, except when the water stands over the natural banks.

Hence, really the practical effect of the levees will be limited to raising the high-water mark, and to slightly increasing the caving. Since the absolute amount of the increased flood-height does not carry the cost beyond the limits of a remunerative investment, it is the part of wisdom to steadily continue work without indulging in groundless fears that the river-bed will rise, or in the equally groundless hopes that it will be sensibly depressed.

Certain indirect agencies, it is claimed, may exert too important an influence upon the levees of the future to be safely neglected—such as an increase in the suddenness of the freshets of the tributaries, owing to the increased cultivation of their valleys. In a great river like the Mississippi no single tributary can produce a flood; and since its destructive overflows are, therefore, always caused by a coincidence of freshets, it is quite impossible to predict whether a greater or a less flood-volume may result from such alleged variations in the regimen of its branches. The change, if any, must gradually develop itself, and it can, therefore, gradually be met.

The prolongation of the delta into the Gulf by the aggregation of sedimentary matter is also assigned as a cause for the ultimate rise of the bed, and hence for a future necessary increase in the height of the levees. A possible secular change of this nature is quite too remote in its effects to merit attention from practical men of the present day. Simple calculation will show that hundreds of years will be required to raise the flood-height at New Orleans an inch from this cause.

In fine, then, we are to conclude that there is no mysterious agency, either favorable or injurious, which may be expected to exert a controlling influence upon the levee system. Experience has shown that the accessions to the volume made at the mouth of any of its large tributaries in flood raise the level of the surface unless immediately drawn off again by crevasses. If we guard against these crevasses by raising and strengthening our levees, an elevation of the high-water mark exactly proportional to the increased volume will be sure to occur. We need have no fear of this normal height being practically increased through the action of any known river-law, and we must expect no reduction from any occult cause. To contain a quart of water a vessel must have exactly the requisite number of cubic inches; and a like principle applies with equal force to water in motion.

It being certain that the alluvial regions of the Mississippi can only be reclaimed by levees, it remains to consider what experience has taught respecting them. The existing system was begun a century and a half ago, near New Orleans, and has gradually extended upward until there are but few points on the river at which it has not been tried. The crops of cotton, sugar, corn, and rice heretofore gathered from the alluvial region, with all the existing wealth represented by lands under cultivation, cities, villages, plantations, and stock, are the direct fruits of this method of protecting the country against overflow. It cannot, therefore, properly be called a failure, and yet the actual condition of the region to-day is such as to demonstrate that the practical application of the system is fatally defective, and that unless some radical improvement be made, no hope remains of opening to cultivation the immense districts of back lands, now exposed to annual inundation through annual breaks in the levees; and also, that only precarious crops can be expected from the narrow fringe of plantations under cultivation now skirting the immediate borders of the Mississippi, and its principal bayous and tributaries. To determine, therefore, in what respects the existing system is defective is highly important. The faults are only too apparent. They are:

1st. Vicious levee organization.

2d. Insufficient heights, in adjusting which, only existing high-water marks have been considered, without remembering that there has never yet been a great flood in the river in which the water has not been greatly lowered by immense crevasses which occur with absolute certainty.

3d. Injudicious cross-sections and construction, which alone would be sufficient to explain many of the frequent breaks, under the combined influence of pressure, seepage, burrowing of craw-fish, &c.

4th. Inadequate arrangements for inspecting and guarding.

5th. Faulty location of the embankments, which are often placed so near caving banks as to insure an early destruction.

Each of the causes of failure will be considered in turn.

Organization.—The marked slope of the country away from the river causes the crevasse-water to pour rapidly into the swamps. The natural drains conducting it southward being only sufficient for ordinary rain-water, soon become engorged, and a vast shallow lake is formed, which gradually rises over the rear of the plantations far and wide. It is therefore evident that the interests of each natural levee district are necessarily an unit, and are quite independent of any political boundaries, whether of parish, county, or State. This proposition, which seems an axiom, has been systematically ignored from the earliest times to the present day.

In Louisiana the charge of the levees, after they ceased to be under purely individual control, was usually vested in the police juries and inspectors of the several parishes, the geographical limits of several of which included both banks of the river. As a break on one side gives immediate relief to the other, the complications thus caused may readily be imagined. Moreover, the law required the riparian proprietors to maintain the levees at their own cost, which was evidently in the highest degree unjust as soon as settlements began to be formed in rear owing, of course, the possibility of their existence to the front levees. Instead of inaugurating a radical reform as the State increased in wealth and population, only half measures were attempted. Certain parishes have arbitrarily grouped into levee districts, for which boards of levee commissioners were appointed and special laws enacted. At the beginning of the late war a most complex and unequal administration was thus in force, which of itself would have been sufficient to insure failure in attempting to carry out any comprehensive system of protection. Since the war various State organizations have been tried, the present plan consisting in levying a general tax on upland and lowland alike, and contracting with a levee company to build all the levees. The allotment of funds and general control is vested in a board of three commissioners, of which one is appointed by the President, one by the State, and one by the company. The work is done according to the specifications and under the supervision of the State engineers, at a uniform price of fifty cents per cubic yard. As the State contains three natural levee districts, the just apportionment of funds among them under this system must be difficult; and the persistent opposition of the parishes not subject to overflow may confidently be expected.

For Mississippi a similar history of county complications might be written. The levees continued under individual control from their commencement in 1840 to 1850, when a grant of the swamp-lands was made by the General Government to supply funds for reclaiming them. For seven years this was attempted under county control, but it becoming evident that, in general, protection depended as much on the levees above as on those in the immediate front, a consolidation of interests took place under direction of a general board of commissioners. This was by far the best organization ever adopted in the alluvial region of the Mississippi, and its fruits were soon seen in good levees, and prompt and energetic action. During the war the embankments suffered from caving and occasional cutting for military purposes; and when peace returned, a step backward in organization was made by constituting two levee districts instead of one. This is the present system.

In Arkansas and Missouri the levee legislation has been so crude and ineffective as hardly to merit notice.

In fine, then, the experience of over one hundred and fifty years has utterly failed to create judicious laws or effective organization in the several States themselves, and no systematic co-operation has been even attempted between them. The latter is no less important than the former, for the river has no respect for State boundaries, and deluges Arkansas through breaks in the levees of Missouri, and overflows Louisiana by floods passing across the Arkansas line.

It is a common and apt figure of speech to personify the Mississippi, and to speak of the conflict waged to protect the country against the inroads of a terrible enemy; and yet the army of defense has always been content to remain a simple aggregation of independent companies, with here and there a battalion under the command of a board of officers. That victory has not more frequently perched upon their banners is surely not surprising.

The British administration of the Indian levees is in striking contrast. The Government takes the initiative, and sends its engineers to survey and estimate for levees at such localities as promise to be remunerative. The reports with detailed maps, plans, and estimates of costs are sent to the collector, who publishes the same and calls for reasons why the improvement shall not be ordered. Unless good reason is shown by the owners of the land to be benefited, the levees are built by the Government and a tax sufficient to pay for the same is laid upon the lands reclaimed thereby. If the sum is large an annual tax for a term of years is collected; if small, immediate payment is required. The enhancement of the value of his land thus precedes any raising of money by the proprietor.

This system is not suggested for adoption on the Mississippi, but is mentioned simply as an illustration that other nations have found by experience that individual efforts cannot successfully combat nature on a grand scale.

Height.—This great problem of the levee system demands scientific investigation quite beyond the operations of ordinary earthwork engineering. To decide, first, how much addition will be made to the present maximum flood volume passing in the river-bed when no water is allowed to escape over the banks, and, second, to infer therefrom how much the river will rise above its present high-water mark at each and every locality throughout the alluvial region, are problems so complex that engineers engaged in constructing the levees have never attempted to solve them. In other words, the height of the embankments has always practically been fixed by guess-work.

As some rule has seemed to be desirable, the arbitrary one of building the levee say one foot, or two feet, or three feet above the highest known water-mark at each locality has usually been adopted. If these rules had all been the same in different places, and if the cross-sections of the embankments had been made sufficient to resist the pressure and wear thrown upon them, the river in floods would have risen sufficiently to pour over the top, and thus give practically the data for a new trial and a new failure. This method of approximation, after a long series of trials, would at length have given a practical solution to the problem; but unfortunately the embankments have always been made so weak that some part has yielded, and the true flood level has never yet been reached or indeed approached. Before the river has risen three feet above the natural level of the high banks many crevasses have been sure to occur and relieve it, and to-day there is not a levee upon the river which is not greatly too low. If the embankments were of unyielding materials, the river in floods would pour over their tops from the head to the foot of the alluvial region.

Appreciating that this problem was beyond the power of the local authorities to solve, the General Government came to their aid, and in 1850 ordered special surveys and investigations to be made. They were conducted for ten years by the Engineer Corps of the Army, under the direction of General Humphreys, then a captain and now the chief of the corps. A far more elaborate series of observations than has ever been attempted upon any other river in the world was patiently carried out, and to-day the results are accessible to all in the report upon the Physics and Hydraulics of the Mississippi, by Humphreys and Abbot.

The proper heights were determined by close calculation from actual measurements made upon the flood of 1858, between Cape Girardeau and the Gulf. These measurements were so exact, so extensive, and so elaborate that the complete history of the great wave which entered the alluvial region in June was traced out, determining where, when, and in what quantities the surplus waters both left and returned to the channel. This enabled a precise estimate to be made of the amount by which the actual measured maximum flood volume, at any point, fell below what it would have been had no water escaped; while a most thorough experimental study of the river rendered it possible to predict with accuracy the height to which the water would have risen above the actual local high-water marks had none left the channel. It was also proved, by extended soundings and measurements, that the bed of the river cannot be deepened by any slight increase in the velocity of its waters; and that no deposit in the channel need be dreaded from any slight reduction in its rate of movement; in other words, that the bed is essentially unchanging in dimensions.

In order to decide whether the flood of 1858 was a safe standard, a most careful analysis of all recorded floods was made; and when the report was published, in 1861, nothing had been left undone to give the best possible solution to the problem of the true height for the embankments. Since that date four great floods have occurred, and it has therefore devolved upon this commission to continue the work by submitting these new floods to the best analysis the facts collected would warrant, with a view to determining whether they suggest any modification in the levee heights previously announced. This task has been performed by Commissioner Abbot, and in Chapter I will be found the detailed analysis and the conclusions resulting therefrom.

Upon this solid foundation the commission rests its opinion that the following heights are necessary to secure the alluvial region from overflow in a first-class Mississippi flood:

Near the mouth of the Ohio the levees should be made about 3 feet above the actual high-water level of 1858, which has been selected as the plane of reference, because more unvarying than the surface of the ground. The height above this level should be gradually increased to about 7 feet at Osceola; thence to Helena the latter height should be maintained; thence to Island 71 the height should be gradually increased to 10 feet; thence to the vicinity of Napoleon it may be gradually reduced to 8 feet; thence to Lake Providence it must be gradually increased to 11 feet; thence to the mouth of the Yazoo it may be gradually reduced to 6 feet, and it should thus be maintained to Natchez; thence to Red River Landing it must be gradually increased to 7 feet; thence to Baton Rouge it may be gradually reduced to 5 feet; thence to Donaldsonville this height must be maintained. At Carrolton 4.7 feet will suffice, with reductions proportioned to the range between high and low water mark for points below. These figures are exclusive of settling, and allow for safety about one foot more than the computed flood-height.

Cross-section.—Several principles should be borne in mind in building a levee.

It has to resist a direct hydrostatic pressure which, when the height is considerable, may be very great. The general law that the pressure exerted by a fluid upon any surface is equal to the weight of a column of that fluid having a cross-section equal to the area in question, and a height equal to the depth of its center of gravity, supplies the means of directly estimating this force in pounds.

The fact that this pressure is exerted in a direction normal to the surface suggests the danger of allowing water to enter the interior of the levee, since a great lifting force may thus be called into action.

Infiltration or seepage also exerts a very injurious effect by tending to render the levee semi-fluid, and thus liable to change its form by yielding to the weight of the superincumbent mass.

A levee exposed to the direct force of the current, or to frequent blows from waves created by wind or the passage of steamboats, will require a much stronger cross-section than one not so attacked.

The soil of which it is composed exerts a marked influence upon its resisting power. A clay levee is vastly stronger than one of equal dimensions made of sand; and owing to the greater tendency of the latter to slide when wet, its slopes must be made much more gentle. Unfortunately most of the embankments of the Mississippi are composed of the sandy loam deposited from its waters, a fact which exacts gentle slopes and massive construction.

In large levees made of sandy soil it is customary and very advantageous to embed a vertical wall of tamped clay in the interior to prevent seepage. Plank fences have also been occasionally tried during the past thirty years, both to prevent seepage and to stop craw-fish and other burrowing animals from endangering the levee. Their cost, and the fact that decay renders it necessary to replace them from time to time, are the chief objections to their adoption.

That the borrow-pits should be made on the exterior of the levee, with occasional bulk-heads to prevent currents and induce deposit; that the bed of the embankment should be loosened and thoroughly cleared from roots and vegetable matter; that a good drainage-ditch should be made parallel to the levee on the inside and not too near, in order to draw off seepage-water; and that the slopes shall be well turfed, and in exposed situations be protected by a growth of bushes in front, are rules observed in all good river embankments.

There has been a marked improvement in the form of the cross-section of the embankments within the last twenty years. In 1851, the old levees of Louisiana usually had the crown equal to the height, with slopes of 1 on 1. The present formula for cross-section is the crown equal to the height, with slopes of 1 upon 3.

The levees of the State of Mississippi have crowns of 5 feet, with slopes 6 to 1 toward the river and 2.5 to 1 toward the swamps. Arkansas levee laws require "for every foot in height, 1 foot wide on top, and in addition 7 feet base." The section recommended in the Physics and Hydraulics of the Mississippi for levees of moderate height is, the crown equal to the height, with slopes of 3 to 1 on the river side, and 2 to 1 on the land side. For the immense levees required to close old bayous it is important to distribute the weight, and a crown of 6 feet with a front slope of 3 to 1 and a rear slope of 4 to 1 seems to be sufficient, unless the soil is very sandy. The last Yazoo Pass levee was 40 feet high and 300 feet long; its crown was 10 feet, with a front slope of 5 to 1 and a rear slope of 3 to 1. The Hushpuckana levee was 43 feet high and 250 feet long; its crown was 8 feet, with slopes of 3 to 1. Both of these levees resisted the flood of 1874.

The following extract from the report upon the Physics and Hydraulics of the Mississippi, giving the dimensions of the principal levees of Europe, is interesting for comparison:

"The French dikes on the Rhine in that part of its course lying between the Black Forest and the Vosges Mountains, where the height is 7 feet, have a width of 10 feet, the slope toward the river being 2 to 1, and toward the land 1.5 to 1. Where the height exceeds 7 feet, the width is increased by a banquette on each side. The area of cross-section of this dike, 7 feet high, is 154 square feet; the area of cross-section of a levee of the State of Mississippi, of that height, is 252 square feet.

"The dikes of the Rhine in Holland, when near the river-bank and when used for the road, have a width of 20 feet on top, when 16 feet high, a slope of 3 to 1 on the river side and a slope of 1.5 to 1 on the land side. The outer slope, when exposed to running ice, is protected by a revetment of brick or fascines. When the dike is not near the river-bank and is not used as a road, the width is only 6.5 feet. The area of cross-section of the first dike is 900 square feet; of the second, 640 square feet; a levee of the State of Mississippi, of the same height, would have an area of cross-section of 1,230 square feet.

"The dikes on the Po (those of the Adige have similar dimensions) are 2.5 feet above the highest flood-mark; usually the width is equal to the height, and the slope of the sides is 2 to 1. When the soil is permeable, they are re-enforced at the height of the mean floods (10 feet below the top of the dike) by a banquette, whose width is 20 feet when the height is 20 feet or over. The area of cross-section of this dike is 1,400 square feet; a levee of the State of Mississippi of the same height would have an area of cross-section of 1,800 square feet. Where the soil is very sandy and has but little cohesion, the dikes of the Po, when 20 feet high and over, have a width at top of 26 feet, two banquettes of 20 feet width, an outside slope of 3 to 1, and an inside slope of 2 to 1. The area of cross-section of this dike, 20 feet high, is

1,840 square feet; a levee of the State of Mississippi, of the same height, would have an area of cross-section of 1,800 square feet. The river-roads are usually upon the levee or the banquette.

"The average height of the dikes on the Vistula is 20 feet. The top of the dike is from 2 to 3 feet above the highest flood; the thickness at the top is 15 feet, or three-fourths of the height, and the slopes 3 to 1 and 2 to 1. The area of cross-section of such a dike is 1,300 square feet; a levee of the State of Mississippi, of the same height, would have an area of cross section of 1,800 feet.

"The highest dike on the Vistula is 28 feet in height. It has a width at top of 18 feet, and an area of cross-section of 2,460 square feet. A levee of the State of Mississippi, of the same height, would have an area of cross-section of 2,660 square feet."

Inspection and guarding.—These duties have always been neglected on the Mississippi, or have been executed in so negligent and unsystematic a manner as to prove of little avail. That they are of the highest importance no one familiar with the subject can question.

Every levee has natural enemies, both human and brute.

The former include every resident and land-owner in the vicinity on the opposite bank of the river, whose selfish interest requires, in times of flood, that some way of escape for the threatening water shall be opened before his own levees break. Of course, among honorable men, no active steps in such a case would for a moment be considered; but where every person, rich and poor, has so strong a common interest, some scoundrel, ready to act, will occasionally be found; and in times of flood, one resolute man, provided with a skiff and shovel, can in a few moments cause a crevasse on any dark night.

There is another class of men called swampers, whose business it was, before levees were attempted, to cut timber for the market in the cypress swamps and low lands bordering the river. This work was done during the dry season; and when the annual floods filled the bottom-lands the logs were rafted out through the net-work of bayous thus rendered easily navigable. Levees have greatly injured this business, but, as in every great flood crevasses are certain to occur, it has not entirely ceased; and many are the breaks attributed to the midnight work of the raftsmen.

Private hostility, especially on the part of the ignorant and degraded classes, finds a ready means of revenge by cutting the levee of a wealthy planter.

Among the brute creation, musk-rats, cray-fish, fiddlers, and other burrowing animals have made many a break by their subterranean labors; and more than one disastrous crevasse has been caused by storms, which, by prostrating a tree across a levee, have opened a way for the ever-ready waters to begin their work of destruction. Sudden caving of the banks, and imperfectly-closed summer roadways over the levee are also fruitful sources of ruin.

In fine, then, nothing but frequent official inspection, and a regular chain of sentinels, will guarantee even a perfect system of levees against unexpected injury. These duties have always been most imperfectly performed on the Mississippi.

In this connection it may be well to consider how other rivers are guarded in times of danger; and the Nile furnishes a good example. This stream is so peculiar and interesting, and is so little known, that a short description, derived chiefly from the writings of Lombardini, is not out of place.

The river is formed by the junction, at Kartoum, of two principal branches; the Blue Nile, which drains the mountainous region of Abyssinia, and the White Nile, which issues from the swamps and lakes of Central Africa. The former discharges at low water 6,000 cubic feet per second, or about one-half as much as the latter, while, in floods, the two are nearly equal, the united volume being about 430,000 cubic feet per second.

The main river first flows through a hilly region, receiving, one hundred and ninety miles below Kartoum, the waters of its last tributary, which in floods contributes about 60,000 cubic feet per second. This portion of the valley is marked by many cataracts, the last being just above Assouan, 1,200 miles below Kartoum. Here the river enters upon the alluvial region liable to annual overflow.

From Assouan to Cairo, a distance of 500 miles, the average breadth of the valley is about 10 miles. From time immemorial this region has been cultivated by aid of irrigation. Front and cross levees, the latter from three to five feet high, cut the land into a succession of basins, which are flooded at will in seasons of high water by sluices opening from a system of main canals. These canals follow the general course of the river near the edge of the desert, and are supplied by large feeders. By cutting the cross levees the water is drawn from basin to basin as desired, and the moisture needed for cultivation is thus supplied. The country having been flooded for thousands of years in this manner, from the rear, the slope away from the river, usual in alluvial regions, is prevented and even occasionally reversed. The total area of this district, usually known as Middle Egypt, is about 5,000 square miles, of which over 3,000 square miles are annually covered by water in this way.

Cairo is situated on the Nile, 12 miles above the head of the delta, marked by the separation of the Rosetta and Damietta branches, which are each about 120 miles in length. The discharge of the main river is here about 12,000 cubic feet per second at low water, and 300,000 cubic feet per second in floods. The area of the delta cultivable, when sufficient water can be provided for the necessary irrigation, is about 4,400 square miles.

The regimen of the Nile is remarkably unvarying. The river is low est in June, rises rapidly until September, and then gradually declines to low water. Unfortunately the range between high and low water mark differs from year to year. Experience has shown that when the range does not exceed 18 feet, famine is inevitable; that with 20 feet the production is insufficient; that with 23 feet the crops are still poor; that with 25 feet they are abundant; and that with 26 feet and upward the flood becomes dangerous, threatening famine and pestilence from the rupture of the levees and drainage too long delayed.

Thus, with water derived from the Nile, upon the system already described for Middle Egypt, the delta could only yield one uncertain crop annually, while with an ample supply three crops could be obtained with certainty. To secure the latter economically from the river, Mahomet Ali inaugurated, in the year 1846, a magnificent system of public works. Where the Nile divides, a barrage or dam of masonry, about 1,600 feet long, crosses each branch. They are so arranged, with four locks and many sluice-gates, as to allow navigation and the free escape of the water during floods, and yet permit its retention at a high level for irrigating purposes. One large canal extends between the branches to the sea, and others on each bank conduct to reservoirs and a system of secondary and tertiary canals by which water is supplied throughout the delta.

The front levees are said to be from 12 feet to 15 feet high near Cairo, and diminish gradually as the sea is approached. They are simple embankments of earth about 12 feet wide on top, and only a few inches above high-water mark. They are used as roadways. Temporary additions were required in the great flood of 1874, to prevent a general inundation. A perfect system of surveillance was employed. During the day the whole population was ordered out by the Khedive upon the levees, and at night lanterns upon poles were placed there at about one hundred yards distance from each other throughout the delta, so that the embankments were briliantly illuminated, while a chain of sentinels kept regular guard. Crevasses were thus prevented which, if allowed to occur, would have proved as disastrous as upon the Mississippi. Evidently some equally efficient plan of local police is essential for the security of our own alluvial region, which should include a comprehensive system of telegraphic communication.

Location.—Faulty location has been a fruitful source of wasteful extravagance from the beginning of the levee system to the present day. In its natural condition, the immediate bank of the river is higher than any of the alluvial land in rear, because it receives a larger amount of deposit in the annual overflows. The average amount of fall is about 7 feet in the first mile. Partly to take advantage of this fact in reducing to the minimum the necessary height of the levee, and partly to facilitate the shipment of crops, the line of embankment has always closely followed the river, thus opening the highest land to cultivation. If the banks of the river were permanent this location would be judicious, but unfortunately the continual caving has rendered the work of repairing the levee onerous and perpetual. A table in Chapter IV, obtained by Commissioner Hébert from the records of the State engineer of Louisiana, places this matter of faulty location in a strong light. It shows that in the eight years between October, 1866, and October, 1874, no less than 107.5 miles of levee caved into the Mississippi in that State alone, the total length of levee being about 800 miles. Clearly such a loss should find no place in a properly-considered plan of construction, and if tolerated with the increased heights of levees which have been shown to be essential to success, the system can never be made either secure or remunerative.

The great extent of the alluvial region induces such variations in physical conditions that no absolute rules for location can be laid down. The following principles, however, are immutable, and should never be neglected:

1st. Caving in general is due to the fact that the banks of the Mississippi contain strata of sand often lying below low-water mark. If the current in high stages impinges upon such a bank, it washes out these strata and thus undermines the mass above, which, as soon as the water falls, topples over by its own weight into the river. The caving, therefore, originates chiefly in the strong currents which mark the period of high water, while the actual sinking of the bank is usually deferred to the early part of the low stage. Any cause which tends to increase or to induce a change of direction of current must, therefore, augment caving.

Accordingly, we find that every great flood is sure to be followed, chiefly in the bends, by unusual caving; every cut-off makes a sensible increase in it for many years, both above and below its site; a wide range between high and low water mark, which necessarily implies a corresponding variation in velocity and direction of currents, is certain to be accompanied by rapidly caving or crumbling banks; finally, the levee-system, when perfected, cannot fail to augment this evil, although not probably to a serious extent. The following figures, derived from the tables in the chapters of Commissioners Hébert and Sickels, give an approximate idea of the annual caving as recently observed (chiefly in the worst bends) in the different parts of the alluvial region. Corresponding additions are made to the opposite points:

Below Bonnet Carré the annual caving is small, not averaging more than 13 feet, and rarely exceeding 25 feet; thence to the mouth of Red River, it averages about 40 feet, rarely exceeding 60 feet; thence to the Arkansas line, it averages 250 feet, rarely exceeding 300 feet; thence to Helena, it averages about 170 feet, and thence to the head of the alluvial region about 100 feet. The excessive caving indicated in the region between Napoleon and Grand Gulf is probably due to the four cut-offs which have occurred there in the last few years.

Although these figures show an alarming want of stability in the banks of the Mississippi, it must not be forgotten that the caving at any particular locality undergoes a secular change, beginning with the disturbing cause, attaining a maximum value, and finally diminishing as the impact of the current lessens or changes its point of application. Evidently no levee can be properly located where this subject has not received the most serious attention.

2. The form to be given to the high-water channel prepared for the river by the artificial embankments cannot be ignored. With the present heights of floods the volume which pours past the levee over the banks in front is small, but with the increased height to which it is certain the river, if successfully restrained to its bed, must rise, the matter is important. Moreover, the security of the levee itself demands that there shall be no sharp, salient angles exposed to the abrading force of the current. The general alignment of the levees must then be carefully considered, both to prevent any undue engorgement of the channel, and to secure the earthwork itself from being swept away.

3. The character of the back country must exercise a controlling influence on the location of the levee. When the bottom-lands are narrow the immediate bank of the river may be too valuable in comparison with the whole to be thrown out; but where an immense area will be opened to cultivation security is the chief consideration, and no risk of speedy destruction by caving should be incurred.

4. At certain points great expense might be requisite to construct the levees sufficiently far back to to promise reasonable security. To meet such cases it is recommended that experiments be tried to stop the caving by appliances and devices which have proved successful on smaller streams. Such works consist of wing-jetties, revetment by hurdles, brush, or stone, &c. Such works* will be absolutely necessary to prevent cut-offs, which are injurious in every way. The sudden change in the regimen of the river which is thus made increases the velocity of the currents and changes their directions so as to much aggravate the evils resulting from caving banks. Success in preventing caving will greatly simplify the problem of giving permanence to levees.

In districts where the caving is excessive a double system of embankments is the only proper solution of the problem. The main levee should be placed at such a distance from caving bends, present or threatening,

* A small pile-jetty, filled in with earth, once stopped a dangerous caving which threatened to carry Natchez-under-the-Hill into the river. Sufficient land was made below the jetty to ultimately overturn it up stream by the pressure thrown upon it when the river fell. The success of the brush and stone revetment near Saint Joseph, Missouri, is well known, but the cost was very great.

as economical considerations may demand, having reference to its relative cost and permanence. It should be constructed in the most substantial manner, and raised to the full height necessary to protect the country against the greatest known floods, a height which, as has been shown, must exceed by several feet the highest of existing levees. Although care should be taken to throw out no more front land than security demands, a considerable area will unavoidably be excluded. To utilize this land advantage should be taken of the fact that the great floods of the Mississippi are comparatively rare, not occurring oftener than once in four years, while the maximum floods do not occur oftener than once in ten years. For three years out of four, therefore, front levees, considerably lower than those at present existing, and following the bends of the river, would open the lands thrown out to limited cultivation in the middle and upper portions of the alluvial basin. Moreover, if the water were excluded from the swamps the river would usually fall soon enough to allow the outside crops to be raised, except in the sugar district, even in flood years.

The advantages of such a levee system are manifest: absolute security would be given to the back country at the minimum cost; three years out of four, crops could be raised throughout the upper portion of the alluvial region ; in flood years, the inhabitants, stock, and movable property on the lands thrown out, would find a secure retreat behind the guard-levees; ample water-way would be supplied for these great floods to pass off between the guard-levees without rising to the extreme height which would be attained if the river were shut more closely to its bed, and the destructive caving due to the increased flood velocity would thus be diminished. The deposit left on the lands thrown out would raise their level sufficiently to materially reduce the heights of the front levees, which unavoidable caving must require to be frequently replaced. This deposit would tend to overcome one of the greatest causes of expense attending the present system, viz, that every hoop made round a caving levee must be built on lower ground; so that the height, and consequently the cost, of levees is constantly increasing. Another advantage of the proposed plan would be that existing embankments would all be utilized, either as guard or front levees, and a return would thus be obtained for outlay already made, much of which would otherwise be lost. Some expense would be required to provide for rain-water drainage for the front lands, but a few carefully constructed culverts, provided with flood-gates, would usually serve all needful purposes.

It is, then, the opinion of this commission that the system of double levees should be adopted wherever applicable, and this would include a considerable area of the valley.

It may be added, that the idea of combining a railroad with the levee, located either on its top or along its side, according to the character of the subsoil, merits serious consideration. The railroad company would be the best possible guard for the levee, as it would be compelled to keep it always in repair. Branch roads would furnish ready transportation for crops from the interior. Finally, the levee, being put to a useful purpose, in addition to its usual passive work of protection, could be made and maintained at relatively less cost.

SURVEYS NEEDED.

The presentation just made of the various elements entering into the practical location of levees, shows that an accurate knowledge of the topography and hydrography of the alluvial region is a prerequisite to making it.

The great amount of essential work already accomplished, in gaining a correct knowledge of the physics and hydraulics of the Mississippi, has determined with reliability the whole history of the floods which subject the region to inundation. The sources from which the waters come, their seasons, periods, ranges, and combinations, have all been investigated, and there is no longer a question as to the height to which the levees must be built to restrain the river within such banks as we may give it.

Notwithstanding this, it is a fact that no continuous topographical and hydrographical survey of the Mississippi River throughout the region between Cape Girardeau, in Missouri, and New Orleans, has ever been made. The only good survey of any considerable portion of it was made under Captain (now General) Humphreys, in 1851, along the west bank of the Mississippi from Red River to Baton Rouge, and thence by both banks to New Orleans.

At this date the changes which have occurred require even this survey to be repeated. There was a reconnaissance map of the bends of the Mississippi, from its mouth up to the junction of the Kaskaskia River, Illinois, made by Lieutenant Ross, of the British army, in 1765, which, though comparatively rude, serves to show the general relations of the bends at that time. There was also a reconnaissance map of the bends of the Mississippi, from Saint Louis to New Orleans, made in 1821, by Captain Young, Captain Poussin, and Lieutenant Tuttle, United States Army, under direction of the board of engineers. The maps were not published, and are on file in the Engineer Department.

We have also the general features of the river as given by the United States land-surveys, which form the basis of existing maps, but these have little practical engineering value now. A few other surveys of localities have been made carefully, but are limited in extent. Lines of levels, for special purposes and for railroad-locations, have also been run in various directions across the alluvial basin, but they are not numerous enough nor sufficiently connected to answer other than general purposes.

The surveys of lines of levees, where built, are generally very partial, and do not furnish the data required for a thorough consideration of the levee question even in their special localities.

In our opinion, therefore, a thorough survey of the river Mississippi and its tributaries should be at once commenced, and be prosecuted as rapidly as practicable throughout the overflowed districts.

This survey should determine all matters relating to the river-beds, such as heights of the banks, the places where caving is taking place or otherwise, and the past history of such changes, as far as it can be made out. The depths at all points of interest should be determined by sounding. Level-lines must be run with greatest care, so as to determine the slopes of the water-surface and of the land, and the elevation of all high-water marks of which the record may still be preserved. Whereever difficulty will be found in disposing of rain-water drainage, the survey should be extended to cover all the country between the river-banks and the high lands, so as to give the extent and elevation of all high ridges and the depths and capacities of all natural water-courses. Borings in some localities will also be required, to determine the nature of the substrata. Wherever the surveys are carried, convenient permanent bench-marks should be established with greatest care, and legal enactments should protect them by severe penalties from being disturbed or removed. Above Memphis, on the Mississippi and along some of the tributaries in the alluvial region, questions of navigation are also to be considered, and the surveys should be made to meet the requirements of such cases.

A careful consideration of the extent and requirements of the survey shows that not less than two years will be occupied, under favorable circumstances, in performing the field-work, and that another year will be required to finish the office-work.

The practical operations on the levees themselves, to meet immediate wants, need not wait for the completion of the surveys. The direction of the surveys should be the same as that of the construction of the levees, and points where levees are most urgently wanted should be surveyed first. The most rapid prosecution of the field-work that is practicable should be made, and a number of fully-equipped parties should enter the field as soon as they can be properly organized.

For doing this work the following general estimate is presented, taken from detailed ones prepared to cover all the items of outfit, and subsistence and payment of employés:

For outfit of instruments, quarters-boats, small boats, and steam-launches....	$60, 000
Field and office work for 2 years, at $100,000....	200, 000
Office-work in third year....	40, 000
	300, 000.

To enter vigorously upon the work, therefore, would require an immediate appropriation of not less than $160,000.

LEVEE-ESTIMATES.

Two distinct estimates seem to be desirable: First. The number of cubic yards required to close the breaks in the existing system, with levees having the same cross-section as those now in their vicinity. Secondly. The number of cubic yards required to construct a permanent system for the reclamation of the alluvial region. Neither of these estimates can be made with any great exactness at present.

Existing system.—The number of cubic yards required to close the breaks actually existing when the examinations were made last summer, is known; but at many other points the levee is in danger of crumbling into the river, and before the repairs can be made more work will, doubtless, be required. Judging by the experience of the last eight years in Louisiana, the annual caving in that State alone will amount to about thirteen miles of expensive levees. Moreover, in making these temporary repairs it must not be forgotten that the present system, even if completed, is quite insufficient to protect the country in great floods. Extensive overflows are certain to occur about once in four years. Still, the raising of crops during ordinary high-water seasons depends upon the closing of these existing breaks; and, practically, they must be closed, or the country will be depopulated before a permanent system, which of necessity must be preceded by suitable surveys, can be constructed.

The full statements in Chapters II, III, and IV, convey all necessary details respecting these estimates. It is sufficient here to state that the gross amount required to close existing breaks, exclusive of the works now under construction, is:

Louisiana....	3, 198, 700 cubic yards;	cost, at 50 cents,	$1, 599, 350
Mississippi....	867, 000 cubic yards;	cost, at 30 cents,	260, 100
Arkansas....	3, 200, 000 cubic yards;	cost, at 40 cents,	1, 280, 000
Missouri....	800, 000 cubic yards;	cost, at 40 cents,	320, 000
Total....	8, 065, 700		3, 459, 450

Permanent system. — In estimating for the permanent system the heights already given, referred to the high-water level of 1858, have been adopted; but the want of proper surveys is severely felt in attempting to reduce them to heights above the ground. Moreover, it is quite impossible to decide how much of the existing levees can be utilized, and how much will only serve for local front levees. What increase in height will be caused by moving the location back sufficiently to secure reasonable permanency, cannot certainly be determined from data now at hand.

The method heretofore employed in such estimates has been to compute the contents of a levee having the requisite height and cross-section, and following, as do most of the existing embankments, the immediate banks of the river. This plan has been adopted by us in making the estimates for Louisiana, assuming that the high water of 1858 was four feet deep along this line. In Mississippi the actual line of levee has been adopted for the estimates, thus throwing out some bad bends. The high-water level of 1858 has been assumed at four feet above the ground. In Arkansas and Missouri the reconnaissance was sufficiently elaborate to give the present location, and the corresponding heights of the levee and of the flood-level of 1874, above the ground. By the use of the table of comparative flood-heights in Chapter I, the latter was reduced to that of 1858, and the estimates were thus made to give, correctly, the contents of a levee of proper height, situated upon the present site.

The form of cross-section adopted has been for levees of ten feet in height and under, the crown equal to the height, with slopes of 3 to 1 and 2 to 1. For heights greater than ten feet the crown has been taken at ten feet, with slopes of 3 to 1 on both sides. The computations are for finished embankments, with no allowance for settling.

We have not deducted the contents of existing levees from these estimates, partly because it is not known how far they can be utilized in the new embankments, and partly because a more retired location, although probably shortening the line, will necessarily increase its height, and thus call for increased cubical contents.

In fact it should be distinctly understood that until extended surveys have been made no really satisfactory estimates of quantities are possible. The following are offered only as approximations, designed to fix some limits for the probable cost. It will be noticed that no items are inserted for extending the system to the valleys of the tributary streams, (except incidentally, the south bank of Arkansas River,) for local front levees, for annual repairs, and for inspecting and guarding the system.

The estimated cost per yard given below is believed to be sufficient to build the levees by employing such mechanical appliances and manual labor as have heretofore been in general use. There is, however, every reason to believe that, with the adoption of a permanent system, such as we have recommended, the certainty which will attend the locations and payments, and the more thorough outfit which will be warranted by large contracts, will enable superior methods of construction to be adopted, and thus will cheapen the price.

Estimates for permanent system.

District.	Contents, cubic yards.	Cost at forty cents per cubic yard.
Saint Francis, bottom-lands	17, 265, 000	$6, 906, 000
White River, bottom-lands	4, 652, 000	1, 760, 800
Yazoo, bottom-lands	31, 188, 000	12, 575, 200
Tensas, bottom-lands	36, 690, 000	14, 676, 000
Louisiana, below Red River, right bank	15, 114, 000	6, 045, 600
Louisiana, below Baton Rouge, left bank	9, 865, 000	3, 946, 000
Total	114, 774, 000	45, 909, 600

The levees contemplated in these estimates are large, much larger than residents of the alluvial lands in general anticipate; but, in the language of General Humphrey's report of 1866, they "would not, when greatest, exceed in magnitude those on the right branch of the Rhine below Arnheim, which protect the most fertile part of Holland. These levees are exposed at high water to as strong a current as that of the Mississippi in flood, and also to the destructive effects of ice. But the occurrence of crevasses, such as take place with every great flood of the Mississippi, are there unknown. Should they happen, the ruin of a large part of the most productive portion of Holland would follow, as extensive tracts protected by the levees are lower than the surface of the sea, and their reclamation from overflow could only be effected by a drainage similar to that which has been applied to the lake of Harlem. The supervision, watching, and repair of these levees is costly, but effective and remunerative. The levees of the Mississippi, as now existing, are trifling compared to the interests they protect, and to the levees of the delta rivers of Europe—the Po, the Rhine, and the Vistula."

With a view to giving exact information as to the extent of the interests dependent upon the levee system at the present day, the commission has had prepared, by Mr. A. D. Banks, a summary statement of the areas of lands situated in the region in question, and under cultivation since 1840, with the corresponding crops. This paper is appended, marked C. It shows that vast interests are already at stake; but with a perfected system the figures will be largely increased. It is estimated that "the total area of the bottom-lands is about 32,000 square miles, of which a mere narrow strip along the main stream and its principal tributaries and bayous has been heretofore open to cultivation. Protected against the river and properly drained this would render available at least 2,500,000 acres of sugar-land, or more than double the amount heretofore planted; about 7,000,000 acres of the best cotton-land in the world, capable of yielding a bale to the acre; and not less than 1,000,000 acres of corn-land of unsurpassed and inexhaustible fertility."

PLAN RECOMMENDED.

In fine, then, in accordance with the terms of the law constituting this commission, we submit the following plan for protecting the alluvial region of the Mississippi River against overflow, premising that, in our judgment, no practical aid can be derived from any diversion of tributaries, or making of artificial reservoirs; that cut-offs are very pernicious; and that artificial outlets, although correct in theory, find no useful application to the Mississippi.

The plan to consist, first, in keeping open the Atchafalaya and the La Fourche, and, if borings shall show it to be safe, in re-opening the Plaquemine; second, in a general levee system extending from the head of the alluvial region to the Gulf, including the valleys of the tributary streams. The requisite laws to be enacted by the several riparian States to give the right of way; to confer the authority to make borrow-pits and bench-marks; to secure the levee from injury from cattle and hogs running at large, and to order out in times of danger, under suitable penalties for non-compliance, the population residing within a reasonable distance from the levees. The main lines of levee to be of sufficient height (as already computed) to restrain the floods, and of the requisite cross-section to resist the action of the water. Where reasonable security against caving requires large areas of front lands to be thrown out, protection against ordinary high waters is to be given by low front levees, closely following the bends. Suitable sluices and gates, in such cases, to be provided in the front and main levee for the rain-water drainage.

The essential conditions which must be considered in devising any proper system of levee administration for our great alluvial valley are the following: The country is divided into six natural drainage-districts: the Saint Francis bottom-lands, comprising the west bank of the river from Cape Girardeau to Helena; the White River bottom-lands, lying between Helena and the mouth of the Arkansas; the Tensas bottom-lands, extending from the Arkansas to Red River; the Yazoo bottom-lands, lying between the bluffs below Memphis and Vicksburgh on the east bank; Louisiana, below Red River, on the west bank; and Louisiana, below Baton Rouge, on the east bank.

Each of these districts, so far as the problem of protection is concerned, is a unit, and should have a responsible chief engineer, clothed with ample powers. He should be provided with necessary funds regularly supplied; be protected by careful legislation granting the right of way for the levees, and the necessary borrow-pits, with full immunity against local injunctions and other interference; in times of flood he should have the power, under prompt, adequate penalties, in case of refusal, to compel the personal attendance and assistance upon the levees of every able-bodied man resident within a reasonable distance of the same, whether such services are needed for guard duty or for repairs; and in turbulent districts he might even require an organized police, independent of the local authorities.

Although each drainage district would thus be under the full control of its chief for all internal matters, certain general relations, which cannot be ignored, exist between them all, and require mutual responsibility; such as the location of the levees on the opposite banks in such a manner as to avoid any local engorgement in floods; co-operation in collecting data, and establishing similar heights of levees in the same vicinity, &c. To secure these ends, a general board of commissioners, composed of a president and the several district chiefs, should have a permanent organization and stated times of meeting. This board should report to and submit its acts to the decision of the supreme authority from which it derives its legal existence, and to which all appeals against the acts of its individual members should be referred.

Without some such strong and simple organization, it is the deliberate opinion of this commission that the alluvial region can never be securely protected against overflow.

How this organization shall be constituted, whether by the General Government or by a mutual compact entered into by the several riparian States, and how its works shall be executed, whether by day-labor or by contract, or through the agency of a company, are matters distinct from the engineering problem, for the solution of which this commission is instructed to submit a plan. They fall within the especial province of legislative action.

To supply the data to carry this plan of protection into effect, the commissioners recommend that an elaborate survey, as above indicated, be made so soon as possible by the General Government.

Pending its completion, any funds that may become available for constructing levees should be applied to repairing such breaks in the existing system as expose large areas to overflow, due regard being had to avoid danger from caving.

It must, however, be distinctly understood that all existing levees upon the Mississippi are graded entirely too low, and that they are certain to be overflowed in any great flood, unless relieved by crevasses.

Whether the funds necessary to carry this system into operation shall be loaned or appropriated by the General Government, or be raised by general taxation in the States interested, or be supplied by the owners of the lands to be reclaimed, does not properly come within the province of this commission to recommend. We are, however, satisfied that in the present impoverished condition of the country, but little can be done, either by the States or by the landed proprietors, unaided by the General Government.

Very respectfully submitted.

G. K. WARREN,
Maj. Eng., Bvt. Maj. Gen. U. S. A., President of Commission;
HENRY L. ABBOT,
Major of Engineers, Brevet Brig. General U. S. Army;
W. H. H. BENYAURD,
Capt. of Engineers, Brevet Major U. S. Army;
JACKSON E. SICKELS,
P. O. HÉBERT,
Commissioners.

CHARLES M. FAUNTLEROY,
Secretary.

CHAPTER I.

ANALYSIS OF MISSISSIPPI FLOODS SUBSEQUENT TO THAT OF 1858.

BY COMMISSIONER HENRY L. ABBOT.

The data available—Flood of 1874—Flood of 1867—Flood of 1865—Flood of 1862—Proper height of levees.

The object of this chapter is to determine what may safely be adopted as the standard flood-volume in devising plans for protecting the alluvial region against overflow, and to deduce therefrom the proper heights for the levees.

DATA AVAILABLE.

The investigations and surveys conducted by General (then Captain) A. A. Humphreys, between the years 1850 and 1861, and fully elaborated in the report upon the physics and hydraulics of the Mississippi, (which constitutes professional paper No. 13 of the Corps of Engineers,) resulted in a definite solution of this problem. In that report the whole subject is thoroughly discussed, and the dimensions of the levees in all parts of the region are computed in detail from the data obtained by actual measurement in the flood of 1858. That flood was adopted as the standard, because a close comparative analysis of all other recorded floods, including that of 1859, proved that in no other would the maximum discharge have been in excess of what would then have occurred had the levees been able to restrain the river to its bed. Hence at the date of that report (1861) the probable difficulty and cost of a perfected system which should give to the plantations upon the banks of the Mississippi the same security that is enjoyed by the fields of Holland was established. The only point left for further investigation was whether the flood of 1858 had been correctly assumed as a standard, a point which time alone could certainly determine.

Since 1859 there have been but four great flood-years, 1862, 1865, 1867, and 1874, the others belonging to the class of ordinary high waters, in which the projected levees would have largely exceeded the requirements of the maximum volume. To decide, therefore, at the present time upon the proper dimensions of levees for the Mississippi, we have only to compare carefully those four great floods with that of 1858 to ascertain whether or not the water-marks and recorded facts indicate a maximum discharge at the head of the alluvial region, or just below the mouths of any of the lower tributaries, in excess of that which would have occurred in 1858 had all the water been confined to the channel from Cape Girardeau to the Gulf. If this question be decided in the negative the flood of 1858 remains a safe standard; if in the affirmative, the estimates in the physics and hydraulics of the Mississippi must be modified to allow for the increased volume to be apprehended.

The first point, then, for attention is the extent of the information which has been preserved respecting the four great floods in question.

When acting as assistant to General Humphreys upon the examination of the levees in the winter of 1865–'66 I made every effort to collect facts respecting the floods of 1862 and 1865. Sufficient high-water marks were found to indicate, with a good deal of precision, the level attained by each of those floods as compared with that of 1858 throughout the alluvial region. Through the kindness of Mr. Augustus V. Taylor, at Cairo, and of Mr. G. W. R. Bailey, at New Orleans, daily records of the stand of the river at those points in 1865 were received. Some meager information respecting the condition of the different tributaries during the two floods was also secured; but the war had distracted attention from river phenomena, and the lapse of time had rendered it impossible to collect as full data as could be desired, especially for the flood of 1862.

Before the flood of 1867 had subsided instructions were issued from the headquarters of the Corps of Engineers to Brevet Brigadier-General McAlester, at New Orleans, to Brevet Colonel Merrill, at Saint Louis, to Brevet Major Burroughs, at Nashville, and to Mr. W. Milnor Roberts, superintending engineer of Ohio River improvements, to collect all possible data respecting the overflow. Circular-letters were accordingly at once addressed to the different civil and military authorities, requesting facts. Many valuable letters were received in reply, and upon this material and a few other data received from Mr. S. Staats Taylor, at Cairo, and from Colonel Merrill, at Saint Louis, the following analysis of this flood is based:

For the flood of 1874, excellent records have been available. In accordance with the resolution of Congress, approved February 21, 1871, nineteen permanent water-gauges have been established, under the direction of the Chief of Engineers, upon the Mississippi River and its principal tributaries; the object being to secure such records as during high water shall be useful for the solution of the levee problem, and in ordinary and low stages shall benefit the steamboat interest. The work has been in charge of Major Merrill, Corps of Engineers, and the results are of great value, particularly as care has been observed to connect the new with the old bench-marks, and thus to secure exact comparisons with former floods. The widely extended system of meteorological observations, supplemented by river-records, taken under the direction of the Chief Signal-Officer of the Army, has also been of much assistance. Daily gauge-records at Rock Island, Ill., and Saint Paul, Minn., have been received from Colonel Macomb and Major Farquhar, Corps of Engineers, respectively. From Major Benyaurd, of the same corps, I have received full information respecting the freshets in Yazoo and Washita Rivers, and a very complete collection of newspaper extracts and personal notes respecting that great flood. Newspaper extracts of value have also been received from General M. Jeff. Thompson, of Louisiana, who also supplied me with an official list of the crevasses in Louisiana, with information respecting the height attained by the floods at various points. From Mr. William H. Bell, city surveyor, records showing the daily level of Lakes Pontchartrain and Borgne, and of the Mississippi River at New Orleans, have been received, with other valuable diagrams and data.

Information bearing upon the discussion has also been freely extracted from the reports of the other members of this commission, which constitute the remaining chapters of this report.

In order to convey a clear idea of the daily condition of the Lower Mississippi in these several floods, I have prepared accompanying Plate I, upon the same scale as that adopted in the report upon the physics and hydraulics of the Mississippi for illustrating the floods there discussed. The daily gauge records, and the notes respecting the several tributary streams, are also appended for future reference, marked D and E. Copies of the precipitation charts of the Signal Service United States Army for February, March, April, and May, 1874, are also added.

Before proceeding to the detailed discussion of the four floods, the following table is presented to exhibit their relative high-water marks, as compared with the floods of 1858 and 1859. It is properly a continuation of the flood-table on page 170, Physics and Hydraulics of the Mississippi. The sign + denotes that the flood in question exceeded the height attained in 1858; and the sign — that it fell short of that height. The numbers following the signs denote the difference in height of the two floods, expressed in feet. In comparing the high-water levels in these different floods, the fact must be borne in mind that five cut-offs have occurred during the period, viz, the American Bend cut-off, on April 15, 1858; the Napoleon cut-off, on April 11, 1863; the Terrapin Neck cut-off, early in March, 1866; the Davis cut-off at Palmyra Bend, on February 10, 1867, and the Council Bend cut-off, on May 10, 1874. Also, that Bayou Plaquemine was closed in 1865, thus adding about 6 inches to the normal flood-height at New Orleans.

Heights of recent floods compared with 1858.

Locality.	1858.	1859.		1862.		1865.		1867.		1874.	
	Date.	Diff.	Date.	Diff.	Date.	Diff.	Date.	Diff.	Date.	Diff.	Date.
		Feet.		*Feet.*		*Feet.*		*Feet.*		*Feet.*	
Saint Louis	June 15			−5.7	Apr. 26	{ −12.0	Apr. 1	−12.6	Feb. 21	−19.2	Apr. 24
						{ −10.3	July 28	− 8.7	May —	−18.7	June 20
Cairo, Ill.	June 21–22	−3.1	May 7	+1.2	May 2	− 1.6	Mar. 17–18	+ 0.9	Mar. 21	− 2.2	Apr. 26
Norfolk, opposite Island 1		−3.9		+0.9		− 2.1		+ 0.7		− 2.4	
Five miles above Osceola	June 17–23			−0.2	May 6			− 0.3	Mar. 20–24		
Memphis	June 23	−0.1	May 12–13	+0.5		− 0.6		+ 0.0	Mar. 26	− 0.3	May 1–3
Head of Cat Island				+0.7		− 0.2					
Foot of Cat Island		−0.3		+0.7		− 0.3					
Cut-off, May 10, 1874.											
Head of Walnut Bend		−2.0		+1.1		− 0.4					
Helena	July 2–6	−1.0	Mar. 22	+1.8		− 0.2		+ 1.2	Apr. 1	+ 1.2	May 11
Friar's Point		−0.6		+1.7		0.0		+ 1.7	Apr. 1–3	+ 2.3	
Wilkinson's Landing, Island 63		+0.1		+0.9		0.0					
Sunflower Landing, Island 66		+0.3		+0.8		− 0.7		+ 0.4	Mar. 15		
Cut-off, April 11, 1863.											
Six miles above Beulah	Apr. 1 and July 8.	0.0	Mar. 22	+1.4	May 4	+ 0.1	Apr. 12	− 0.4	Mar. 14		Apr. 30
Napoleon	Apr. 6–7	+0.3	Mar. —	+2.1	Apr. 20	+ 1.8		+ 1.3	Apr. 3	+ 2.0	
Ten miles below Napoleon										+ 1.6	
Luna, (bend above Greenville)										− 1.3	
Columbia, (bend above Greenville)										− 1.9	
Argyle Landing, Island 83								− 3.1		− 2.1	
Greenville				−1.4				− 4.3	Apr. 1		
Sunnyside, foot Island 84				−1.0				− 3.4		− 3.8	
Cut-off, April 15, 1858.											
Grand Lake Landing, Island 89								− 1.6		− 2.5	
Providence	Apr. 8	+0.8	Apr. 25–28			− 1.0					Mar. 20–23
Cut-off, March, 1866.											
Vicksburg	June 26–27	+1.3	r. 21–30	+2.2	Apr. 27	− 0.5		− 0.1		− 3.2	May 1–5
Cut-off, February 10, 1867.											
Natchez	June —	+1.2	May 2	+2.1				− 0.3		− 2.6	Apr. 20
Baton Rouge		+0.2	May 6	+1.3						+ 1.5	Apr. 16
Carrollton	May 10–12	+0.4	May 6	+0.8						+ 1.0	Apr. 16
Algiers		+0.2		+0.7							

In this connection, the attention of levee-engineers should be invited to the unfortunate fact that the local high-water marks of the flood of 1858 are rapidly disappearing. The highest water-level of that flood constituted the datum-plane to which all the computations for heights of projected levees were referred in the Mississippi survey of 1850–'61; and it is, therefore, a matter of primary importance that the actual local high-water level of that year shall be carefully preserved by permanent benches. To aid in approximately re-determining the marks when lost, as well as to compare the more recent floods with each other, the following table has been prepared for points where the marks of 1858 have disappeared. The arrangement is the same as the last, to which it is supplementary, the only difference being that for each locality, the letters B. M. indicate the flood whose high-water plane has been selected for comparison with the rest. It is greatly to be regretted that the loss of the flood-mark of 1858 prevents a consolidation of these two tables.

Indeed, as a preliminary to the systematic construction of levees throughout the alluvial region, a careful survey, including accurate lines of levels on both banks, frequently connected with each other, should be extended from the forts to Cape Girardeau, and permanent iron or stone benches should be established at short intervals, protected against injury by stringent legislation. As the survey advanced, every authentic high-water mark, and all exact data as to the rate of caving in the bends, would, of course, be noted and recorded for permanent reference hereafter. With such a survey as a basis, and with numerous water-gauges placed in connection with it, and observed daily, the work of properly constructing a grand system of levees might be undertaken with confidence. Without it, everything must be uncertain; some levees will be built too high, and others too low, in spite of the best efforts of the superintending engineer. Flood-levels are too varying and uncertain to serve as a proper datum for works of construction of this magnitude.

Comparison of recent floods—reference to 1858 lost.

Locality.	1862.		1865.		1867.		1874.	
	Diff.	Date.	Diff.	Date.	Diff.	Date.	Diff.	Date.
					Feet.		*Feet.*	
New Madrid	B. M.				-0. 7	Mar. 25-27	-2. 0	
Osceola	B. M.				-0. 3	April 1		
Cut-off, May 10, 1874.								
Yazoo Pass					B. M.		+0. 4	
Delta					B. M.		+0. 3	
Fort Penny, (opposite Friar's Point)	B. M.						+2. 0	
Australia Landing							(*)	(*)
Concordia	B. M.				-0. 6	March 28	(*)	(*)
One mile above White River	B. M.				-1. 7	March 30		
Turene	B. M.						(†)	(†)
Three miles below White River	B. M.				-0. 9	March 30		
Cut-off, April 11, 1863.								
Bolivar Bend, (Island 75)	B. M.		-0. 7				(†)	(†)
Cat Fish Point‡							+1. 8	
Island 82, (below Gaines Landing)	B. M.						-1. 0	
Choctaw Bend, (Island 83)	B. M.		-0. 5		-0. 8	March 20		
Egg's Point, (foot of American Bend Cut-off)							(*)	(*)
Hilliard Landing, (near Louisiana line)					B. M.		-1. 0	
Bunche's Bend	B. M.				-2. 1			
Skipwith's Landing	B. M.						-4. 0	
Wade's Landing, (Island 93)	B. M.				-1. 5	April 8		

Comparison of recent floods, &c.—Continued.

Locality.	1862.		1865.		1867.		1874.	
	Diff.	Date.	Diff.	Date.	Diff.	Date.	Diff.	Date.
					Feet.		*Feet.*	
Providence	B. M.				−1.6		−3.5	
Ben Lomond, (opposite Providence)	B. M.				−2.0		−5.0	
Hay's Point, (eight miles below Providence)	B. M.				−3.0		−4.5	
Cut-off, March, 1866.								
Mouth of Yazoo River	B. M.				0.0			
Island 104, (Diamond)	B. M.				−1.0			
Cut-off, February 10, 1867.								
Foot of Davis's Cut-off	B. M.				+1.0			
Hard Times	B. M.				+1.0			
Red River Landing			(§)	(§)	B. M.		+0.4	April 16
Morganza	B. M.						+1.1	April 16
Duvall's, (Island 124)	B. M.		−3.5					

* Below 1858 and subsequent floods. † Highest since 1857. ‡ Any flood since 1857. § Equal 1862.

FLOOD OF 1874.

As the records of this flood are more complete than of either of the others, it will be considered first.

The appended copies of the War Department monthly precipitation-charts for February, March, April, and May, reveal at a glance the meteorological conditions which caused the flood. In February, the rain-fall throughout the alluvial region was not unusual, and, as appears from Plate I, the river was generally about at mid-stage. In March, heavy rains prevailed throughout the lowlands below Cairo, thus filling the swamps and swamp-rivers, and rapidly raising the Mississippi itself. In April, these rains became excessive, and extended eastward over the valley of the Tennessee and Cumberland Rivers. The character of this deluge is well shown by the following tables, which fully account for the general overflow, and confirm the opinion, derived from the study of former floods, that the greatest inundations of the Lower Mississippi are caused by precipitation near the parent stream, and not among the distant mountains. The May map sufficiently explains the early subsidence of the river by showing that an unusual drought prevailed throughout the submerged district; thus permitting the rapid emptying of the swamps and consequent drainage of the cultivated lands.

The following monthly rain-records were furnished by the Signal-Service. The average precipitation at the same localities is quoted, for comparison, from the Physics and Hydraulics of the Mississippi:

Average precipitation.

Station.	Number of years observed.	Downfall of rain in inches.				
		Spring.	Summer.	Autumn.	Winter.	Year.
Memphis	3	11.0	7.8	7.9	15.0	41.8
New Orleans	24	11.1	16.6	11.8	12.0	51.5
Saint Louis Arsenal	19	12.8	13.8	8.8	6.2	41.6
Vicksburg	15	11.7	11.2	10.9	15.0	48.9

Rain-fall in inches, Lower Mississippi Valley.

Date, 1874.	Cairo, Ill.				Memphis, Tenn.				Vicksburg, Miss.				New Orleans, La			
	February.	March.	April.	May.	February.	March.	April.	May.	February.	March.	April.	May.	February.	March.	April.	May.
1									0. 18	0. 34			0. 08	0. 05	0. 68	
2									0. 08				1. 51			
3		0. 23		0. 08	0. 13			0. 07				0. 02				
4				0. 03				0. 03								
5		2. 06			0. 02	0. 05	0. 01		0. 63		0. 01		0. 10		1. 34	
6	0. 47	0. 79	0. 40		0. 27	2. 22	0. 01		0. 04	1. 23	0. 03		0. 85	0. 54		
7			0. 06				1. 00				2. 00			0. 19	0. 70	
8			1. 77				1. 65				4. 46				0. 73	
9			1. 85				1. 22				0. 39				0. 02	
10		0. 01				0. 14				0. 18						
11						0. 05				0. 91				0. 12		
12	0. 01															
13	2. 36		0. 64		0. 37		0. 04		0. 32		0. 03		0. 12		0. 08	
14			0. 77			0. 02					0. 01		0. 01	0. 62		
15		0. 17	0. 68	1. 12		0. 26	3. 60	0. 11		1. 95	4. 18	0. 06	0. 02	0. 23		
16		0. 03	0. 08							0. 78	0. 92	0. 03		0. 84	3. 84	
17	0. 14				0. 64				0. 19	0. 02	0. 05			0. 19	1. 80	
18		1. 36				0. 90	0. 11				1. 04				0. 10	
19	0. 01	0. 30	0. 95			0. 52	1. 52			0. 06	4. 45				1. 98	
20	0. 71		0. 01		0. 18	0. 45				1. 01			0. 01			0. 01
21	2. 12				0. 27	0. 53			0. 84	0. 11			0. 02			
22	0. 90		0. 15		0. 77		0. 86	0. 30	0. 59	0. 96	2. 89		0. 02			
23	0. 05		0. 21		0. 01					1. 05			0. 70	0. 40	0. 56	
24							0. 01		0. 55		1. 40		0. 09	0. 07	1. 75	
25	0. 02				0. 03				0. 05		0. 02		0. 15	0. 21	0. 04	
26		0. 02										0. 03		0. 72		
27		0. 98			0. 01											
28	0. 59			0. 21	1. 53		0. 13			0. 13	0. 36	0. 02		0. 94		0. 02
29				0. 07		0. 55				0. 49				1. 31		
30		0. 25		0. 04		0. 49		0. 02								
31		0. 48				0. 30		0. 10		0. 64				1. 14		1. 19
Total	7. 38	6. 68	7. 57	1. 55	4. 10	6. 61	10. 16	0. 63	3. 47	9. 86	22. 24	0. 16	3. 68	7. 57	13. 62	0. 22

Rain-fall in inches, valleys of tributary streams.

Date, 1874.	Saint Louis, Mo.				Louisville, Ky.				Shreveport, La.			
	February.	March.	April.	May.	February.	March.	April.	May.	February.	March.	April.	May.
1	0. 24	0. 02				0. 01	0. 05		0. 06	0. 24		
2				0. 05					0. 04			0. 03
3		0. 19		1. 84				0. 21				0. 01
4		0. 03		0. 55		0. 18		0. 09				
5		1. 01	0. 47			0. 35	0. 32		1. 90			
6	0. 02	0. 47	0. 25		0. 47	1. 71	0. 16		0. 03	1. 00		
7					0. 01	0. 10	0. 32				2. 18	
8			0. 08				0. 14				2. 00	
9							1. 09				0. 08	
10				0. 02						0. 80		
11				0. 06						0. 02		
12	0. 12			0. 05				0. 26				
13	1. 40		0. 09		2. 12		0. 04		0. 89		0. 85	
14			0. 06	0. 39			0. 75			0. 29	0. 09	
15		0. 07	0. 01	0. 09		0. 03	0. 84	0. 20		1. 02	1. 66	0. 02
16		0. 16	0. 37			0. 20	0. 08			0. 91	0. 11	
17		0. 01				0. 07	0. 03	0. 02	0. 25		0. 03	
18		0. 49			0. 03	0. 88					0. 12	
19	0. 02	0. 07	1. 83	0. 01		0. 28	1. 45			0. 60	0. 08	
20	0. 13	0. 01	0. 06	0. 20	0. 48		0. 13			1. 18		
21	1. 14				1. 31				0. 43	0. 49	0. 65	
22	0. 24		0. 10		0. 23		0. 03		2. 16	0. 06	1. 80	
23			0. 01		0. 41		0. 11	0. 39		1. 92	0. 41	
24							0. 07					
25					0. 10		0. 10					
26		0. 02			0. 02							0. 25
27		0. 07	0. 10			0. 65	0. 19		0. 78			
28	0. 35			0. 43		0. 10	0. 11		0. 50		0. 58	0. 59
29				0. 01						0. 52		0. 02
30		0. 90				0. 13						
31		0. 84				1. 95				0. 22		
Total	3. 66	4. 36	3. 43	3. 70	5. 18	6. 63	6. 01	1. 17	7. 04	9. 27	10. 64	0. 92

The following data respecting the downfall at Baton Rouge were communicated by Mr. Waller, who has done so much by his careful records to preserve the history of important meteorological and river facts: The total rain-fall in March, 1874, was 7.2 inches, and in April, 18.1 inches. During the night of the 15th and morning of the 16th of April, 7.9 inches fell. During the four and one-half days from April 15th to April 19th, the unprecedented amount of 15.4 inches fell; during the twenty-eight days from March 23d to April 19th, this quantity was 22.5 inches.

The following facts and tables convey correct information respecting the crevasses which were open in this great flood. They are derived from the reports of Commissioners Sickels, Benyaurd, and Hébert, which constitute the remaining chapters of this report.

In Missouri and Arkansas these breaks were so numerous that it is unnecessary to recapitulate them in detail here. Suffice it to say that, between Commerce, Mo., and New Madrid, there were 23.9 miles of crevasses and breaks; thence to Helena there were 68.2 miles; thence to Great Cypress Bayou, below Napoleon, there were 20.5 miles; and thence to the Louisiana line there were 23.9 miles.

The following tables exhibit the crevasses in the States of Mississippi and Louisiana in detail:

Yazoo bottom crevasses—flood of 1874.

Locality.	Date of discharge.		Maximum width.	Maximum depth at high water.	Remarks.
	Beginning.	Ceasing.			
			Feet.	*Feet.*	
Trotter's Point, opposite Helena.	May 10	....	760	12	Broke in evening.
Maynard, ½ mile above Friar's Point.	May 10	....	750	13	Broke at daybreak.
Miller, ¾ mile below Friar's Point.	May 10	....	150 800	20 8	Broke at sunrise.
Garth, 7 miles below Friar's Point	May 10	....	640	14	
McCloud, 12 miles below Friar's Point.	May 10	....	780	14	From McCloud's to Robinson's the river poured over tops of levees 6 to 7 feet high.
Beard, 13 miles below Friar's Point.	May 10	....	470	12	Do.
Hurlburt, 15 miles below Friar's Point.	May 10	....	600	14	Do.
Robson, 22 miles below Friar's Point.	May 10	....	1,820	15	Do.
Malone, opposite Island 66	May 10	....	600	16	
Bell Beulah, (old river)	Apr. 30	....	232	6	Do.
Cook, 4 miles above Bolivar Landing.	Mar. 20	....	1,360	5	
Bolivar Landing	Mar. 15	....	1,900	8	Kept at 300 feet wide for four weeks, then closed to 250 feet.
Connolly, Cat-fish Point..........	Apr. 28	....	700	20	Abandoned.
Utopia, Washington County	....	....	......	......	Small break.
Miller's, Washington County	....	....	......	......	Do.
Griffin, Washington County	....	....	......	......	Do.
Cammack, near Tallula..........	(*)	(*)	15,000	3	
Christmas, above Island 97	(†)	(†)	10,700	1	
Dumbarton, near Island 98	....	....	......	......	Small break.

* Open many years. † Open since the war.

Louisiana crevasses—flood of 1874.

Locality.	Parish.	Bank.	Date of discharge. Beginning.	Date of discharge. Ceasing.	Maximum width.	Depth at high water.	Remarks.
					Feet.	*Feet.*	
Ashton	Carroll	R.			14, 000	4	Has been running for several years.
Bass, Upper	....do	R.	Mar. 13		3, 310	4½	Two breaks.
Bass, Lower	....do	R.	Mar. 13		1, 100	4½	
Diamond Bend	Madison	R.			35, 000	—	Has been running for several years.
Point Pleasant, Upper.	Tensas	R.	Mar. 22		2, 000	½	Ten or twelve breaks.
Point Pleasant, Lower.	....do	R.	Apr. 16		620	4	Eleven breaks.
Buckridge	....do	R.			1, 200	4	
Hardtimes, Upper	....do	R.	Mar. 8		260	9	For nearly 3,000 feet water ran 2 feet deep over levee.
Hardtimes, Lower	....do	R.	Mar. 22		1, 400	9	
Disharoon	....do	R.	Mar. 25		3, 000	4	
Water-proof, Upper	....do	R.	Apr. 17		380	7	Hole in crevasse 40 feet deep and 160 feet wide.
Water-proof, Lower	....do	R.	Apr. 17		980	7	Hole in crevasse 40 or 50 feet deep and 900 feet wide.
Green's	Concordia	R.	Apr. 28				These crevasses, although broken, cannot be considered as discharges, because the water ran into the river from the rear.
Glasscock's	... do	R.	Apr. 28				
Lake side	Point Coupee	R.	Apr. 16		410	6	
Morganza	....do	R.	Apr. 16		1, 710	16	Front crevasse. Rear crevasse measured 4,730 feet.
Morrison's	....do	R.	Apr. 15		180	5	
Point Marrow	West Baton Rouge.	R.	Apr. 6		2, 630	5	Five breaks.
Hereford	....do	R.	Apr. —		835	4	Four breaks.
Lobdell's	....do	R.	Apr. —		280	4	
Hickey	....do	R.	Apr. 16		2, 500	8	
McCullum's	East Baton Rouge.	L.	Apr. 11	Apr. 26	705	6	Three breaks on front levee.
Sauve's	Iberville	R.	Apr. 16	Apr. 19	40	3	
Bonnet Carré	St. John	L.	Apr. 11		1, 670	52. 7	Average about 22.5 deep at high water, 1874.
Bellechasse	Plaquemine	R.	Apr. 17	Apr. 29	96	10½	
Greenwood	....do	L.	Apr. 7	Apr. 28	320	4	Two breaks.
Orange Grove	....do	L.	Apr. 8	Apr. 10	60	8	
St. Rosalie	....do	R.	Apr. 7	Apr. 10	70	2	
Bohemia	....do	L.			120	2	
Point à la Hache	....do	L.			170	2	

The condition of the great northern tributaries next claims attention. The Upper Mississippi and Missouri were both low, as is sufficiently shown by the gauge-record at Saint Louis, where the water remained, with slight oscillations, about 25 feet below the high-water level of 1844. In other words, the river at Saint Louis only attained a medium stage during the flood of 1874.

In the Ohio River, above Louisville, there were several successive rises, but nothing like a flood. At Cincinnati there were four principal rises, culminating, on January 11, at 14.6 feet; on February 26, at 18.3 feet; on April 13, at 18.6 feet; and on May 1, at 16.5 feet below the great flood of 1832. These were all of short duration, and the river rapidly subsided between them. At the head of the falls at Louisville, the gauge averaged about 10 feet during March, and 12 feet during April, 19 feet being the maximum reading. The great flood of 1832 read 40.76 feet on this gauge. At Paducah, however, the contributions of the Tennessee, the Cumberland, and the other lower tributaries, produced a considerable freshet, which culminated on April 25–26 at a point only

6.1 feet below the great flood of 1867. A previous rise had reached a level less by 4 feet on March 10, and the river had then subsided 15 feet.

The flood in the Tennessee River was excessive. At Florence it was divided into two rises, with a fall of 12 feet between them, the first culminating, on March 24, at 12.7 feet, and the second, on April 17, at 5.1 feet below the great flood of 1867. A 6-feet rise also occurred in the first week in March. By the middle of May the water had subsided 20 feet.

A great freshet also occurred in the Cumberland River; the highest point (estimated at 50 feet above low-water mark) was attained at Nashville, on April 17, a point 11.7 feet lower having been reached on March 25, with a fall of 26.9 feet between them. An earlier rise had culminated on February 24, only 1.4 feet below that in March.

The Cairo gauge-curve (see Plate I) shows to the eye the aggregate effect of these freshets at the entrance to the low country. This city is a particularly important locality in all floods, being situated so near the head of the alluvial region, that, when the source of supply is known, a relative estimate of the maximum discharge into that district may be formed from a judicious study of the gauge indications there; but, in this connection, it is well to call attention to the following facts, which were fully established by repeated observations upon the Mississippi, and which, paradoxical as some of them may appear, are in perfect accordance with the laws governing flowing water. (See page 324, Physics and Hydraulics of the Mississippi.)

1. For any given level there is much more water passing when the river is rising than when it is falling.

2. At any given gauge-reading there is usually more water passing in a long and rapid than in a short and slow rise, but this is not always the case, the discharge being governed by the relative stage of the water in the channel above and below.

3. The maximum discharge, in any normal rise, occurs when the has reached a point a few inches below the highest point attained.

4. If, when a freshet has culminated, and the water either comes to a stand or begins to fall, a second rise occurs, it will cause the surface to rise considerably higher than would have been the case had the same volume passed without a previous diminution of supply. For instance, in the flood of 1851 the Mississippi, at Red River Landing, attained a certain stage, with a measured discharge of 1,200,000 cubic feet per second. It had ceased to rise and was just ready to begin to fall, with a discharge reduced to 1,160,000 feet, when the volume again increased to 1,200,000 cubic feet, raising the water-level to a point *two feet higher than before.* This was no isolated case, but was in strict accordance with general river-laws, as is fully explained on page 363, Physics and Hydraulics of the Mississippi.

It is therefore carefully to be borne in mind that the maximum discharges of two floods are by no means necessarily proportional to the relative water-levels attained in them. Under some circumstances the lesser discharge may cause the higher water-mark. These principles being understood, the facts connected with the flood of 1874 at Cairo will be considered.

A glance at Plate I makes it apparent that, neither in maximum volume nor in duration, was this flood comparable with that of 1858. It consisted of two rises—one culminating on March 11, and the other on April 26, with a fall of 10.7 feet between them. The first rise shows by its broken crest that its greatast height, 6.1 feet below high water of 1858, exceeded by several inches that due to the same volume had it been delivered without a check in the supply. The second swell rose uniformly, 14 feet in 18 days, to the highest points attained, (2.7 feet below high-water of 1858.) After remaining within 3 feet of this level for 20 days, the river declined very rapidly to a low stage.

Comparing these facts with those noted in 1858—when the daily discharge was accurately measured—and remembering that the Upper Mississippi being low in 1874, no water worth considering could have entered the Saint Francis bottom-lands between Cape Girardeau and Cairo, we are able to decide with tolerable precision that the maximum volume discharged into the head of the alluvial region, in the latter overflow, was about 1,225,000 cubic feet per second, as compared with 1,475,000 cubic feet in 1858—difference, say, 250,000 cubic feet.

Clearly, then, a judicious levee system, based on the flood of 1858, would hardly have been tested in 1874 at any point above the mouth of the first tributary below the Ohio. This tributary is the Saint Francis River, entering ten miles above Helena. Unfortunately, in 1874 the conditions determining the high-water mark at this locality were not a little intricate.

First of all, the cut-off at Council Bend, situated a few miles above, must be considered. It occurred on May 10, 1874. On May 19, Mr. J. B. Miles, gauge-observer at Helena, under instructions from Colonel Merrill, proceeded up the river to learn the facts concerning it. He reports as follows: It began to make at 10 a. m., and in a few hours the entire river passed through the new channel, the current round the bend almost ceasing. At Dr. Peters's plantation, just below the cut-off, the river rose 6 inches, and then began to fall, as it also did at Helena on the morning of May 11. At Commerce, one mile above the cut-off, the people reported that the river fell 24 inches in twenty-four hours. A few miles higher, a fall of 15 inches on May 11 was reported. At twenty-five miles above the cut-off this fall was 8 inches, and at President's Island, nine miles below Memphis, 4 inches. The river was about at a stand when the cut-off occurred, and the shortening did not exceed twelve miles.

The normal effect of a cut-off has been well established to be the following: The water-level is raised just below it by an amount equal to half the fall of the river, in a straight portion equal in length to the shortening of the channel, and is lowered just above it by an equal amount, plus the fall required to overcome the resistance due to the curvature of the bend. The following computation is based on data furnished in the Physics and Hydraulics of the Mississippi.

The fall per mile in a straight portion of the river between Memphis and Helena was, in this flood, 0.24 foot, which, in twelve miles, amounts to 2.88 feet. For the resistance due to the curvature, we have:

$$\frac{v^2 \sin^2 a}{134} = \frac{36 \times 3.0}{134} = 0.8 \text{ foot.}$$

Hence the lowering above the cut-off should equal, $\frac{2.88}{2} + 0.8 = 2.24$ feet or 27 inches.

And the raising below should equal $\frac{2.88}{2} = 1.44$ feet or 17 inches.

The former accords well with the reported fall, viz, 24 inches, but the latter indicates a discrepancy of $17 - 6 = 11$ inches, for which an explanation should be sought. It will be found in the following facts.

Although the levees along the Saint Francis front were in a worse condition in 1874 than in 1858, the crest of the wave sweeping past Cairo was so much lower that it lost far less into the swamps. But the extraordinary rain-fall during March and April, amounting at Memphis to 16.77 inches, or more than double the usual quantity, had already filled them; and the volume returned through the Saint Francis River and over the banks in the vicinity is reported as immense. The levees below at first resisted better than usual, and, until the morning of May 10, no crevasses had occurred within 25 miles of Helena. On this day, however, nine broke into the Yazoo bottom, and, two days later, another on the right bank, near Fort Penny, opposite Friar's Point. The effect of these breaks was not only to check the rise due to the cut-off at and below its site, but even to produce a sudden and anomalous fall in the river, which, at Friar's Point, amounted to ten inches. It is more than probable from the coincidence in dates that the incipient rise occasioned by the cut-off was an important cause of the general and sudden destruction of the levees; but it should be noted that two of the breaks had already occurred a few hours before.

What, then, must be decided respecting the relative high-water discharges in 1858 and 1874, at Helena? The latter flood actually rose 1.2 feet higher, but it is certain that the normal discharge was much less. In 1858 the Yazoo Pass and other immense crevasses in the vicinity were open when the great rise occurred, and accurate measurement established that, in consequence of the increased local slope due to these outlets, the volume actually passing Helena failed to attain its normal height by 3.2 feet. The statement of Mr. Miles—confirmed by the gauge-records at Memphis and Helena—that the river was about at a stand on May 10, when the cut-off and crevasses occurred, would indicate that the high-water mark of 1874 was not sensibly affected thereby. But the gauge-record at Helena shows that the river nearly came to a stand after the real crest of the flood-wave passed, and again began to rise rapidly a few days later, as the discharge poured from the swamps. Judging by the measured effect of the similar occurrence at Red River Landing in 1851, already mentioned, this would indicate that the actual height attained was not less than a couple of feet in excess of that due to the discharge. Hence, all the facts lead to the belief that the actual maximum discharge in the two years was 1,334,000 cubic feet per second for 1858, and say 1,160,000 cubic feet for 1874; difference, 174,000 cubic feet.

This result implies that the mingled rain and returning Mississippi water received from the Saint Francis bottom-lands just above Helena, at the date of high water there, more nearly than usual equaled the loss from crevasses and channel-filling experienced by the crest of the wave after passing Cairo; and hence, that these swamps hardly served as a reservoir during the flood, but simply delayed the date of high water at Helena about two weeks. This is perfectly consistent with all the recorded facts: that the crevasse loss was small; that the rise at Cairo was unusually prolonged; that the swamps were so full of rain-water as alone to raise the Saint Francis over its banks; and lastly, that the volume poured into the Mississippi at high water was enormous. The rain-water alone, thus contributed to the flood, may safely be estimated at 60,000 cubic feet, or double that received in 1858.

If the river had been confined to its bed by levees, the maximum discharge would have been much more reduced by channel-filling, between Cairo and Helena, than was actually the case; and the anomalous rise from the interference with normal changes of slope at Helena would not have occurred. Levees constructed to restrain the flood of 1858 must, then, have been largely in excess of the requirements in 1874, at least as far down as the mouth of the Arkansas.

Below Helena the occurrence of so many cut-offs between 1858 and 1874, and the lack of exact data respecting the discharge of the numerous and immense crevasses in the latter year, render any close analysis of the actual high-water marks too much a matter of speculation to merit confidence. Fortunately, however, the condition of the several tributaries is known from daily gauge-records, kept above the influence of back-water from the Mississippi; and it is therefore quite possible to submit the flood to a discussion which will reveal what its maximum discharge would have been, as compared with that of 1858, had no crevasses occurred in either year; and hence what would have been the relative strain upon a perfected levee system, based upon the flood of 1858 as a standard. Neglecting, then, for the present, the actual overflow, the conditions which would have presented themselves if the river had been confined to its bed in 1874 will be considered.

The floods of 1858 and 1874 were of essentially different character, both in respect to origin and local results. In 1858 an immense wave entered the head of the alluvial region, but received on its passage only small contributions from the lower tributaries. It deeply flooded the Yazoo bottom-lands, but comparatively spared the Tensas and Atchafalaya basins. In 1874 the volume entering the low lands was greatly smaller; but on its passage it was largely re-enforced by freshets from all of the lower tributaries. Moreover, it spared the Yazoo district, and worked ruin in the Tensas and Atchafalaya regions. Each flood was a good standard of a distinctive class of overflows, and levees sufficient to restrain both would afford all reasonable protection to the country.

The gauge records show that, in 1874, the date of maximum discharge with perfected levees would have fallen between April 20 and May 10; and that the wave from the Ohio would probably have encountered the maximum contributions of the year from most of the lower tributaries. In other words, there would have been an unusual and most dangerous coincidence in floods throughout the entire alluvial region. The first step is to decide what these several contributions would have been from the daily gauge-records and notes contained in the appendices, and from the known capacity of the rivers, as set forth in the Physics and Hydraulics of the Mississippi.

There was no great flood—properly speaking—in the Arkansas in 1874. The highest rise of the season occurred at Little Rock on April 25, being then reported as 8 feet below the high-water level of 1857, which, itself, was considerably below that in the latter part of March, 1858, when the river stood 5 feet below its highest recorded stand, (1833,) 3 feet below the great flood-mark of 1844, and 1 foot above that of 1867.

In White River there was a destructive overflow. The stream rose rapidly at Jacksonport in the latter part of February, and remained fluctuating at a high stage until, on April 23, it culminated 1.78 feet below high water of 1867. It then fell slowly to low-water mark. The flood of 1858 in this river was probably at least equal to that of 1874; as it attained at Des Arc, on April 10, a point only 1 foot below the great inundation of 1844. The want of exact comparative marks, however, is much to be regretted.

Now, the combined flood-discharge of these two rivers in 1858 was actually measured, and found to be 160,000 cubic feet per second. In 1874 the above facts show that it must have been decidedly less, and its contributions to the supposed flood-wave, with levees perfected, will accordingly be assumed at 130,000 cubic feet per second.

The Yazoo River is next to be considered. Fortunately, Major Benyaurd succeeded in collecting valuable and accurate information respecting it, which is given in full in Appendix A. There was a great freshet in 1874, the largest on record, due to rain-water alone. It culminated at Greenwood on April 22, at 0.2 feet above the high-water mark of 1867, when the Yazoo Pass was open, and the Mississippi was contributing a large volume to the discharge.

The following considerations lead to an approximate estimate of the maximum rain-water contributions of this tributary in 1874:

An inspection of plate 1 will show that while the Mississippi remained after March 20 sensibly at a stand at Lake Providence, it rose gradually at Vicksburg 3 feet, culminating on May 1–5. It then began slowly to fall, and had declined over a foot before May 21, when the Mississippi gauges above began to indicate a marked reduction of discharge in the channel. But the crevasse-water, flowing through the swamps to the Yazoo River, steadily increased in volume during this period, both from the formation of new and the enlarging of old breaks, (see list of crevasses.) Evidently, then, the *increase* of Yazoo rain-water discharge, during the freshet of that river, must have raised the Mississippi in full flood at Vicksburg 1.5 feet, which would indicate its volume as about 50,000 cubic feet, or, adding the usual rain-water drainage, say 90,000 cubic feet, per second, of rain-water, quite independent of any returning crevasse-water, at the top of the Yazoo freshet. What the crevasse-water was, may be thus inferred. The combined rain and crevasse discharge from the Yazoo, which raised the Mississippi, at Vicksburg, 3 feet during the last three weeks of April, must, at its maximum, have equaled 110,000 cubic feet per second. Hence 110,000 – 90,000 = 20,000 cubic feet per second, came from the crevasses on May 1, and this volume increased gradually for many days thereafter.

These figures, although to a certain extent speculative, accord perfectly with the following facts, and therefore merit confidence: In 1858 the contribution of the Yazoo River at the top of the Mississippi flood was accurately measured, and it proved to be 129,000 cubic feet per second, of which only 30,000 cubic feet was rain-water. The maximum rain-water discharge of the Yazoo River in its great April rise of 1858 was measured, and was 70,000 cubic feet. The rain-fall at Vicksburg in 1874 was, in March, 9.86 inches; and in April 22.24 inches—amply sufficient to account for so enormous a rain-water discharge from the Yazoo, which more than once before has, unsuspected, worked ruin upon the country below.

We must, then, admit that the crest of the flood-wave, with perfected levees, would have received 90,000 cubic feet per second from this tributary.

The Red River next claims attention. The daily gauge-records at Shreveport, Alexandria, Camden, and Trinity, in Appendix E, supply exact information, and prove that this tributary played a chief part in the flood in Lower Louisiana.

At Shreveport, the river began rising in January, attained a high stage in the latter part of March, culminated on April 29 to May 1, at a level only 2.8 feet below high-water mark, (flood of 1849,) and then soon declined.

At Alexandria the river rose steadily 23.4 feet between February 1 and April 4, thus attaining a very high stage, which continued, with slight oscillations, until May 12, when the water rapidly subsided. The highest stand was on May 8–10, but it did not vary more than 2 feet from this level for fifty days. The highest mark was 1.6 feet below that in 1866; but, unfortunately, the relative stand, as compared with the great floods of 1849, 1851, and 1858, is not reported.

In the Washita, the greatest flood on record occurred. The river at Camden was very high during the whole of March, and reached its highest point on April 19, after which it rapidly subsided.

These facts show that there was a coincidence in the floods, although probably not in the maximum discharges, of the Red and Washita Rivers in 1874, and that their united contribution to the great flood-wave from the Ohio would have been very formidable had the levees been perfected. The data at hand do not justify a direct estimate of this volume in cubic feet, but the following known facts give an approximation. In 1851, the united maximum discharge of these rivers and their tributaries, accurately measured, was 220,000 cubic feet per second, and in 1858 it was 180,000 cubic feet per second, no crevasse-water in either case being included. These floods were the second and third, in height, on record; and the fact that in 1874 the Red River plantations above the influence of the Mississippi were not much damaged, does not indicate that the maximum discharge, even allowing for a greater volume from the Washita, exceeded, if indeed it equaled, the smaller of the two. However, to avoid underrating the difficulties to be overcome, it will be assumed as equal; that is, as 180,000 cubic feet per second.

Respecting the outlet bayous the following facts have been collected: An official report of a commission of engineers to the governor of Louisiana, in 1872, states that no material difference, either in depth or width, has occurred in the Atchafalaya in the past 22 years. This result was reached by a comparison of actual surveys, which, repeated by the commission in 1873, led to the same conclusion, except that a very gradual abrasion of the channel and bank near the upper mouth was noted. These measurements, confirming the results obtained in 1851 and 1859 by the Mississippi survey, show that the discharge of the Atchafalaya at any given stand now may safely be estimated upon the same basis as in 1858.

Bayou Plaquemine was closed in the autumn of 1865, thus increasing the flood-discharge of the Mississippi below its mouth 35,000 cubic feet per second. Mr. G. W. R. Bayley states that this was necessary on account of the rapid cutting in holes of the blue-clay layer which protects a deep sand stratum in the bed of the bayou, thus threatening an enormous enlargement of its capacity, and the consequent submergence of an extensive district.

Bayou La Fourche remains unchanged in capacity as a relieving outlet of the Mississippi.

The following table, based upon the foregoing data, gives a comparative idea of the maximum volume which a perfected levee system would have confined to the channel of the river, throughout the alluvial region, in the floods of 1858 and 1874. The same allowance for channel-filling is made for both floods, as the absolute oscillation upon which this depends would probably have been equal in the two years. Although not claiming numerically the accuracy of similar tables in the Physics and Hydraulics of the Mississippi, these figures are based upon well-established facts, and the general conclusions to which they point can hardly be doubted.

Flood of 1874 compared with that of 1858.

Locality.	Actual maximum discharge per second.			Maximum discharge per second with levees perfected.		
	Flood of 1858.	Flood of 1874.	Difference.	Flood of 1858.	Flood of 1874.	Difference.
	Cubic feet.	*Cubic feet.*	*Cubic feet.*	*Cubic feet.*	*Cubic feet.*	*Cubic feet.*
Head of alluvial region	1, 478, 000	1, 225, 000	+253, 000	1, 478, 000	1, 225, 000	+253, 000
Helena	1, 334, 000	1, 160, 000	+174, 000	1, 369, 000	1, 145, 000	+224, 000
Napoleon	1, 221, 000			1, 418, 000	1, 265, 000	+153, 000
Vicksburg	1, 245, 000	1, 125, 000	+120, 000	1, 430, 000	1, 340, 000	+ 90, 000
Red River Landing	1, 238, 000			1, 338, 000	1, 395, 000	– 57, 000
Baton Rouge	1, 238, 000			1, 338, 000	1, 395, 000	– 57, 000
Donaldsonville	1, 197, 000			1, 328, 000	1, 385, 000	– 57, 000
Carrollton	1, 188, 000			1, 328, 000	1, 385, 000	– 57, 000

The table explains itself. It is evident that levees sufficient to restrain the flood of 1858 would have been ample to protect the country in 1874, nearly as far down as the mouth of Red River. Here and below they would probably have failed, and crevasses would have relieved the channel. Another fact, moreover, must not be forgotten. The maximum discharge, with levees perfected, in 1858, at Donaldsonville and Carrollton, has been increased 31,000 cubic feet above the estimates and computations of the Physics and Hydraulics of the Mississippi, which were based on the supposition that Bayou Plaquemine would be kept open. Its closure, which has been allowed for in the foregoing table, has increased the flood-discharge below its mouth 35,000 cubic feet per second, a serious matter, involving an increase in the height of the levees throughout the whole region, amounting to 6 inches at New Orleans.

Having thus obtained a proper understanding of the formidable nature of the flood of 1874, it only remains to consider the phenomena actually presented below Helena.

As already stated, the levees in Tunica County, Mississippi, resisted the flood, and those in Coahoma County broke so late that only local damage resulted. Bolivar County, less fortunate, suffered severely from a rise in Arkansas and White Rivers in March, but by drawing off the surplus water from the Mississippi it aided in the saving of the rest of the Yazoo front; the Sunflower Valley was flooded from these breaks. As usual, the White River swamps and Desha and Chicot Counties, Arkansas, were deeply flooded.

The gauge at Vicksburg shows that the actual volume which reached the mouth of Yazoo River by the bed of the Mississippi did not probably at any time exceed 1,000,000 cubic feet per second.

The channel-filling in this part of the valley is very small as compared with that above. Hence, it is evident that the amount discharged by crevasses below Helena and above Vicksburg must have nearly equaled 1,160,000+130,000−1,000,000=290,000 cubic feet per second. The greater part of this volume, which is about double the flood-discharge of the Connecticut River, passed through the crevasses in Carroll Parish, La., and over the Arkansas line into the Tensas bottom-lands already well filled by rain. Re-enforced by dangerous additions from the crevasses below Vicksburg, it encountered near Trinity an extraordinary flood from the Washita, exceeding that of 1828, and thence poured onward in a huge wave to meet the flood of the Red River at and near the mouth of the Black. What the result would have been cannot for a moment be doubtful, even if the levees of Lower Louisiana had been intact, but they had already succumbed. The sea of water poured unresisted into Grand Lake, through and near Bayou Atchafalaya, and through the Morganza, Hickey, and other smaller crevasses; into Lake Pontchartrain through the great Bonnet Carre crevasse, and into the La Fourche basin and Saint Bernard Parish through the breaks below New Orleans.

The immediate cause of the great Morganza and Hickey crevasses—the most destructive of the year—was unusual. The March rise of the Ohio had found all the lower tributaries swollen by local rains, and under their combined influence the rise at Red River Landing was rapid. By April 15 the river then had attained a very high stage, when a wide-spread and extended rain-storm occurred. The downfall at Memphis on April 15 was 3.6 inches; at Vicksburgh on the 15th and 16th it was 5.1 inches; at Baton Rouge on the 15th and 16th it was 7.9 inches, and at New Orleans on the 16th and 17th it was 5.6 inches. In consequence of this storm the Mississippi at Red River Landing rose 6 inches in twenty-four hours, and immediately the Point Coupee levees gave way. The sudden fall which ensued at points below was scarcely less unusual, and is well shown by the curves on Plate I.

The almost tropical rain storms which occur occasionally on the Mississippi have more direct influence than is generally supposed upon its local level. An instance of the kind came under the personal observation of the writer, at Friar's Point, on March 13, 1866. There was a furious tempest at 4 p. m., followed during the night by a literal deluge. At 9 a. m., on March 13, the river stood 5.20 feet below high water of 1865, having fallen 0.10 foot in the preceding twelve hours. At 9 a. m. of March 14 it stood 5.00 feet below the same bench-mark, after having fallen nearly an inch since daylight. No wind affected these readings; and it is evident that the rain which fell on the water-surface temporarily raised the local level 4 or 5 inches. Happening at very high water, such a rise might well prove disastrous, as, indeed, the above facts show was the case in 1874 below Red River Landing.

The overflow of the Atchafalaya basin was extreme in this flood. Bayou Teche was deeply inundated from Saint Martinsville down. At Brashear City, on Berwick's Bay, on April 19, the streets became impassable. The water continued to rise, gaining 11 inches in the forty-eight hours ending April 25, thus reaching a point 4.2 feet above its ordinary stand. On May 2 it was reported as only 1.6 feet below the flood-mark of 1867, and it rose 0.5 foot after that date. This elevation, although 2.1 feet below the high-water mark of 1828, was extraordinary for a flood of so short duration. In 1850, when the numerous crevasses continued actively discharging for more than four months, the water at Brashear City rose only to a point about 3 feet below the level attained in 1828.

The records of the city surveys of New Orleans, kept at Magnolia street, on the new canal, show that the effect of the Bonnet Carre crevasse was to raise Lake Pontchartrain, suddenly, about 2 feet, beginning on April 17, and to keep it at this increased level for about ten days, when it rapidly subsided nearly to its accustomed height. The crevasse at the same place in 1871 produced a similar effect.

Evidently the facts recorded as to the overflow in 1874 corroborate the inferences derived from the foregoing analysis.

The following discussion of the floods of 1862, 1865, and 1867 is largely taken from a report addressed by me to the Chief of Engineers in 1869, and published in Senate Miscellaneous Document No. 8, Forty-first Congress, first session:

FLOOD OF 1867.

In some respects its origin was peculiar. The winter of 1866–'67 was marked, throughout the southern portion of the Ohio Valley, by an unusual downfall of snow and rain; while in the region drained by the Upper Mississippi and Lower Missouri the season was remarkably dry. A sudden thaw with warm rains in February caused moderate floods in the Alleghany and Monongahela Rivers, and in the smaller tributaries of the Ohio heading near the main stream; and a great flood, second only to the flood of 1858, in the Wabash. The combined effect of those freshets was to cause a very sudden rise in the Ohio, which culminated at Louisville on February 22, where it was only 8 feet below the high water of 1832; and at Caseyville, below the mouth of the Wabash, on March 1, where it was half a foot above the high water of 1832, the greatest of the recorded floods at that locality.

The same climatic influences extended over the valleys of the Illinois River and other southeastern tributaries of the Upper Mississippi, producing a moderate freshet in the Mississippi at Saint Louis. The rise there began on February 13, the river being 25.5 feet below the city directrix; it culminated on February 21, at 9.3 feet below this bench. After remaining four days sensibly at a stand the river gradually subsided, until on March 21 it was 21 feet below the directrix. The freshet at Saint Louis was by no means a large one, being 16.9 feet below the high water of 1844, and 12.6 feet below that of 1858; still, it is evident that it almost exactly combined at Cairo with the February rise in the Ohio, and thus did its maximum of injury to the alluvial regions. The downfall at Saint Louis was 2.3 inches in January, 4.8 inches in February, and 2.4 inches in March, showing a slight indication of the great February rains, but none whatever of those in March.

Such was the condition of the rivers when, in March, a wide-spread series of furious rain-storms occurred. The belt containing them extended from the head-waters of the Washita and White Rivers of Arkansas eastward across the States of Arkansas, Missouri, Kentucky, Tennessee, western North Carolina, and western Virginia; but it was in the mountain region, where heads the Tennessee River, that the greatest deluge occurred. The downfall here was entirely beyond precedent, raising the Tennessee River at Chattanooga, on March 11, 53 feet above low water, or 15.5 feet above any known water-mark. With the Cumberland, the Kentucky, the Green, and, indeed, all the lower southern tributaries discharging full floods into the Ohio before the February rise had had time to pass away, this sudden Tennessee River flood raised the Lower Ohio to the highest stand ever attained. Fortunately the immense wave found the Mississippi burdened only with the previous rise, the Upper Mississippi, the Missouri, and the Arkansas all being low. The Washita, White, Saint Francis, and Yazoo Rivers were swollen from the same rains, but probably not sufficiently to produce much effect upon the great wave from the Ohio, which arrived rather too late to coincide with their freshets. This flood in the Ohio was no less remarkable for duration than for extreme height—matters of equal importance in effecting a flood in an immense channel like that of the Lower Mississippi. For thirty-two consecutive days, at Cincinnati, (February 16 to March 19,) the mean channel-depth was 51.3 feet, the greatest being 55.8 feet and 57.3 feet, on February 22 and March 14 and 15, respectively, and the least being 44.6 feet, on March 2 and 3. So long a continuance at this stage is beyond precedent.

In order to facilitate the comparison of this flood with that of 1858, I have prepared the curves shown on Plate I. It is much to be regretted that no daily records for the lower river are available.

At Cairo, on February 1, the river was at an ordinary low-water stage, the water-surface reading 3.9 feet on the gauge of the Cairo City Company. On the morning of the 2d it had begun to rise rapidly. The February freshets in the Upper Ohio culminated at Louisville on February 22, being eight feet below high water of 1832; that in the Wabash at Vincennes on the same date rising half a foot above all known water-marks, and that in the Mississippi at Saint Louis on February 21–25 being 12.6 feet below high water of 1858. The combined effects of these floods arrived at Cairo on March 1, bringing the river to a stand at about the level of the high water of 1858, (0.2 foot above that level at the foot of Twentieth street, and 0.3 foot below it near the junction of the two rivers.) This rise of 36.7 feet in 28 days was unprecedented. The river then gradually declined until, on March 8, it had fallen 0.9 foot: it then again slowly swelled until, on March 21, it reached its highest stand, 1.4 feet above high water of 1858 and 0.1 foot above high water of 1862, at the foot of Twentieth street, and 0.9 above the high water of 1858, and 0.3 foot below the high water of 1862, near the junction of the two rivers. These discrepancies in flood-level must always be expected at Cairo, unless the water-surface is taken at the *junction* of the two rivers. Thus, Mr. Hely, city engineer, reports that on March 18, 1867, he found the Ohio water to be 11.5 inches above that of the Mississippi at the north junction of the Cairo levees, the stations being 60 feet apart. This second swell was, of course, due to the arrival of the combined Upper Ohio, Cumberland, and Tennessee rise. After culminating, the river at Cairo fell nearly as rapidly as it had risen. (See plate.)

What do these facts indicate respecting the maximum discharge into the head of the alluvial region in the flood of 1867? This discharge must plainly have occurred *late in February, just before the first swell culminated*, for the conditions at Red River Landing in 1851 were repeated in the second rise. The height attained in the first swell was not quite equal to the high-water level of 1858; but, since the rise was longer and more rapid, it will not be safe to estimate the discharge at Cairo at a less amount than it was in that year, which, accurately measured, was 1,420,000 cubic feet per second. Since there was no overflow into the Saint Francis bottom between Cape Girardeau and Cairo in 1867, this amount represents the whole of the maximum volume poured into the alluvial region near its head in that year. In 1858, at the date of maximum discharge at Cairo, 35,000 cubic feet per second were passing through Cape Girardeau Inlet, and 20,000 cubic feet over the banks between Commerce Bluffs and Cairo—giving a total maximum discharge into the alluvial region of 1,475,000 cubic feet per second, or 55,000 cubic feet more than in 1867.

Without claiming exact accuracy for this estimate of the maximum volume to be kept in the channel in 1867 by a perfected levee system, it is hardly possible that any error equaling 55,000 cubic feet per second can exist in it. Clearly, then, levees computed for the flood of 1858 would have restrained that of 1867, at least as far as the mouth of the first tributary below the Ohio. To this point, Helena, we may therefore turn our attention.

At Helena the first rise culminated about March 14, standing one foot above high water of 1858, and 0.8 foot below high water of 1862. The river then subsided about 0.3 foot, but again swelled to its highest point during the year on April 1, being then 0.2 foot above the mark of the first rise. In the next 20 days it gradually subsided about five feet, remained steadily at this level for three weeks, and then fell rapidly. (See plate, both Helena and Friar's Point.)

These facts strongly confirm the inference derived from the Cairo records, that the maximum discharge in 1867 was materially less than in 1858. In the latter flood the highest water was due to the immense wave which poured through the Saint Francis bottom-lands into the river, already swelling with water from above. This sudden influx, combined with the previous breaking of several immense crevasses immediately below Helena, lowered the actual high-water mark anomalously about 3.2 feet. (See page 406 Physics and Hydraulics of the Mississippi.) In 1867 the records indicate no such influences. The Saint Francis River in 1858 was contributing 30,000 cubic feet per second of rain-water to the Mississippi at the time when the great wave, if restrained to the channel, would have passed; and there is no reason for estimating a larger supply in 1867. Hence, had no anomalous influence lowered the high water of 1858 at this locality, the river would have risen 3.2—1.0—say two feet above the level attained in 1867. But the actual maximum discharge in 1858 was 1,334,000 cubic feet per second; two feet lower, it would normally be about 1,234,000 cubic feet per second, which was probably the maximum discharge in 1867. Hence, for the volume in 1867, lost into the swamps and absorbed in filling the bed of the river between Cairo and Helena, as the wave-crest swept down, we have 1,420,000—1,234,000=186,000 cubic feet per second. The *actually measured* amount of channel-absorption between these two points in the March rise of 1858 was 140,000 cubic feet per second, (see page 349 Physics and Hydraulics of the Mississippi.) Admitting an equal amount in 1867, we still have 46,000 cubic feet per second for the excess of crevasse losses over the receipts from the swamp-drains near Helena, a result entirely probable. In fine, then, the conclusion reached from the Cairo records, that the head of the alluvial region received about 55,000 cubic feet per second less water at the date of maximum discharge in 1867 than at the same time in 1858, is confirmed by all the facts noted at Helena.

The next point where an accession to the flood-wave could have occurred is Napoleon, just below the joint mouths of the Arkansas and White Rivers. The oscillations at Beulah (see plate) represent very nearly those which must have occurred at this locality. Unfortunately the cut-off which was made here in 1863 renders it impossible to apply a close analysis to the water-marks of the two floods. It is a matter of record that there was a moderate freshet in both of the tributaries (particularly in White River) in March, 1867, but that at the date of highest water at Napoleon, (April 3,) the current of the Arkansas was almost checked for 53 miles above its mouth, by back-water from the Mississippi. In 1858 the maximum flood-wave, if confined to the channel, would have received about 60,000 cubic feet per second from these two tributaries, making its volume 197,000 cubic feet per second larger than the actual maximum discharge. Starting with 55,000 cubic feet per second less, and being much more depleted on its passage by the necessity of filling a comparatively empty channel, the flood-wave of 1867, if confined by levees, would have required immense contributions from the Arkansas and White Rivers to raise its volume to that of 1858 at Napoleon. Such contributions we know, from the recorded facts, it could not have received. Indeed there is little doubt that its maximum discharge would have fallen short of that of 1858 from 50,000 to 100,000 cubic feet per second at Napoleon. By no possibility could it have equaled that flood.

Vicksburg, below the mouth of the next tributary, Yazoo River, is now to be considered. The two cut-offs recently made in this vicinity, Terrapin neck in March, 1866, and the Davis cut-off in February, 1867, render any close analysis of this flood by studying the water-marks impossible. There are indications that, at the date of highest water, the Yazoo River was discharging a considerable volume, the supply probably consisting, as is usually the case, largely of water returning from the swamps. In 1858 the great flood-wave, if confined to the channel, would have received about 30,000 cubic feet per second of rain-water from this tributary, and the facts reported do not lead to the conclusion that this contribution would have been much, if any, exceeded in 1867. Certainly any possible excess would have fallen far short of the amounts required to produce an equality of discharge in the floods.

In Red River there was a considerable flood in June, and probably a moderate rise in March, due chiefly to contributions from Washita River. Precise facts, however, have not been secured respecting this tributary, which is the last that enters the Mississippi.

The Atchafalaya basin was deeply flooded through a break in the grand levee near Morganza. The Teche country was under water, and at Brashear City the flood-mark was one of the highest on record, being only 1.0 foot below high water of 1828.

In fine, then, the information collected respecting the flood of 1867 renders it certain that a thorough levee system, based upon the flood of 1858, would have been amply sufficient to protect the whole alluvial region from overflow. At no point would the water have risen to within 1 or 2 feet of the mark which would have been left by the flood of 1858 had it been strictly confined to the channel. Yet the actual water-mark of 1867 was, in general, a little higher than that of 1858. This apparent discrepancy is easily understood when it is remembered that there has never yet been a high-water mark not lowered by crevasses discharging into the swamps, the amount of the lowering varying greatly with the locality and with the peculiar conditions of the flood. The more perfect state of the levees in 1858 kept the swamps comparatively empty early in the season, and thus left a reservoir which, when they broke, at date of maximum discharge, served to reduce the high-water mark more than was the case in 1867, the swamps having been early filled in that year. No more palpable error can therefore be committed than to attempt to estimate the relative difficulty of restraining different floods to the channel by simply comparing their actual water-marks. It is only by an analysis like the preceding that any well-grounded opinion can be formed upon such a matter.

FLOOD OF 1865.

Occurring just at the close of the war, no facts have been preserved upon which to base a close analysis of this flood. The foregoing table exhibits how its water-marks compare with those of 1858. Rising to a less level at Cairo by 1.6 feet, there is no probability that the flood of 1865 equaled that, or even the flood of 1867, in maximum discharge into the head of the alluvial region, upon which, of course, the difficulty of restraining floods primarily depends.

The daily oscillations at Cairo and at New Orleans, the former recorded by the engineers of the Cairo City Company, and the latter by Mr. Bayley, are represented upon the accompanying Plate I. They give a good general idea of the flood, which seems to be remarkable for duration rather than for extreme volume of maximum discharge. Applying the principles and table given upon page 133, Physics and Hydraulics of the Mississippi, to the New Orleans curve, the total annual discharge there in the river-year, November 1, 1864, to October 31, 1865, is found to be 20,788,000,000,000 cubic feet, much less than that usual in great flood-years, (about 27,000,000,000,000 of cubic feet.)

The facts collected respecting the action of the chief tributaries are meager. There was a great flood of the Upper Ohio in the middle of March, which, at and above Cincinnati, seems to have compared favorably with those of 1862 and 1867. It probably received relatively small contributions from the Wabash, the Cumberland, and Tennessee, for at Cairo its height was materially less. There was no great flood in that year in the Upper Mississippi or the Missouri, since the record at Saint Louis shows that the river there hardly rose above ordinary stages in any month except in the latter part of July and August, when a little freshet occurred, causing the river for about five weeks to average 10 feet above its usual stage at that season. No records of any flood in the Arkansas or White River are in my possession, but they are too defective to render it certain that none occurred. In Upper Red River a freshet in June is mentioned, and the fact is recorded that, at the mouth of Bayou Tensas, the flood rose 1.8 feet above all previous marks, a circumstance no doubt explained by the immense crevasses in Carroll and Madison Parishes. It is also a matter of record that Bayou Teche overflowed its banks in low places as far up as Franklin, and that the water at Brashear City, on Berwick's Bay, was very high. These facts, due also to crevasses, probably explain the small annual discharge at New Orleans as compared with other flood-years.

In fine, then, we may confidently place the overflow of 1865 in the second class of great floods in which the maximum discharge with perfected levees would have fallen far short of that quantity in 1858, or even in 1867.

FLOOD OF 1862.

Beyond a doubt this was one of the greatest floods which ever occurred upon the Mississippi, and it is extremely to be regretted that the war raging at the time has so obliterated all records that it must always remain classed with the traditional overflows of 1815 and 1828, respecting which we do not possess the data to permit a close analytical comparison with the standard flood of 1858. Even the engineers of the Cairo City property, whose daily river-records have done so much for the proper understanding of the hydraulics of the Mississippi, failed to record the history of this flood, only preserving its extreme high-water level, (attained on May 2,) to remain a standing subject of perplexing speculation for future students of the river.

We know that there was a very great flood in the Ohio River at Cincinnati, and also in the Cumberland River, some time in the spring of 1862, and a destructive overflow in the Wabash in February. There was also a moderate flood in the Mississippi at Saint Louis, which began to rise on March 12, from a stand 26 feet below the city directrix, and culminated on April 26 at 2.4 feet below that bench. It then gradually subsided until, on June 9, it stood 15 feet below the directrix. It remained above and within two feet of this level until July 26, when it slowly subsided to the usual low-water stage, (about 25 feet below the directrix.)

At Cairo, the highest water occurred on May 2, and was 1.2 feet above the high water of 1858. Its date evidently corresponds to that of the freshet at Saint Louis; but this freshet, 5.7 feet below the high water of 1858, could only have produced such a rise at Cairo by combining with the great Ohio flood. How did these freshets meet? If, as was the case in 1858, they united so exactly at Cairo as to raise the river uniformly for the last 8 or 10 feet up to high-water mark without any intermediate stand or slight fall like that at Red River Landing in 1851, or at Cairo in 1867, then the maximum discharge must have exceeded that of 1858 by about 50,000 cubic feet per second. But even supposing this to have been the case, it is very certain that a flood 5.7 feet below that of 1858 at Saint Louis could not have risen nearly so high at Cape Girardeau, and thence to Cairo; and hence could not have lost the 55,000 cubic feet per second, or any large part of it, into the Saint Francis bottom-lands. Under no supposition, then, could the flood of 1862 have discharged a larger volume into the head of the alluvial region than the flood of 1858. If, as in 1867, there was a slight recession at Cairo just before the extreme high-water mark was attained, due to a slight want of coincidence in the floods of the two rivers, it is probable that, as in that year, the maximum volume contributed to the alluvial region fell short of the discharge in 1858 by perhaps 50,000 cubic feet per second. The want of recorded facts at Cairo must always leave this a matter of doubt, and the most unfavorable theory must therefore be adopted, namely, that the two floods were equal in maximum discharge into the head of the alluvial region, (1,475,000 cubic feet per second.)

Between Cape Girardeau and Napoleon, then, we may safely consider that levees raised to the grade required to retain the flood of 1858 would have been severely taxed in 1862, but that they would have been sufficient. The only supposable conditions to cause their failure would be that the flood-wave had found the lower river more full than it was in 1858, which, under the conditions of the latter flood, would be extremely improbable.

At Napoleon the flood-wave in 1862 received a moderate freshet from the Arkansas, and probably from the White River also. This is established not only by the records, but also by the recorded date of high water, April 20. It is plain that the Arkansas flood was the earlier of the two; and very possibly if the river had been confined by levees no dangerous coincidence would have occurred. In the condition of the records, however, this must always remain a matter of doubt.

It is believed that there was no flood in the Yazoo or Red Rivers at date of high water in 1862, (except water returning from the swamps,) but the records are too defective to render this certain.

In fine, then, as already stated, the flood of 1862 must probably always remain a source of anxious perplexity to engineers having the direction of the levee system of the Mississippi. The actual high-water marks of that year generally exceed those of any other by several inches, (see table already given;) but, as fully explained above, this proves absolutely nothing respecting the relative difficulty of restraining these floods had the levee system been perfected at their date. In my judgment, the only conclusion which the facts will warrant is that the two floods were essentially equal in the strain to which they would have subjected a general levee system.

PROPER HEIGHTS OF LEVEES.

The foregoing discussion renders it reasonably certain that, during the sixteen years which have elapsed since 1858, only three high waters have occurred which would have tested a proper system of levees based on that flood, viz: those of 1862, 1867, and 1874; that in the last only have we reason to believe that the embankments would have failed in any part of the valley; and, finally, that even in 1874 they would have been amply sufficient for all points above the influence of Red River. While, therefore, the so frequent recurrence of these great floods imperatively forbids any reduction in the height of the levees recommended in the Physics and Hydraulics of the Mississippi, the recent history of the river shows them to be sufficient for the entire region above Natchez.

For points below Natchez, the table already given, of the maximum discharge which would have occurred in 1874, had the river been confined to its bed by a perfected levee system, has received the same mathematical analysis as was employed in the similar discussions of the Physics and Hydraulics of the Mississippi, where the methods are so fully explained as to require no notice here. The resulting flood-heights, estimated above the high-water level of 1858, are, for Red River Landing, 4.7 feet; for Baton Rouge, 3.7 feet; for Donaldsonville, 3.7 feet; for Carrolton, 3.5 feet.

Combining, then, the computations for the floods of 1858 and 1874, we have the following result for the proper heights of the levees throughout the alluvial region:

"Near the mouth of the Ohio, they should be made about three feet above the actual high-water level of 1858, which has been selected as the plane of reference, because more unvarying than the surface of the ground. The height above this level should be gradually increased to about 7 feet at Osceola; thence to Helena, the latter height should be maintained; thence to Island 71, the height should be gradually increased to 10 feet; thence to the vicinity of Napoleon, it may be gradually reduced to 8 feet; thence to Lake Providence, it must be gradually increased to 11 feet; thence to the mouth of the Yazoo, it may be gradually reduced to 6 feet, and it should be thus maintained to Natchez."

From Natchez to Red River Landing, the height of the levees above the flood-plane of 1858 must be gradually increased to 7 feet; thence to Baton Rouge, it may be gradually reduced to 5 feet; thence to Donaldsonville, it must retain this height of 5 feet. At Carrollton, 4.7 feet will suffice; with reductions, proportioned to the range between high and low water mark, for points below. These figures are exclusive of settling, and allow about one foot for safety, above the computed height.

Respectfully submitted.

HENRY L. ABBOT,
Member of the Commission.

CHAPTER II.

LEVEES IN THE STATES OF MISSOURI AND ARKANSAS.

By Commissioner Jackson E. Sickels.

Little data showing the present condition of the levees in the States of Missouri and Arkansas, on the Mississippi River, could be obtained from the official records in these States. Hence a thorough reconnaissance, necessarily rapid, was made, the results of which are presented. This extended from the bluffs at Commerce, which is at the head of the alluvial region, to the Louisiana line, comprehending, also, an examination of the levees on the south bank of the Arkansas River, below Auburn.

The levee system begins about five miles below Commerce. Between this point and New Madrid, seventy-three miles, the length of the breaks and gaps in the levee is thirty-two and one-half miles. From a point opposite the lower end of Island No. 8 to New Madrid, I suggest the abandonment of the old line of levee. Very little of the levee remains, and the rapid caving of the banks in the bends above and below Donaldson's Point makes an interior line advisable, throwing this point outside of the levee. From New Madrid to the boundary-line between Missouri and Arkansas, a distance of fifty-four and one-half miles, the breaks and gaps in the levee amount to thirty and one-half miles. Between New Madrid and Point Pleasant, ten miles, the formation is diluvial, and is from 10 to 15 feet above overflow. Just below Point Pleasant, the banks of the river again become submerged, and the escaping floods of the Mississippi drain westward into the valley of the Saint Francis. The bank at Little Cypress Bend, five miles below Point Pleasant, is caving seriously at the upper end of the bend, and has reached back to Cushion Lake. In Prairie Bend, opposite Gayoso, the bank is also caving rapidly; hence an interior line was examined, passing to the west of Cushion and Big Lakes, and joining the old levee about one mile below Gayoso. This line would place outside of the levee about 10,000 acres of land, of which only a small portion is cultivated. More thorough examinations, however, may show a line for the levee nearer the river, and promising reasonable permanency.

The levees in Missouri are built with slopes of about five to one, and have a crown of from 6 to 8 feet. To complete the levees to the Arkansas line, filling the breaks and gaps and building, the levees on the new routes indicated will require 800,000 cubic yards of embankment.

Between the State line and Osceola, thirty-two miles, about two-thirds of the levee remains. Excepting a very small percentage this is sufficiently distant from the river to form a part of a more permanent system. Between these points the river is exceedingly direct, and the banks are caving only in the bends opposite Rucker's Point and Island 30.

Between Osceola and Mrs. Lanier's, distant by direct line twelve and a half miles, along the outer curve of the bends, the levee is practically gone. In view, therefore, of the small portion of existing levees which could be utilized and the rapid caving of the banks on this portion of the river, two interior lines were examined. The first of these leaves the river at Captain Erwin's, four miles below Osceola, and crosses the neck opposite Fort Pillow, to Lanier's, three and a half miles. The distance around the point is nine miles. The second interior line leaves the river at the Nodina place, two and a quarter miles below Lanier's, and crosses the narrow neck opposite Randolph to Mrs. Lanier's, two and a half miles. A considerable portion of this line is above overflow. The distance around the bend is fifteen miles. The land thus exposed to overflow is mostly swamp. At Shaneeville, opposite Island 37, there are four miles of high land from 6 to 8 feet above overflow. Between Mrs. Lanier's and Hopefield, opposite Memphis, twenty-six miles of levee embankments, amounting to forty-five per cent. of the whole distance, will be required.

From Hopefield to the Saint Francis River, $70\frac{1}{2}$ miles, about $39\frac{1}{4}$ miles of levee remain which could be made part of a new line. This contemplates, however, a line two miles in length, crossing the neck between Council and Walnut Bends. The distance around the point is 8 miles; and the recent cut-off at Council Bend, which sends the current directly against this point, the bank of which is caving rapidly, suggests the interior line.

Between the high lands at Helena and the lower end of Laconia circle, 66 miles, about 12 miles of levee will be required. This will include the length of levee on a line 2½ miles across the neck opposite Island 66. Considerations similar to those already presented in other like cases suggested the interior line.

Auburn, on the south bank of the Arkansas River, 56 miles above the mouth, is the point which is the limit of the influence of the back-water of the Mississippi at its highest flood, and is the point, approximately, at which the levee system may properly terminate. Between Auburn and Red Fork, 27 miles, the breaks and gaps will amount to ½ mile. Between Red Fork and Napoleon, at the mouth of the Arkansas River, the breaks and gaps, taking a line going behind Lake Jefferson, will require 7 miles of levee; most of this will consist of very high embankment.

South from Napoleon to Cypress Bend, following the old line of levee, 23 miles, the levee is virtually gone. Considering the length and cost of the levee required between Red Fork and Cypress Bend, and the insecurity of large portions of the existing levee owing to its proximity to the river at the caving bends, it may be found advisable to adopt an interior line. Such a line may be traced from the town of Red Fork, following the high ground along Red Fork Bayou, to the line of the Little Rock, Pine Bluff and New Orleans Railroad, 5 miles. Thence making that company's road-bed a levee to Cypress Bend, on the Mississippi River, distance 17 miles. Such a location would, however, expose a large area to inundation, and it is contemplated only as a possible expedient.

From Cypress Bend to the Louisiana line, 68 miles, the length of the breaks and gaps is 22½ miles. In the bend below Gaines's Landing and in the bend above Luna the banks are steadily caving; also below Luna and in the bend opposite Island 84. Two back lines were therefore examined, throwing outside of the levee—Point Comfort and Point Chicot—the points between these bends. The aggregate length of these proposed interior lines is 4½ miles. The length of the line following the bends of the river is 21 miles, on which only about 7 miles of levee remain.

The following table gives in detail the breaks and gaps in the existing levee-system on the west bank of the Mississippi from Commerce, Mo., to the Louisiana line, and on the south bank of the Arkansas from its mouth to Auburn:

Tabular statement showing breaks and gaps in the levee along the Mississippi and Arkansas Rivers, in the States of Missouri and Arkansas.

Length, in feet.	Average height, in feet.	Remarks.
500	5	Head of Big Lake.
200	00	South side of Big Lake.
200	1	
100	1	
500	1	
500	1	
500	00	
1,000	1	
1,000	1½	

Tabular statement showing the breaks and gaps, &c.—Continued.

Length, in feet.	Average height in feet.	Remarks.
9,000	3½	Opposite Cairo.
9,000	5	Opposite Island Number 1.
5,000	1	Above Hunter's Landing.
2,000	3	
1,700	2	Opposite Island Number 4.
500	½	Below Lucas Bend. (Interior line.)
15,000	2	Above Island Number 6.
400	8	
21,000	1	Above Island Number 8. (Interior line.)
100	25	Bayou Saint James.
200	12	Dry Bayou.
10,500	3	Opposite Island Number 8.
1,000	3	
1,000	3	
5,800	3	Interior line to New Madrid, north and west of Hubbard Lake.
18,400	8	Interior line to New Madrid, north and west of Hubbard Lake—Saint John's Bayou.
20,800	3	
100	25	
20,000	1	Interior line from Port Pleasant to Caruthersville, west of Big Lake and Bayou—west of Gayoso.
4,000	2½	
100	15	
14,000	2	
2,500	4	
8,000	3	
800	4	Opposite Linwood Bar.
7,600	3	
300	2½	Opposite Island Number 16.
200	2	
100	2	Head of Island Number 18.
500	2	Opposite Island Number 18.
1,700	2½	
200	15	Half-Moon Bayou.
5,000	4	Below Cottonwood Point—Pemiscot Bayou
100	15	
12,000	6	
6,000	2½	Head of Island Number 21.
24,000	3	Opposite Island Number 21.
100	15	
21,500	4	Above Island Number 25.
300	5	Opposite Island Number 25.
250	5	
13,000	6	Opposite Island Number 26.
120	7	
300	5	
200	6	
100	20	Mill Bayou,
2,700	4	Below Mill Bayou.
2,000	2	Opposite Island Number 30.
600	3	
18,500	4	Across Neck, opposite Flower Island
500	5	
1,400	3	Across Neck, below Island Number 34.
7,800	3	
26,300	3	Opposite Island Number 35.
5,500	4½	Opposite Dean's Island.
1,500	3	
600	5	
200	4	Opposite Island Number 37.
2,500	4½	
150	20	Old River Bayou, below Plumb Island

Tabular statement showing the breaks and gaps, &c.—Continued.

Length in feet.	Average height, in feet.	Remarks.
100	3	
20,000	4	
2,500	$2\frac{1}{2}$	Opposite Brandywine Bend, (slough.)
100	15	
6,000	$2\frac{1}{2}$	
100	10	Fogleman's Bayou.
100	15	Bayou at Mound City.
100	15	
16,000	4	Above Hopefield.
50	10	
100	12	Opposite Vice-President's Island.
300	5	
1,000	3	Opposite lower end of President's Island.
5,500	4	
70	12	Merryweather's.
150	4	
5,000	$2\frac{1}{2}$	Scanlin's.
7,500	$2\frac{1}{2}$	Below Scanlin's.
100	5	
200	$2\frac{1}{2}$	
200	3	Opposite Cat Island.
2,500	2	
6,500	$2\frac{1}{2}$	
150	6	
100	20	Lost River Bayou.
300	4	
9,000	$2\frac{1}{2}$	
9,800	$1\frac{1}{2}$	Opposite Blue's Point.
7,800	10	
3,500	$1\frac{1}{2}$	
7,000	$\frac{1}{2}$	Above Bledsoe's.
100	20	Bayou at Bledsoe's.
21,000	$2\frac{1}{2}$	Council Bend.
70	13	
1,000	4	Below Hamlin's.
11,000	3	Across neck, opposite cut-off to Walnut Bend.
550	3	Walnut Bend.
1,500	$4\frac{1}{2}$	Above Saint Francis Island.
1,200	8	Fort Penny.
150	35	Old Town Bayou.
700	7	Six miles below Old Town Bayou.
200	8	
1,700	5	Foot of Island Number 63.
7,000	6	Below Island Number 63.
17,500	5	Opposite Island Number 65.
10,500	4	Mrs. Offit's.
26,500	5	Opposite Islands Numbers 67 and 68.
600	5	Napoleon Crevasse of 1874.
12,000	5	
12,000	8	Between Napoleon and Cypress Creek.
15,000	4	
3,000	6	
400	12	Great Cypress Bayou.
1,000	5	
400	12	Between Chicot City and Cypress Creek.
28,000	6	
500	5	Alligator Bayou.
300	4	Crevasse at Chicot City.
120	9	Opposite lower end of Island Number 79.
180	6	Below Eunice.
200	4	

Tabular statement showing the breaks and gaps, &c.—Continued.

Length in feet.	Average height, in feet.	Remarks.
7,000	8	Above Island Number 82.
1,500	6	
2,000	9	
3,000	5	
7,000	2	
7,000	1	
10,000	3	Below Island Number 22.
7,000	$3\frac{1}{2}$	
600	8	One mile above Luna.
4,000	$3\frac{1}{2}$	Gap between bends, throwing out Point Chicot.
3,000	12	Opposite Island Number 84. Whisky Chute Bayou.
7,000	2	Opposite Island Number 84.
2,500	7	American Bend.
1,000	9	Just below Island Number 87.
2,000	1	
2,000	8	
2,000	7	
3,000	5	
6,000	$4\frac{1}{2}$	
4,000	3	
4,000	$4\frac{1}{2}$	East of Willow Lake, from Sterlingworth.
600	7	
8,000	3	
730	6	One mile from Louisiana line. Made by United States gunboat.
500	$6\frac{1}{2}$	One-half mile from Louisiana line.
		ARKANSAS RIVER.
1,050	7	Bayou and crevasses at and near Red Fork.
260	$5\frac{1}{2}$	
700	9	
180	6	
2,000	8	Opposite Rosemary Landing.
5,000	4	
2,500	4	Across Rollin's Bend.
14,000	2	Around Lake Jefferson, south side.
6,000	5	
5,000	4	
1,100	4	Near road to Napoleon, crevasse of 1867.

Summing up preceding details, it appears that the aggregate length of levees in the States of Missouri and Arkansas along the Mississippi, and on the south bank of the Arkansas extending up to Auburn, is $295\frac{1}{2}$ miles. The aggregate length of breaks and gaps is 192 miles.

In order to determine what measure of permanence could be secured to levees placed at reasonable distances from the river, every effort was made to ascertain accurately the annual rate of caving in the worst bends. The data on this point must be taken simply as a close approximation, for only in a few instances are they the result of exact measurement.

Statement of caving banks on the Mississippi River, in States of Missouri and Arkansas.

From Greenfield's Landing to Ohio City, opposite Cairo, caving rapidly. Bird's Island entirely gone. The current sets hard against the shore.

At Prickett's, in bend above Belmont, caving slowly.

In Lucas's bend, opposite Island No. 4, caving 100 feet annually.

In bend, opposite Island No. 8, caving slowly.

In bend, just below Island No. 8, caves from 50 to 75 feet annually.

In New Madrid Bend, caves 50 feet annually.

Just below Point Pleasant, caves 25 feet annually.

In Little Cypress Bend, above Island No. 14, has caved nearly one mile within 20 years.

Opposite Gayoso, caving from 25 to 40 feet annually.

Opposite lower end Island No. 18, caves slowly.

At Craighead's, ten miles below Osceola, caves 150 feet annually.

Opposite Island No. 40, caves from 100 to 150 feet annually.

Just above Hopefield, opposite Memphis, caves from 100 to 125 feet annually.

At Grayson's, opposite lower end Vice-President's Island, caves from 50 to 75 feet annually.

From Bledsoe's to Hamlin's, caves about 100 feet annually.

Walnut Bend, caves very little.

At Fort Penny, opposite Friar's Point, no cave in 20 years.

At Old Town, no caving.

Opposite Islands 67 and 68, caves 100 feet annually.

In Cypress Bend, twenty miles below Napoleon, caves from 40 to 100 feet annually.

At Eunice, above Island No. 80, has caved 1,500 feet in last 16 years.

Opposite Point Comfort, above Island No. 82, east bank has caved 3,960 feet (by actual measurement) in 24 years.

At Columbia, bank caves slowly.

Opposite Island No. 84, from 1840 to 1870, caved about one mile; no caving since 1870.

Nine miles above Louisiana line, caving 100 yards annually.

Opposite Willow Lake, five miles above Louisiana line, caves 100 yards annually.

Ashton, State line, since 1840, a sand-bar two miles wide has formed in front, and this represents caving on east bank of river.

In the States of Missouri and Arkansas are three clearly-defined levee districts. The first of these extends from the Commerce Bluffs to the Saint Francis River. The levees within this district evidently should be under one supervision and control, since any defect in their construction or lack of proper watchfulness, would threaten large areas of the district below. Thus, flood-waters breaking through the levees along the Mississippi in the State of Missouri would, besides endangering portions of the levee which it would attack in the rear, inundate the back country down to, if not below, the line of the Memphis and Little Rock Railroad. In connection with a perfected levee system for this district, provision must be made for the rainfall. Extended instrumental surveys alone can determine whether culverts with flood-gates, through the main levee, or drainage westward to the Saint Francis, should be provided.

Between Helena and the mouth of White River are the distinctly marked limits of another levee district. Flanked by Crowley's Ridge on the north, this district is perfectly protected from overflow from above, but the lower portion will be liable to inundation from the back-water of the Mississippi.

The alluvial region between the Arkansas River and the Louisiana line is, for purposes of protection against inundation, a part of the levee district which includes all of Northern Louisiana down to the Red River and should be under one jurisdiction. Though other plans have been proposed to protect the upper parishes of Louisiana from the floods of the Arkansas and from the back-water of the Mississippi, it is believed that the simplest and certainly most effective remedy will be found in maintaining the levees along the south bank of the Arkansas River, continuing them up the river to a point about ten miles above Auburn. The existing levees between this point and Red Fork are located, excepting in one instance, at secure distances from caving bends; and a comparatively trifling addition to their height will be required to make them a part of the proposed perfected system. When so built they will permanently reclaim within the counties of Lincoln, Desha, and Chicot thousands of acres of the choicest cotton-lands in the Arkansas and Mississippi bottoms.

The estimated cost of repairing and perfecting existing levees in the above-described districts is as follows:

District.	Cubic yards.	Price.	Amount.
Saint Francis district, from Commerce, Mo., to Saint Francis River.	2, 250, 000	$0 40	$900, 000
Helena district, between Helena and White River.	750, 000	40	300, 000
Upper portion of Tensas district, from Arkansas River to Louisiana line	1, 000, 000	40	400, 000
Total	4, 000, 000	....	1, 600, 000

In estimating for the perfected levee system, the height of the embankments is fixed with reference to the flood-line of 1858, giving to them such additional heights as the increased volume of water confined between these artificial banks will render necessary. The crown of the levee will be uniformly 10 feet in width. The slopes will be 5 to 1 for all levees 10 feet or less in height, and 6 to 1 where the levee is over 10 feet. It is to be understood that the following estimate is to be accepted only as an approximate one:

District.	Cubic yards.	Price.	Amount.
Saint Francis district, from Commerce, Mo., to Saint Francis River.	17, 099, 000	$0 40	$6, 839, 600
Helena district, between Helena and mouth of White River	4, 652, 000	40	1, 860, 800
Upper portion of Tensas district, from Arkansas River to Louisiana line	14, 767, 000	40	5, 906, 800
Total	36, 518, 000	....	14, 607, 200

The following statement and data give all the information obtained with reference to high-water marks on the Mississippi and Arkansas Rivers:

Statement of high-water marks of 1874, *as compared with previous floods.*

At Commerce, Mo., from 4 to 5 feet below 1867.

At Norfolk, Mo., the following records were kept and are kindly furnished by Mr. Mercer:

1874	0. 0	1868	—2. 3	1862	+3. 4
1873	—2. 9	1867	+3. 0	1861	—2. 3
1872	....	1866	—2. 3	1860	—5. 9
1871*	....	1865	+0. 4	1859	—1. 5
1870	—2. 3	1864	—2. 7	1858	+2. 5
1869	—3. 6	1863	....		

* At Christmas lowest water ever observed—Bacon Rock 3 feet out of water.

At New Madrid high water of 1867 was 16 inches higher than that of 1874.

Col. Sam. Tate, president of the Memphis and Little Rock Railroad

Company, furnished the following table of elevations of high water for the years and at the points indicated on the line of his railroad, west from Hopefield:

One mile west:
1867. Elevation of high water above datum 101.82
1869. Elevation of high water above datum .... 100.
1871. Elevation of high water above datum 100.96
Three and a half miles west:
1871. Elevation of high water above datum 101.81
Four miles west:
Elevation of high water above datum 100.9
Nine and three-quarter miles west:
1867. Elevation of high water, &c 97.2
1870. Elevation of high water, &c 95.4
1871. Elevation of high water, &c 96.2
Fifteen miles west:
1867. Elevation of high water 95.7
1871. Elevation of high water 89.82
Sixteen miles west:
1867. Elevation above datum 95.13
Eighteen miles west:
1871. Elevation above datum 89.12
Twenty-one miles west:
1874. Elevation above datum ....
Twenty-three and twenty-four miles west:
1871. Elevation, &c 88.26
Twenty-eight and twenty-nine miles west:
1874. Elevation, &c 93.00
Thirty-two miles west:
1874. Elevation, &c 91.50

At Widner's Station, 37 miles west, high water of 1874, sixteen inches below high water of 1867.

Table of high-water marks on Mississippi and Arkansas Rivers, with reference to 1874.

Year.	Opposite Island 39.	Sunnyside, foot Island 84.	Columbia, bend above Greenville.	Luna, bend below Greenville.	Opposite Island 82.	10 miles below Napoleon.	Napoleon.	Opposite Lake Jefferson, Arkansas River, 15 miles above mouth.	Hilliard's Landing, near Louisiana line.
1844	....	....	....	....	0.0	....	....	−3.0	....
1858	2.5	3.8	1.9	1.3	....	−1.6	−2.0	−1.5	....
1859	....	....	....	....	....	....	....	−1.4	....
1862	....	2.8	....	....	1.0	....	....	....	....
1867	0.9	0.4	....	....	....	....	−0.9	−0.5	+1.0
1868	....	....	....	....	....	....	....	....	+1.6
1874	0.0	0.0	0.0	0.0	0.0	0.0	0.0	0.0	....

There is also submitted herewith (see Appendix F) a table of relative heights of high-water, levees and ground, from Commerce, Mo., to Louisiana line, and on south bank of Arkansas River, from its mouth to Auburn.

The system of continuous embankments or levees along the lower Mississippi seems to offer the only practical solution of the problem of reclaiming its alluvial basin from inundation.

The diversion of tributary streams and the opening of cut-offs and outlets constitute, in connection with levees, other methods of protection, which have ardent advocates.

These special auxiliary plans would, however, involve an enormous, and in some cases an indefinite cost, and are, to say the least, of questionable practicability and utility; while a comprehensive levee system, traversing the whole lower valley, secures every possible advantage, for it would be at once efficient, simple, and, considering results, economical.

Yet the States immediately interested could not carry out the system proposed. The States of Arkansas, Mississippi, and Louisiana are too impoverished to repair even their present temporary and imperfect systems, much less to assume the burden of a work having the magnitude of the system in view.

Superadded to these financial obstacles are certain grave political ones. As the system must be independent of and ignore all State boundaries, is it practicable for the States to cede such jurisdiction or control to a common head—to make such full and indissoluble engagements with each other as are indispensable to the construction, supervision, and maintenance of this system? The creation of such executive and administrative authority would certainly constitute an anomaly in our politics, as it would also be the exercise of a power on the part of the States not known to, if not, indeed, directly prohibited to them by the Federal Constitution.

This being so, it would appear that as this great public improvement is to redeem millions of acres of the richest territory on this continent, now a waste or a jungle, and make it tillable and habitable, and will thereby add largely to the national wealth and prosperity, and as the *means* and the *power* to do this are to be found in the General Government alone, upon it must the task devolve if it is to be accomplished.

Respectfully submitted.

JACKSON E. SICKELS,
Member of the Commission.

CHAPTER III.

STATE OF THE LEVEES IN MISSISSIPPI.

BY COMMISSIONER MAJ. W. H. H. BENYAURD, UNITED STATES ENGINEERS.

In accordance with the resolution of the commission calling for information concerning the condition of the levees, number, location, and size of existing crevasses, records of high-water marks of different floods, and such other information pertaining to the question of the reclamation of the overflowed lands, so far as applicable to the Yazoo Basin, the following report is submitted to the commission:

The shortness of the time in which to collect the necessary information, and the limited means at our disposal, precluded anything in the way of an instrumental survey being attempted. An examination ot the entire line of levees along the front of the Yazoo Basin was made by Mr. Jas. M. Searles, civil engineer. Reports and letters were received from Mr. M. L. Alcorn, president board of levee commissioners, first district; Mr. W. G. Myers, president, and I. McD. Vernon, chief engineer, board of levee commissioners second district; Mr. R. A. O'Hae, and others. From these examinations and reports much valuable information was obtained concerning the present system of levees in the State of Mississippi and the changes necessary to completely protect the lands of that section from annual overflow.

The counties bordering upon and near the Mississippi River are divided into two levee districts, known as the first and second. In the former are the counties of De Soto, Tunica, and Coahoma. The latter district comprises the counties of Bolivar, Washington, and Issaquena. Warren County, the most southern in the basin bordering on the river, is without any organization, and has but few miles of levees.

In the first or upper district, the line commences in De Soto County, at the hills which border the southern shore of Horn Lake; thence running westwardly, it approaches the Mississippi River in the vicinity of Norfolks, and from that point it runs, at a safe distance from the bank, to the northern line of Tunica County. The length of the line in De Soto is about eighteen miles; it is in good condition and has no breaks. It stood about two feet above the high water of 1874. The average height of the levees is about six feet, with crown equal to height, and with side-slopes of 3 and 2 to 1.

In Tunica County the line is about thirty-seven miles long, and is favorably located by leaving out three large river points. The levees in this county have an average height of 8½ feet, with crown of 6 feet and side-slopes of 4 and 2 to 1. The river banks are caving badly along the whole front of this county, particularly so in the vicinity of the village of Commerce, and a new location of the line is rendered necessary. The only crevasse that occurred in this county during the flood of 1874 was at Trotter's, near Eagle Lake. It had a length of 760 feet and depth of 12 feet. In Coahoma County the line is fifty-five miles long, with an average height of 12 feet, crown of 6 feet, and with side-slopes of 4 and 2 to 1. The rapidly-caving banks along the front of this county necessitates a new location of the levee-line. The Yazoo Pass and Hushpuckana levees are located, respectively, near the upper and lower end of these counties.

The dimensions of the former, as reconstructed in 1859, were, height, 40 feet; crown, 10 feet; side-slopes of 5 and 3 to 1, and with a length of 300 feet. Across a willow flat adjoining there was constructed during the same year a levee 25 feet high, 5,000 feet long, crown 10 feet, and with side-slopes of 4 and 3 to 1. These levees stood 4 feet above the high water of this year, (1874.) The Hushpuckana was closed in 1871. It is 250 feet long, 43 feet high, crown of 8 feet, and with side-slopes of 3 to 1 on both sides. This levee is still intact. It stood 6 feet above high water of 1874. A crevasse occurred this year in one of the wings; the opening was 300 feet long and about 12 feet deep. Though this levee is in the upper district, its preservation is so essential to the protection of the lands in the lower district that its construction and repair is taken in charge by the board of levee commissioners of the latter district. The following crevasses occurred in Coahoma during the flood of 1874:

Name.	Locality.	Length.	Depth.	Date of occurrence.
		Feet.	*Feet.*	
Sanders	½ mile above Friar's Point	750	13	Daybreak, May 10.
Miller	¼ mile below Friar's Point	150	20	Sunrise, May 10.
Do	do	800	8	May 10.
Garth	7 miles below Friar's Point	640	14	Do.
McCloud	12 miles below Friar's Point	780	14	Do.
Beard	13 miles below Friar's Point	470	12	Do.
Hurlbert	15 miles below Friar's Point	600	14	Do.
Robson	22 miles below Friar's Point	1,820	15	Do.
Malone	Opposite Island 66	600	16	Do.

From the fifth to the eighth break, the flood passed over the unbroken line of levee at a depth of about six feet.

In the counties of Bolivar, Washington, and Issaquena, comprising the second district, there are one hundred and ninety-seven miles of levees. The average height is about eight feet, with a crown of six feet, and with side-slopes of four and two to one. The following crevasses occurred in Bolivar County during flood of 1874:

Name.	Locality.	Length.	Depth.	Date of occurrence.
		Feet.	*Feet.*	
Cook	4 miles above Bolivar Landing	1,360	5	March 20.
Bolivar	Bolivar Landing	1,900	8	March 15.
Connolly	8 miles below Bolivar Landing	700	20	April 28.
Bell	12 miles above Bolivar Landing	232	6	April 30.

Besides various small breaks in the vicinity of Cat-fish Point.

There were no crevasses in Washington and Issaquena Counties this year, though there were two in the latter county left open from previous years. They are known as the Cammack and Christmas breaks. The former is three and a quarter miles long, with an average depth of thirteen feet; the latter is about two and a quarter miles long, with an average depth of eight feet. The levees in the lower district are generally favorably located, except in some few localities, but new sites will be required to insure a comparative degree of permanency.

In Warren County the only remaining one of the basin fronting on the Mississippi River, a small levee of three feet elevation extending from the county-line to a point near Eagle Bend, a distance of about seven miles, is all that this county has. The expense attending the reclamation of the lands in this county, on account of the difficulty of securing proper drainage arising from the back-water up the Yazoo River, has hitherto precluded any attempts at securing immunity from the floods.

The following table shows the number of cubic yards necessary for the reconstruction of the levees at the several points indicated, and according to the plan and location of the levees as now being constructed in the State:

Name of levee.	County.	Cubic yards.
Trother's	Tunica	15,000
Sanders'	Coahoma	17,000
Miller	....do	7,500
Miller	....do	7,600
Garth	....do	16,600
McCloud	....do	20,000
Beard	....do	9,000
Hurlbut	....do	15,500
Robson	....do	54,000
Malone	....do	20,000
Hushpuckana wing	....do	6,000
Bell	Bolivar	7,000
Cook	....do	25,000
Bolivar	....do	32,000
Connolly	....do	28,000
Catfish Point, small openings	....do	20,000
Utopia	Washington	20,000
Miller's	....do	54,000
Griffin	....do	17,000
Cammack	Issaquena	427,000
Christmas	....do	133,000
Dunbarton	....do	96,000
Total		1,049,000

In the lower district upward of 200,000 cubic yards have been contracted for, to be finished in February, 1875. In the upper district, however, no means have yet been undertaken to close up the worst of the existing breaks, and the line is still in the condition that the flood of 1874 left it. It is estimated that about 867,000 cubic yards will be required to finish the line as it was originally constructed; this, at 30 cents per cubic yard, amounts to $260,000.

The Yazoo Basin presents many advantages for reclamation over the other districts now needing protection from the floods of the Mississippi, on account of the natural drainage afforded by the various streams that flow toward the Yazoo River. All of these, with the exception of one or two minor ones, flow toward the Yazoo. Their banks are generally above overflow, while their slope is sufficient to carry off the rain-fall. A continuous line of levee may be built along the front of this basin, and, with proper height and cross-section, made to protect the back lands from the disastrous effects of the flood. In the upper counties, the river-bank being of a light sandy nature, and caving badly, a new location is necessary, particularly at the Yazoo Pass, as the breaking of the line at this point would entail great damage upon the Yazoo Basin. It might be found necessary to go east of Moon Lake, and from that point continue down east of Friar's Point; thence, by way of Port Royal Ridge, east of Lewis's Swamp, and down the Totten Ridge, crossing the Hushpuckana below the present levee. In Bolivar the line should be relocated, commencing at the lower end of Vermillion Lake, and keeping down the east side of Bolivar, omitting Catfish Point; then keeping down through Washington and Issaquena Counties, at a safe distance from the banks, and avoiding the larger bends entirely. In case it be found necessary, these latter might be protected by low levees upon something of the same system as now adopted. In Warren County a levee along the river-front would afford only a limited protection, as the lands would be overflowed from the back-water of the Mississippi up the Yazoo. The lower portion of the county could only be effectually reclaimed by leveeing up the banks of the tributary branches, and at the same time providing measures for draining the rain-fall. The distance up which we must levee the tributary branches can only be determined after a thorough instrumental survey has been made, as the increased height to be given to the levees on the Mississippi front, arising from restraining the flood-waters within narrower limits than at present, will necessarily cause the back-water to set higher up the tributary streams. The new line, as before described, can only be an approximation, and is so intended, as its correct position can only be determined after the thorough and comprehensive survey above alluded to has been made. The increased height and cross-section arising from restraining the flood, and from the levee being retired from the bank, can then be more accurately determined, as well as what portion of the existing system can be used in the new one.

The estimated length of the line is about 262 miles, and the estimated amount of material required is about 31,188,000 cubic yards.

For a comparison of the flood-marks of different years, the following table is added:

Locality.		Authority.
Helena	High water of 1858, 22 inches below 1862	J. B. Miles.
	High water of 1859, 12⅓ inches below 1858	Do.
	High water of 1862, highest ever known	Do.
	High water of 1867, 7 inches below 1862	Do.
	High water of 1874, 7 inches below 1862	Do.
rair's Point	High water of 1858, 18 inches above 1844	J. G. Miller.
	High water of 1859, 11 inches above 1844	Do.
	High water of 1862, 38 inches above 1844	Do.
	High water of 1867, 38 inches above 1844	Do.
	High water of 1874, 45 inches above 1844	Do.
	High water of 1874, 7 inches above 1867	M. L. Alcorn.
Delta, Miss	High water of 1874, 3 inches above 1867	Do.
Yazoo Pass	High water of 1874, 5 inches above 1867	Do.
Australia	High water of 1874, below 1858, 1859, 1862, and 1867	I. McD. Vernon.
Concordia	High water of 1874, below 1858, 1859, 1862, and 1867	Do.
Terene	High water of 1874, above 1858, 1859, 1862, and 1867	Do.
Prentiss	High water of 1874, above 1858, 1859, 1862, and 1867	Do.
Niblett's	High water of 1874, above 1858, 1859, 1862, and 1867	Do.
Catfish Point	High water of 1874, 22 inches above any water known	Do.
Greenville	High water of 1874, below 1858, 1859, 1862, and 1867	Do.
Eggs Point	High water of 1874, below 1858, 1859, 1862, and 1867	Do.
Skipwith's	High water of 1874, 48 inches below 1862	Do.
Ben Lomond	High water of 1874, 60 inches below 1862	Do.
	High water of 1874, 36 inches below 1867	Do.

Council Bend cut-off, above Helena, occurred May 10, 1874.

Original map is on file in the Engineer Bureau of the War Department.

Respectfully submitted.

W. H. H. BENYAURD,
Captain Engineers.

CHAPTER IV.

CONDITION OF THE LEVEES IN LOUISIANA.

BY COMMISSIONER P. O. HÉBERT.

I have the honor to submit the following:

1. Map showing changes of river from Sargent's Bend to twenty miles below, since the Davis cut-off in 1867. On a scale of one mile to 3 inches. (Original on file in Engineer Department, United States Army.)

2. Map showing changes of river since 1828, from the Arkansas line to Providence, on a scale of one mile to 1½ inches. (Original on file in Engineer Department, United States Army.)

3. Map of Bonnet Carré Bend, showing the crevasses of 1871 and 187 , at that point, on a scale of 1,200 feet to an inch. (Original on file in Engineer Department, United States Army.)

4. Table of crevasses that have occurred in Louisiana since 1864 to the present time, with their maximum dimensions, dates of beginning to discharge, and ceasing to discharge.

5. Table of high waters—having reference to high water of 1858, as per Humphreys and Abbot's report—and

6. Table of rate of caving at 100 different places, being every locality where cavings have taken place since 1866, from the Arkansas line down to tide-water.

7. Estimate of levees needed for 1874–'75, over and above those ordered by commission of engineers of Louisiana, amounting to 3,198,700 cubic yards of earth. To this must be added at least 250,000 cubic yards of earth for repairs. All these levees are left out, simply for the want of means to construct them.

Levees in the State of Louisiana are constructed, annually, under a contract between the State and a chartered "levee company." A commission of engineers determine, on the 1st day of October, the number and sites of levees to be built, and issue orders to the levee company in accordance therewith, accompanied with maps and all necessary specifications. After the levees are constructed another board, styled a "commission of persons," passes upon them, after proper examination. Upon their certificate the "levee company" is paid by the treasurer of the State. The "levee tax" is now limited by law to two mills for "construction," and one mill for "repairs," upon the dollar. These two taxes have, this year, been consolidated by the commission of State engineers, upon "construction." It will be perceived that the quantity of levees constructed depends upon the amount of the tax collected, the "levee company" being simply the agent of construction for the State. Without entering into tedious and unnecessary details, I would say that the State of Louisiana is at this moment in a deplorable condition in regard to protection from inundation.

With ruined finances and an impoverished people, the State of Louisiana cannot protect herself against her remorseless enemy, the Mississippi, at its annual high floods. The General Government *must* come to the rescue; otherwise, the fairest and most fertile portion of the Valley of the Mississippi must be abandoned and become depopulated. There is no illusion in this. It is simply a fact.

So far back as the year 1846, when chief engineer of the State of Louisiana, in my report to the legislature, I uttered the opinion that all improvements, including levees, upon the Mississippi, belong to the General Government, as it is a *national river*.

The system for the protection of the alluvial lands of the Mississippi should be based upon accurate scientific surveys and examinations, and include the whole valley of the river; and, once adopted, to be carried out through a series of years, if necessary, annual appropriations to be made by the Government, as for other works of national utility.

The mode of accomplishing this must, necessarily, be left to congressional legislation.

Table of crevasses that have occurred in Louisiana since 1864, with their dimensions when they can be had.

[Compiled November, 1874, by A. F. WROTNOWSKI, assistant engineer United States levee commission.]

No.	Locality.	Parish.	Right or left bank.	Date of discharge.		Maximum width.	Maximum depth at high water.	Velocity per second.	Area of crevasse.	Remarks.
				Commenced.	Ceased.					
				1864.		*Feet.*	*Feet.*	*Feet.*		
1	Ashwood	Tensas	Right			13,000	2			
2	Point Pleasant	do	do							
3	Disharoon to Simms	do	do			22,600	3			
4	Bondurant to Saint Joseph	do	do			12,000	3 to 4			
				1865.						
5	Brown and Johnson	Madison	Right							
6	Kempe	Tensas	do			4,200	10			
7	Waterproof	do	do			750	6			Two breaks.
8	New Carthage	do	do			600	5			
9	Surget	Concordia	do			400	5			
10	Scott	Point Coupee	do			600	7			
11	Chinn and Robinson	West Baton Rouge	do			700	8			
12	Bouligny	Orleans	do							
				1866.						
13	Ashton	Carroll	Right							
14	Elton	do	do							
20	Bass	do	do			11,100	8			Six breaks.
21	Miller and Morancy	do	do			500	4			
22	Duckport	Madison	do			2,000	4			
23	Marengo	Concordia	do			2,000	5			
24	Racourci	Point Coupee	do							
25	New Texas	do	do							
26	Morganzia	do	do							
27	Grand Levee	do	do							
28	Chinn and Robinson	West Baton Rouge	do							
30	Bouligny	Orleans	do			240	7			Two breaks, 36 days running.
31	Poydras	Saint Bernard	Left			300	4			Seven days running.
32	Scarsdale	Plaquemine	do			300	4			Nine days running.
				1867.						
33	Ashton	Carroll	Right							
34	Savage	do	do	April 5		1,350	2½			
35	Diamond Bend	Madison	do							
36	Point Pleasant	Tensas	do							Cut-off occurred opposite.
37	Buckner's	do	do			600	12			
38	Kempes	do	do	April						
39	Delta	Madison	do			1,000				

Table of crevasses that have occurred since 1864, with their dimensions when they can be had—Continued.

No.	Locality.	Parish.	Right or left bank.	Date of discharge.		Maximum width.	Maximum depth at high water.	Velocity per second.	Area of crevasse.	Remarks.
				Commenced.	Ceased.					
				1867.		*Feet.*	*Feet.*	*Feet.*		
40	Duckport	Madison	Right							
41	Marengo	Concordia	do							
42	Chinn and Robinson	West Baton Rouge	do							
43	Hickey	do	do							
44	Roman	Saint James	do							
45	Poydras	Saint Bernard	Left							
46	Pistola	Plaquemine	Right							
47	Boudreaux, (Lafourche)	Lafourche								On Bayou Lafourche.
48	Aubert, (Lafourche)	do	Left			225	6			Do.
				1868.						
49	Ashton	Carroll	Right			13, 000	6			
50	Illawara	do	do			5, 300	7			
51	Hawes and Harris	do	do			1, 500	3½			
52	Young's Point	Madison	do			1, 200	4			
53	Diamond Bend	do	do				2½			
54	Point Pleasant	Tensas	do			5, 500	2½			
55	Wilson's	do	do			7, 000	4			
56	Brown's, (Ship's Bayou)	do	do			600	4			
59	Disharoon	do	do			3, 000	3			Three breaks.
60	Bondurant	do	do							
61	Gillespie	do	do			500	4			
62	Saint Joseph	do	do							
63	Kempes	do	do			8, 000	12			
64	Marengo	Concordia	do			2, 400	5			
65	Glasscock	do	do				3			
66	Grand Leveee	Point Coupee	do			6, 400	9			
				1869.						
67	Ashton	Carroll	Right			13, 000	5			
68	Miller	do	do			100	4			
69	Wilton	do	do				4			
70	Diamond Bend	Madison	do				2½			
71	Point Pleasant	Tensas	do				2			
72	Wilson's	do	do				4			
73	Disharoon	do	do				3			
74	Hardtimes	do	do				7			
75	Hardscrabble	do	do				2			
76	Bondurant	do	do							
77	Kempes	do	do				11			

78	Marengo	Concordia	do				5			
79	Glasscock's	do	do				3			
80	Hermitage	Point Coupee	Right.			387	10			
81	Point Manoir	West Baton Rouge	do			250	6			
82	Turner's Bayou, (Atchafalaya)	Avoyelles	do			520	35			
83	Stockett's Bayou, (Atchafalaya.)	do	do			60	14			
84	Marine Bayou, (Atchafalaya)	Point Coupee	Left.			450	35			
85	Stokes Bayou, (Atchafalaya)	do	do			75	14			
86	Harvey's Bayou, (Atchafalaya)	Saint Landry	Right.			120	10			
87	Currant Bayou, (Atchafalaya)	do	do			225	20			
88	Ashland	Ascension	Left.			70	5			
89	Roman	Saint James	Right.			800	8			
90	Stevenson's	Saint John	do			45	10			Ran 3 days.
91	Gaudet, (Lafourche)	Lafourche	do			140	6			
92	Villere	Saint Bernard	Left.			220	4			
				1870.						
93	Ashton	Carroll	Right.							
94	Diamond Bend	Madison	do							
95	Bordalon, (Atchafalaya)	Point Coupee	Left.							
96	Marine Bayou, (Atchafalaya)	do	do							
				1871.						
97	Ashton	Carroll	Right			13,000	4			
98	Elton	do	do			60	1.5			Ran 2 days.
99	Airlie	do	do	Mar. 20		250	4			Ran about 30 days.
100	Point Manoir	West Baton Rouge	do			250	4			
101	Bordelon, (Atchafalaya)	Point Coupee	Left			7,000	4			
102	Saint James	Saint James	Right							
103	Wallis	do	Left			150	5			Ran 6 days.
104	Comas and Canty	Ascension	do							
105	Bonnet Carre	Saint John	do	Apr. 19		2,400	18	13		
106	Fashion	Saint Charles	Right							
107	Louisa	do	do			60	5			Two days running.
108	Taylor	do								
109	Palmer's									
110	Sparks	Jefferson	Right							
111	Villeré	Saint Bernard	Left	Apr. 12	Apr. 16	90	3			
112	Marero	do	do			60	3			Ran about 4 days.
113	McDonough	Plaquemines	Right			40	4			Two days running.
114	Poverty Point	do	Left			650	2½			Ran about 15 days.
115	Lagarde, (Lafourche)	Lafourche	do			220	8			Ran about 40 days.
				1872.	1872.					
116	Ashton	Carroll	Right			13,000	4			
117	Diamond Bend	Madison	do			33,000	4			
118	Kimball's Bayou, (Tensas)	Concordia	do			200	20			
119	Bordelon, (Atchafalaya)	Point Coupee	Left			7,000	4			
120	Harang, (Lafourche)	Lafourche	do			70	2			
121	D. R. Head, (Lafourche)	do	do			60	2			
				1873.	1873.					
122	Ashton	Carroll	Right			13,500	4			
123	Diamond Bend	Madison	do			33,000	4			

Table of crevasses that have occurred since 1864, *with their dimensions when they can be had*—Continued.

No.	Locality.	Parish.	Right or left bank.	Date of discharge.		Maximum width.	Maximum depth at high water.	Velocity per second.	Area of crevasse.	Remarks.
				Commenced.	Ceased.					
				1874.	1874.	*Feet.*	*Feet.*	*Feet.*		
124	Ashton	Carroll	Right	....	....	14,000	4	....	....	Two breaks; new levee.
126	Bass, Upper	do	do	Mar. 13	....	3,310	4½	....	....	
127	Bass, Lower	do	do	Mar. 13	....	1,100	4½	....	....	
128	Diamond Bend	Madison	do	....	....	35,000	4	....	....	Ten or twelve breaks.
139	Point Pleasant, Upper	Tensas	do	Mar. 22	....	2,000	1½	....	....	Eleven breaks; new levee.
150	Point Pleasant, Lower	do	do	Apr. 16	....	620	4	....	....	New levee.
151	Buckridge	do	do	....	....	1,200	4	....	....	For nearly 3,000 feet water ran over levee 2 feet deep; levee just finished when broke.
152	Hardtimes, Upper	do	do	Mar. 8	....	260	9	....	....	
153	Hardtimes, Lower	do	do	Mar. 22	....	1,400	9	....	....	
154	Green's	Concordia	do	Apr. 28	....	....	....	....	....	The Green and Glasscock cannot be considered as discharges, because the water ran into the river from the rear.
155	Glasscock's	do	do	Apr. 28	....	....	....	....	....	
156	Lakeside	Point Coupee	do	Apr. 16	....	410	6	....	....	Front crevasse; rear crevasse 4,730 feet wide.
157	Morganzia	do	do	Apr. 16	....	1,710	16	....	....	
158	Morrison	do	do	Apr. 15	....	180	5	....	....	
159	Callihan's, (Atchafalaya)	do	Left	....	....	220	3	....	....	
160	Doherty's, (Atchafalaya)	do	do	....	....	250	8	....	....	
161	Sword's, (Atchafalaya)	do	do	....	....	156	9	....	....	Bayou; new dike.
162	Marine, (Atchafalaya)	do	do	....	....	450	35	....	....	Old crevasse.
163	Bordelon, (Atchafalaya)	do	do	....	....	7,000	4	....	....	
164	Norwood, (Atchafalaya)	Avoyelles	Right	....	....	....	....	....	....	
165	Hetherwick, (Atchafalaya)	do	do	....	....	....	....	....	....	
166	Farmer Bayou, (De Glaize)	do	Left	....	....	....	....	....	....	
167	William's, (Red River)	Red River	Right	....	....	200	5	....	....	Sixty days running.
168	Wilson, (Red River)	Rapides	do	....	....	330	14	....	....	Do.
169	Echo Log, (Red River)	do	do	....	....	550	14	....	....	
170	Machorie, A'Lourse, (Ouachita)	Ouachita	Left	....	....	180	20	....	....	
171	Pargoud, Upper, (Ouachita)	do	do	....	....	....	....	....	....	
172	Pargoud, Lower, (Ouachita)	do	do	....	....	....	....	....	....	Five breaks.
177	Point Manoir	West Baton Rouge	Right	Apr. 6	....	2,630	5	....	....	Three breaks.
180	Hereford	do	do	....	....	835	4	....	....	Two breaks.
182	Lobdell	do	do	....	....	280	4	....	....	
183	Hickey	do	do	Apr. 17	....	2,500	8	....	....	Three breaks.
186	McCullam's	East Baton Rouge	Left	Apr. 8	Apr. 26	705	6	....	....	

187	Lauve	Iberville	Right	Apr. 16	Apr. 19	40	3			
188	Bonnet Carré	Saint John	Left	Apr. 11		1,370	53		34.895	Average depth at high water, 22.5.
189	Moreau, (Lafourche)	Lafourche	do	Apr. 10	May 3	430	6			
191	Selby, (Lafourche)	do	do			115	5			Two breaks; ran about 1 day.
192	Parr, (Lafourche)	do	Right	Apr. 5		130	7			
193	Belle Chasse	Plaquemines	do	Apr. 17	Apr. 29	96	10½			New levee.
194	Greenwood	do	Left	Apr. 7	Apr. 28	320	4			Do.
195	Orange Grove	do	do	Apr. 8	Apr. 10	60	8			
196	Saint Rosalie	do	Right	Apr. 6	Apr. 9	70	2			Three days running.
197	Bohemia	do	Left	Apr. 4		120	2			
198	Point à la Hache	do	do			170	2			

NOTE.—The Ashton and Diamond Bend crevasses have been left open for several years, and the volume of water is yearly reduced on account of heavy sediment which deposits itself in and behind the crevasse. The difficulty of obtaining accurate data for date of ceasing to discharge, and velocity of the crevasse current, the compiler has thought proper to leave those columns mostly blank, except where the data is authentic. In the widths and depths of crevasses, (with the exception of 1871 and 1874,) the dimensions are merely approximate, and are sufficiently reliable for a general estimate. In addition to the above list, a number of crevasses occurred, at different periods, on the Red, Ouachita, and Atchafalaya, of which there is no knowledge sufficient to record.

Table of high waters, based on high water of 1858.

Authorities: General W. E. Merrill, United States Engineers; Humphreys and Abbot Report, from 1828 to 1861; papers board of State engineers of Louisiana, compiled by A. F. Wrotnowski, assistant engineer United States Levee Com. 1874.

Figures marked thus (?) are questionable.

Locality.	Elevation above Gulf, high water of 1858.	Depth at high water of 1858.	Width at high water of 1858.	Gauge and basis of high water of 1858.	Years.													
					1828.	1844.	1849.	1850.	1851.	1852.	1853.	1854.	1855.	1856.	1857.	1859.	1860.	1861.
Saint Louis	408				−0.70	+4.30			−0.40									
Cairo	322			49.58														
Columbus	310	96	2,240	40.90		−0.90	−1.60	−2.70	−5.00							−2.10		
Memphis	221	83	3,360	34.28	−1.30	−1.00	−3.26	−0.60	−1.00	−1.20						−0.10		
Helena		71	4,080	42.41	−1.50	−2.40	−1.80	−1.80	−4.80							−1.42		
Napoleon				?45.30		−1.70		−2.40	−2.90							+0.30		
Lake Providence		87	3,580	?43.00				−2.60	−2.10							+0.30		
Vicksburg		101	2,660	46.65	−0.60	−0.80	−0.60	+0.10								+1.30		
Natchez	66	118	4,540	?47.04	+0.70	+0.10	−0.30	−0.50	−0.70							+1.20		
Red River Landing	50	126	3,500	43.33				+1.80	+0.70	−1.80								
Baton Rouge	34	108	2,350	34.63	+0.20	−0.60	+0.40	0.00	−0.08	−4.63						+0.50		
Plaquemines		128	2,700		+0.30	−0.90	0.00	−0.60	+0.10									
Donaldsonville	25.8	103	3,300	?30.00			+0.10	−1.20	+0.30	−1.60	−2.10	−2.40	−11.20	−3.80	−3.40	+0.50		
Bonnet Carre Bend	*20.21	†64	†3,700				0.00		+0.20							+0.40		
Carrollton	15.6	137		15.10	+0.10	−0.60	+0.10	−1.30	+0.30	−1.00	−0.10	−0.40	−9.10		−1.80	+0.40	−1.90	
New Orleans				†15.40														
Fort Saint Philip	5.1	151	2,400															

* High water of 1871. † High water of 1874.

Table of high waters, based on high water of 1858—Continued.

Figures marked thus (?) are questionable.

Locality.	Years.													Oscillation.	Remarks.
	1862.	1863.	1864.	1865.	1866.	1867.	1868.	1869.	1870.	1871.	1872.	1873.	1874.		
Saint Louis														41.39	Some of these heights are not supposed to be strictly accurate from want of proper comparative bench-marks.
Cairo						+1.39							−2.18	50.96	
Columbus															
Memphis						+0.52							+0.72	35.95	
Helena	+1.79					+1.21							+1.19	46.40	
Napoleon						?+1.70								46.80	
Lake Providence	?−3.30					−3.71						?−6.88	−4.59	44.72	
Vicksburg	+4.45					+2.37							−2.15	52.40	
Natchez	?−3.07					−0.32	−4.32	−2.16	−4.07				−3.84	52.70	
Red River Landing	?−2.37					?−2.37		−4.37		−4.20			+1.30	45.25	
Baton Rouge	+1.25												+1.62	36.25	
Plaquemines															
Donaldsonville	−0.32							−1.67		−0.33			−0.32	24.80	
Bonnet Carre Bend													*+1.00	22.00	
Carrollton										+0.30			+0.55	17.55	
New Orleans	−0.80									−0.60			0.00	14.70	Mean low-water oscillation daily, 1.08 - 15.78.
Fort Saint Philip															

* Above high water of 1871.

Table showing the rate of caving for different years on the Mississippi

[Compiled from notes of Board of State Engineers of Louisiana, by

Locality.	Parish.	1867.		1868.		1869.		1870.	
		Maximum length of cave.	Maximum depth of cave.	Maximum length of cave.	Maximum depth of cave.	Maximum length of cave.	Maximum depth of cave.	Maximum length of cave.	Maximum depth of cave.
		Feet.	*Feet*	*Feet.*	*Feet.*	*Feet.*	*Feet.*	*Feet.*	*Feet.*
Ashton	Carroll							20,000	2,550
Elton	....do			2,500	350	5,000	200	5,500	950
Bass	....do			9,500	400			11,000	1,000
Transylvania to Savage	....do								
Savage	....do								
Hawes Harris	Madison								
Omeiga	....do								
Morancy	....do								
Milliken's Bend	....do								
Young's Point	....do							6,000	800
Grant's Canal, upper end	....do								
Diamond Bend	....do								
Point Pleasant	Tensas							5,600	1,100
Wilson's or Buckridge Landing.	....do								
Alligator Bayou	....do								
Hardtimes	....do					10,000	1,000		
Disharoon	....do							4,000	400
Hardscrabble	....do								
Bondurant	....do								
Harper's and Kempe's	....do			9,200	1,350	11,500	650	13,500	1,400
Waterproof	....do					12,000	450	5,000	270
L'Argent	Concordia								
Marengo	....do			25,000	3,000				
Vidalia	....do								
Green's	....do								
Glasscock's	....do							6,000	800
Bourgiere or Union Point	....do					5,000	600		
Hog Point	Point Coupee					2,500	200		
New Texas	....do	5,000	260						
Morganzia	....do								
Red Store	....do			6,800	130	2,000	180		
Colomb	....do								
Waterloo	....do					2,000	170		
Point Manoir	West Baton Rouge								
Lobdell	....do								
Chinn and Robinson	....do								
Carolina	....do								
Williams	....do								
Walker's	....do								
Hebert	....do								
Hickey	....do								
Newcome	East Baton Rouge								
Conrad's	....do								
Daigle	....do								
Thuillet	Iberville, right bank								
Shlaghter	....do								
Evergreen	....do								
Stone's	....do								
Bayou Goula	....do								
White Castle	....do								
Saint Gabriel	Iberville, left bank								
Point Clair	....do								
Landry	Ascension, left bank								
New River	....do								
La Croix	Ascension, right bank								
Buena Vista	Saint James, right bank								
Webre	....do					6,000	140		
Roman	....do					2,500	140		
Cantrelle	....do					2,000	120		

River, in the State of Louisiana only, based on surveys made in 1866.

A. F. Wrotnowski, assistant engineer United States Levee Commission.]

1871.		1872.		1873.		1874.		Average depth of cave per year.	Remarks.
Maximum length of cave.	Maximum depth of cave.	Maximum length of cave.	Maximum depth of cave.	Maximum length of cave.	Maximum depth of cave.	Maximum length of cave.	Maximum depth of cave.		
Feet.	*Feet.*	*Feet.*	*Feet.*	*Feet.*	*Feet.*	*Feet.*	*Feet.*	*Feet.*	
18, 000	150	......	....	17, 000	230	16, 000	80	376	Bend of river and crevasse since 1867.
5, 000	600	5, 000	500	7, 000	320	8, 000	400	415	Gentle curve of river and sandy soil.
10, 000	350	......	....	12, 000	300	20, 500	250	287	Bend, sandy soil, crevasses in 1867 and 1872-'74.
......	.....	21, 000	900	......	......	6, 000	350	156	Bend, slight gradual wave, full force of current.
......	.....	12, 000	850	......	......	6, 000	350	150	Do.
......	.....	9, 000	900	......	......	9, 000	1, 400	287	Cave caused by Terrapin-Neck cut-off, 1868.
......	.....	7, 000	250	......	......	8, 000	800	131	Bend, current striking, effected by Terrapin cut-off.
.....	.....	13, 000	800	......	......	12, 000	1, 200	250	Do.
......	.....	......	.....	......	......	12, 000	1, 400	175	Bend, effect of cut-off above.
......	.....	......	.....	......	......	......	....	200	Opposite Yazoo River.
......	.....	4, 000	700	......	......	7, 000	600	162	Big bend, full force of current.
......	.....	......	....	35, 000	1, 000	......	......	142	Big bend, full force and effect of cut-off.
6, 200	1, 050	......	.....	11, 200	2, 000	12, 000	650	600	Water through cut-off (Davis) striking with full force, sandy.
10, 000	1, 550	......	.....	......	......	14, 000	2, 100	456	Effect of Davis cut-off, sandy.
......	....	......	.....	......	......	8, 000	340	42	Slow wave.
7, 000	500	......	.....	......	......	12, 000	600	262	Big bend, full force of current.
......	.....	7, 000	600	......	......	7, 000	300	162	Bend.
......	.....	1, 800	300	......	......	6, 000	500	100	Slight bend.
......	.....	......	.....	......	......	11, 000	600	75	Do.
14, 500	550	10, 500	450	9, 000	4, 000	......	.....	1, 200	Full force of current at upper end of bend.
......	.....	......	.....	......	......	19, 000	800	190	Big bend and full force of current, crevasses in 1874.
......	.....	......	.....	......	......	2, 500	250	31	Bend, gradual wave.
......	.....	......	.....	25, 000	1, 400	......	......	628	Big bend, full force of current, sandy.
......	....	......	.....	......	......	2, 000	300	37	Sink or slough.
......	.....	......	.....	7, 000	200	6, 000	750	119	Full force of current.
......	.....	......	....	......	......	27, 000	500	162	Full force of current and big bend, crevasses in 1870-'71-'74.
......	.....	......	.....	......	......	15, 000	600	150	Bend.
......	.....	4, 000	750	......	......	5, 500	200	143	Upper end of Raccourci cut-off and caused by same.
......	.....	......	.....	......	......	4, 000	150	51	Gradual wave, gentle curve.
......	.....	......	.....	......	......	13, 000	550	68	Bend, gradual wave caused by crevasses.
4, 800	135	......	.....	......	......	6, 500	180	78	Slight bend, but receives full force of current.
5, 000	40	......	.....	6, 000	280	8, 000	100	52	Do.
......	.....	......	.....	......	......	6, 500	40	26	Washing and wearing slowly.
......	.....	......	.....	......	......	3, 000	1, 100	137	On point, big eddy, and sandy soil.
......	.....	......	.....	......	......	6, 000	280	35	In bend, full current striking.
......	.....	......	.....	......	......	3, 500	460	57	Big bend, full current striking.
......	.....	......	.....	......	......	3, 000	280	35	Straight course, gradual wave opposite city of Baton Rouge.
......	.....	......	.....	......	......	14, 000	220	27	Sunken bank and straight river.
......	.....	......	.....	......	......	4, 000	320	40	Sunken bank about six feet above bend.
......	.....	......	.....	......	......	2, 500	250	31	In bend and receives full force of current.
......	.....	......	.....	......	......	6, 000	250	31	In bend and receives full force of current, loam and sandy soil, crevasses in 1867 and 1874.
3, 000	250	2, 000	100	......	......	......	......	58	In slight bend and receives full force of current, crevasse just above in 1874.
......	.....	......	.....	......	......	1, 800	200	25	Above point, gradual wave.
......	.....	......	.....	......	......	3, 500	220	27	Straight course above bend.
......	.....	......	.....	......	......	12, 000	240	30	Slight bend, full force of current.
......	.....	......	.....	......	......	4, 000	80	10	Do.
......	.....	......	.....	......	......	14, 000	340	42	Do.
......	.....	......	.....	......	......	15, 000	250	31	Do.
......	.....	......	.....	......	......	7, 000	350	43	Big bend, full force of current.
......	.....	......	.....	......	......	3, 500	70	9	Slight point, current strikes.
......	.....	......	.....	......	......	17, 000	100	12	Bend, current strikes.
......	.....	......	.....	......	......	5, 000	70	9	Above point, current strikes.
......	.....	......	.....	......	......	8, 000	420	52	Bend, current strikes with full force.
......	.....	......	.....	......	......	13, 000	130	16	Slight bend, current strikes.
1, 800	170	......	.....	......	......	......	......	34	Do.
8, 000	200	......	.....	......	......	......	......	40	Do.
......	.....	......	.....	......	......	......	......	47	Above bend, current strikes.
......	.....	......	.....	......	......	......	......	47	Above bend, current strikes, crevasse in 1867-'69.
......	.....	......	.....	......	......	......	......	40	Do.

Table showing the rate of caving for different years on the Mississippi River,

Locality.	Parish.	1867.		1868.		1869.		1870.	
		Maximum length of cave	Maximum depth of cave.	Maximum length of cave.	Maximum depth of cave.	Maximum length of cave.	Maximum depth of cave.	Maximum length of cave.	Maximum depth of cave.
		Feet.	*Feet.*	*Feet.*	*Feet.*	*Feet.*	*Feet.*	*Feet.*	*Feet.*
Union	Saint James, left bank.								
Fairchild	Saint James, right bank								
Stevenson's	Saint John's, right bank								
Bonnet Carre Church	...do								
Carroll	...do								
Angelina	Saint John's, left bank.								
Saint Peter's Church	...do								
Below Bonnet Carre crevasse of 1874.	...do								
Ramson	Saint Charles, right bank.								
Zoelly	...do								
Ashton	...do								
Zeringue	...do								
Pecou	Saint Charles, left bank								
Ormond	...do								
Sarpy	...do								
Frellsen	...do								
Waggaman	Jefferson, right bank								
Labranche or Kennedy's	...do								
Westwego Railroad depot	...do								
Wall's	...do								
Oakland	Jefferson, left bank								
Kennerville	...do								
Trudeau	...do								
Sauve	...do								
Soniat	...do								
Mason	...do								
Carrollton	...do								
McDonoughville	Orleans, right bank								
Orleans	...do								
Villere	Saint Bernard								
Walker's	...do								
Story's	...do								
Poydras	...do								
Carnearvon	Plaquemines, left bank								
Scarsdale	...do								
Greenwood	...do								
Belair	...do								
Fairview	...do								
Point a La Hache	...do								
Bellechasse	Plaquemines, right bank								
Myrtle Grove	...do								

in the State of Louisiana only, based on surveys made in 1866—Continued.

1871.		1872.		1873.		1874.		Average depth of cave per year.	Remarks.
Maximum length of cave.	Maximum depth of cave.	Maximum length of cave.	Maximum depth of cave.	Maximum length of cave.	Maximum depth of cave.	Maximum length of cave.	Maximum depth of cave.		
Feet.	*Feet.*	*Feet.*	*Feet.*	*Feet.*	*Feet.*	*Feet.*	*Feet.*	*Feet.*	
2, 000	90	......	......	......	......	......	......	18	In bend, current strikes with full force.
......	......	......	......	......	......	3, 000	120	15	Slight bend, current strikes.
......	......	......	......	......	......	2, 000	20	3	Slight force of current.
......	......	......	......	......	......	1, 500	30	4	Do.
......	......	......	......	......	......	3, 500	30	4	Slight bend.
......	......	......	......	......	......	2, 000	80	10	Do.
......	......	......	......	......	......	2, 500	130	16	Straight course.
......	......	......	......	......	......	3, 000	150	18	Bend, full force of current, crevasses in 1871 and 1874.
......	......	......	......	......	......	3, 000	70	9	Slight bend.
......	......	......	......	......	......	2, 000	70	9	Do.
......	......	......	......	......	......	2, 500	80	10	Do.
......	......	......	......	......	......	2, 500	90	11	Do.
......	......	......	......	......	......	2, 000	200	25	Do.
......	......	......	......	......	......	1, 500	300	37	On point, caused by eddy.
......	......	......	......	......	......	11, 000	300	37	Bend, current strikes.
......	......	......	......	......	......	11, 000	120	15	Slight bend, current strikes.
......	......	......	......	......	......	3, 500	180	22	Big bend, current strikes.
......	......	......	......	......	......	12, 000	110	13	Straight river, current strikes.
......	......	......	......	......	......	4, 500	60	8	Bend, current strikes, eddy caused by wharf built for railroad depot.
......	......	......	......	......	......	1, 500	30	4	Bend, current strikes.
......	......	......	......	......	......	5, 000	200	25	Slight bend, current strikes.
......	......	......	......	......	......	3, 000	180	22	Do.
......	......	......	......	......	......	4, 000	60	8	Do.
......	......	......	......	......	......	5, 000	180	22	Do.
......	......	......	......	......	......	2, 000	50	6	On point, eddy.
......	......	......	......	......	......	4, 000	30	4	Straight course, gradual wave.
......	......	......	......	......	......	6, 000	40	5	Bend, current striking.
......	......	......	......	......	......	7, 000	220	27	Do.
......	......	......	......	......	......	3, 000	200	25	Do.
......	......	......	......	......	......	2, 000	20	3	Slight bend, current striking, crevasse in 1869-'71.
......	......	......	......	......	......	1, 800	30	4	Slight bend, current striking.
......	......	......	......	......	......	3, 000	60	8	Do.
......	......	......	......	......	......	6, 000	220	27	Big bend.
......	......	......	......	......	......	6, 000	40	5	Slight bend, current striking.
......	......	......	......	......	......	1, 500	30	4	Do.
......	......	......	......	......	......	1, 800	160	20	Slight bend, current striking, crevasse in 1874.
......	......	......	......	......	......	3, 000	20	3	Slight bend, current striking.
......	......	......	......	......	......	2, 500	40	5	Straight course, current striking.
......	......	......	......	......	......	7, 000	30	4	Straight course, gradual wave, crevasse in 1874.
......	......	......	......	......	......	3, 500	80	10	Bend, current striking with full force, crevasse in 1874.
......	......	......	......	......	......	6, 000	30	4	Do.

Table of levees caved into the Mississippi River, from caving banks alone, in Louisiana, from October, 1866, *to October*, 1874.

[Compiled from notes in the office of board of State engineers of Louisiana, by A. F. Wrotnowski, assistant engineer United States Levee Commission.]

Locality.	Parish.	Right or left bank.	Wing-levees, in feet.	Curtain-levees, in feet.	Total wing-levees caved.	Total curtain-levees caved.
Ashton	Carroll	Right	1, 718	13, 410		
Elton	do	do	3, 475	11, 364		
Bass	do	do	3, 590	18, 870		
Point Lookout	do	do	389	1, 310		
Transylvania	do	do	1, 320	4, 920		
Airlie	do	do	1, 210	3, 250		
Goodrich	do	do	910	1, 100		
About Illawarra	do	do	2, 010	10, 010		
Newman	do	do		780		
Hawes Harris	do	do		7, 490		
Total in Carroll					14 622	72, 504
Morancy	Madison	Right	1, 010	9, 310		
Milliken's Bend	do	do		5, 980		
Duckport	do	do		2, 280		
Young's Point	do	do	750	2, 080		
Upper end of Grant's Canal	do	do		1, 870		
Diamond Bend	do	do	750	11, 300		
Kellogg's	do	do	550	6, 900		
Total in Madison					3, 060	39, 720
Point Pleasant	Tensas	Right	4, 055	16, 340		
Wilson's	do	do	1, 010	18, 270		
Brown's	do	do	650	1, 350		
Hardtimes	do	do	1, 690	4, 510		
Disharoon	do	do	1, 620	4, 970		
Hardscrable	do	do	260	2, 820		
Bondurant	do	do		6, 680		
Kempe's	do	do	7, 010	21, 630		
Waterproof	do	do	3, 050	11, 600		
L'Argent	do	do		430		
Total in Tensas					19, 345	88, 600
Marengo	Concordia	Right	125	450		
Vidalia	do	do	120	1, 150		
Green's	do	do	1, 650	13, 250		
Glasscock's	do	do	2, 150	17, 500		
Bourgiere	do	do	370	4, 500		
Total in Concordia					4, 415	36, [illegible]50
Hog Point	Point Coupee	Right	1, 400	2, 950		
Fisher's Landing	do	do		1, 100		
New Texas	do	do	800	3, 400		
Morganzia	do	do	250	1, 900		
Grand Levee	do	do	720	7, 100		
Cooley's	do	do	300	4, 300		
Red Stone	do	do	750	6, 300		
Colomb's	do	do	400	750		
Van Wickle's	do	do	50	1, 820		
Waterloo	do	do	240	2, 520		
Fausse River, Lower	do	do	1, 250	1, 500		
Total in Point Coupee					6, 160	33, 640
Point Manoir	West Baton Rouge	Right	350	1, 050		
Cain	do	do	850	7, 500		
Barrow	do	do	550	2, 750		
Lobdell's	do	do	370	3, 050		
Buhler's	do	do	220	530		
Brady's	do	do	60	1, 036		
Bird's	do	do	60	360		
William's Point	do	do		300		
Ferry Landing	do	do	270	1, 250		
Patrick's	do	do		300		
Brusle Landing	do	do	210	1, 050		
Walker's	do	do	770	2, 340		
Hebert's	do	do	150	820		
Hickey's	do	do	880	3, 156		
Australia	do	do		750		
Total in West Baton Rouge					4, 760	26, 242

Table of levees caved into the Mississippi River, &c.—Continued.

Locality.	Parish.	Right or left bank.	Wing-levees, in feet.	Curtain-levees, in feet.	Total wing-levees caved.	Total curtain-levees caved.
Newcome	East Baton Rouge.	Left	200	3, 230		
Conrad	....do	....do	200	850		
Martinez	....do	....do	220	450		
Lopez	....do	....do	300	1, 800		
Daigle	....do	....do	50	1, 050		
Walker's	....do	....do	1, 030	2, 950		
Total in East Baton Rouge					2, 000	10, 330
Ventress	Iberville	Left	660	1, 420		
Gourier	....do	....do	150	650		
Stingle Store	....do	....do	60	750		
Saint Gabriel	....do	....do	320	1, 180		
Le Blanc	....do	....do	300	980		
Brown's Store	....do	....do	150	1, 040		
Berry's	....do	....do	340	1, 340		
Walsh	....do	....do	....	350		
Thuillet	....do	Right	300	1, 650		
Wood's	....do	....do	780	6, 750		
Slaughter's	....do	....do	....	1, 040		
Gay's	....do	....do	200	660		
Evergreen	....do	....do	450	4, 680		
Landry's	....do	....do	580	3, 000		
Stone's	....do	....do	250	6, 750		
Hebert's	....do	....do	100	750		
Rooney's	....do	....do	150	700		
Hall's	....do	....do	....	750		
Braud	....do	....do	....	300		
Bayou Goula	....do	....do	120	450		
Tally Ho	....do	....do	450	2, 760		
Dubuclet	....do	....do	250	2, 020		
White Castle	....do	....do	....	750		
Total in Iberville					5, 610	40, 720
Burnside	Ascension	Left	....	410		
New River	....do	....do	....	2, 050		
Doyal	....do	....do	200	2, 310		
Landry	....do	....do	1, 180	3, 650		
Bringier	....do	....do	125	1, 200		
Marchand	....do	....do	450	1, 200		
Riverton	....do	....do	90	600		
Duffel	....do	Right	50	250		
Legare	....do	....do	60	450		
Barrowville	....do	....do	40	150		
Lacroix	....do	....do	120	800		
Manning's	....do	....do	600	2, 200		
Pedesclaux	....do	....do	350	1, 250		
Total in Ascension					3 265	6, 520
Hebert	Saint James	Right	....	1, 900		
Buena Vista	....do	....do	220	2, 750		
Turcuit	....do	....do	50	750		
Le Bœuf	....do	....do	100	450		
Webre	....do	....do	360	1, 120		
Roman	....do	....do	80	1, 070		
Cabahanocy	....do	....do	160	1, 560		
Union	....do	Left	130	880		
Poche	....do	....do	130	400		
Nichol's	....do	....do	....	900		
Jacob's	....do	....do	120	1, 020		
College Point	....do	....do	....	1, 200		
Laiche	....do	....do	150	780		
Humphries	....do	....do	....	510		
Duplantier	....do	....do	160	1, 060		
Total in Saint James					1 660	16, 350

Table of levees caved into the Mississippi River, &c.—Continued.

Locality.	Parish.	Right or left bank.	Wing-levees, in feet.	Curtain-levees, in feet.	Total wing-levees caved.	Total curtain-levees caved.
Lebourgeous to Tregor's	Saint John	Left	110	860		
Godberry's	do	do	240	2, 200		
Godberry's to Reserve	do	do	490	2, 480		
Saint Peter's	do	do	340	1, 410		
Jaubert	do	do		1, 150		
Bonnet Carre to Gipsey	do	do	1, 030	1, 380		
Good Hope to Sarpy	do	do	420	4, 060		
Ormond	do	do		2, 310		
Pecan Grove	do	do	120	7, 000		
Frellsen	do	do	900	9, 710		
Parish Line	do	Right	690	2, 080		
Devil's Store	do	do	300	960		
Stephenson to Rousell's	do	do	590	2, 180		
Bonnet Carre Church	do	do	130	1, 840		
Hymel	do	do	60	250		
Zoelly to Killona	do	do	120	2, 360		
Whitehead to Davenport	do	do	465	1, 750		
Newman and Fausse	do	do	400	1, 830		
Ramson to Ashton	do	do	580	2, 980		
Lone Star to Louisa	do	do		2, 820		
Zeringue to Freret	do	do	550	2, 980		
Total in Saint John					7, 535	54, 590
Waggaman to La Branche	Saint Charles	Right	660	3, 320		
Oakland to Kennerville	do	Left	700	5, 240		
Trudeau and Sauve	do	do	1, 050	4, 500		
Soniat	do	do	50	800		
Total in Saint Charles					2, 460	13, 860
Deblieux and Augustine	Jefferson	Left	100	600		
Fazende and Wall's	do	Right	120	1, 710		
Total in Jefferson					220	2, 310
Orleans	Orleans	Right	90	760		
Lepretre	do	do	580	4, 050		
Villere's	do	do	250	1, 300		
Total in Orleans					920	6, 110
Villere's	Saint Bernard	Left	60	360		
Story and Merritt	do	do		5, 940		
Ducros and Poydras	do	do	660	2, 350		
Total in Saint Bernard					720	8, 650
Carnaervon	Plaquemines	Left	620	3, 570		
Corn's	do	do	170	450		
Sawyer to Greenwood	do	do	450	2, 870		
Belair to Fairview	do	do	200	1, 070		
Poverty Point	do	do	350	4, 810		
La Hache to Bohemia	do	do	690	3, 150		
Kernachon	do	do		800		
Bellechasse to Concord	do	Right	155	1, 050		
Star to Myrtle Grove	do	do	60	2, 070		
Oakland	do	do	40	1, 500		
Total in Plaquemines					2, 735	21, 340
Total linear feet					79, 487	488, 336
Total right bank					64, 022	383, 056
Total left bank					15, 465	105, 280

Estimate of levees needed for 1874–'75 over and above those ordered by commission of engineers of Louisiana.

Locality.	Parish.	Stream.	Right or left bank.	Contents in cubic yards.	Remarks.
Ashton	Carroll	Mississippi	Right	167, 000	Crevasse; has been opened for several years; chief State engineer's estimate.
Omeiga	do	do	do	24, 000	Estimate of commission of engineers of Louisiana.
Diamond Bend to Kellogg's	Madison	do	do	860, 000	Crevasse; has been running several years; estimate across neck to Vidal Bayou.
Point Pleasant	Tensas	do	do	60, 000	Estimate of commission of engineers of Louisiana.
Buckridge	do	do	do	40, 000	Estimate of commission of engineers of Louisiana—low-grade levee; for full grade, plus 355,000.
Hardtimes, (Upper)	do	do	do	34, 000	Estimate of commission of engineers of Louisiana.
Hardtimes, (Lower)	do	do	do	45, 500	Do.
Glasscock	Concordia	do	do	580, 000	Crevasse; estimated for permanent line, from Henderson levee to Brabston's, 39,000 feet long.
Morganzia	Point Coupee	do	do	205, 000	Estimate of commission of engineers of Louisiana.
Bonnet Carre	Saint John	do	Left	290, 000	Do.
Willard's Bayou	Bossier	Red River	do	20, 000	Estimate of W. C. Melvin, assistant State engineer of Louisiana.
Wilson's	Rapides	do	Right	40, 000	Do.
Echo Landing	do	do	do	40, 000	Do.
Mouth to Muscle Bayou	Point Coupee	Atchafalaya	Left	398, 000	Estimate of J. V. Van Pelt, chief engineer Louisiana Levee Company.
Mouth to Petit Prairie	Avoyelles Saint Landry	do	Right	380, 200	Do.
La Fourche	La Fourche	La Fourche	Right and left	15, 000	Approximate.
Total				3, 198, 700	

NOTE.—The Ashton, Diamond Bend, and Glasscock are not included in the estimate of the commission of engineers of Louisiana; and these would reduce the amount actually needed to 1,591,700 cubic yards over and above the amount ordered by the commission of engineers of Louisiana for the year 1874–'75.

I have the honor to be, very respectfully, your obedient servant,

P. O. HÉBERT,
Of the Commission of Engineers.

APPENDIX A.

REPORT OF C. M. FAUNTLEROY, SECRETARY OF THE COMMISSION, UPON THE APPLICATION OF THE RESERVOIR SYSTEM TO THE VALLEY OF RED RIVER.

WASHINGTON, D. C., *December* 7, 1874.

SIR: In the interim between the receipt of your letter of instructions of the 21st of September last and the present, I have devoted the time in ascertaining, in the Red River Valley of Louisiana, as much positive information as I could about the extent of the lakes and other low areas in the bottom-lands of Red River that might be made available as reservoirs to restrain the floods of this stream; and, altogether, such information as I have been able to collect, will, I trust, be of that kind that shall conform as near as practicable to the exact requirements of your instructions.

The time allowed me, and the appliances available, have not sufficed for that critical personal investigation of the subject of artificial reservoirs within the natural basins of the upper-lake regions which would justify me in attempting more than some general observations in connection with the facts imparted to me by those who have for a long period of time been familiar with this interesting problem.

With regard to the second branch of the subject submitted for my report, I have less embarrassment, for, having resided upon the banks of Red River for some years back, and having very frequently traversed the stream in its extent, from its mouth to Shreveport, to and fro, my attention has long been earnestly directed to the question of the most advantageous method of protecting the alluvial lands of this region from overflow. Proceeding to treat the several propositions as they have been presented, the lake country comes first in review; and here I would present some views of Mr. W. C. Melvin, civil engineer, (who is, and who has been for a number of years, assistant State engineer for the Red River district of Louisiana;) but before doing so, I will take occasion to say that I came in contact with no individual in that section who possessed, by general consent, a greater amount of practical knowledge bearing upon the subject of my investigations than did this engineer. The United States engineer-steamer Sterling having been placed at my command for the purpose of examining the lake country with the view to this report, Mr. Melvin very kindly accompanied me. Unfortunately for my purpose and personal satisfaction, we were prevented by extreme low water from proceeding further in that direction than to Gold Point, on Soda Lake, opposite to Albany.

In response to my inquiry for reliable information Mr. Melvin writes:

"I beg leave to submit to you only such facts as come within my individual knowledge. With the view of forming a basin or basins to retain a portion of flood-water to supply the river during the low-water seasons, I believe that one basin, embracing all the lakes from Springbank down to Couchatta, and thence in a direction southwest-by-west, below Sewal's Canal, crossing Peace's Bayou and Black Bayou to Irvin's Bluff, below Harrison's saw-mill, with *locks* at Black Bayou to be constructed to supply Clear Lake, and thence through to Ferry Lake and Cypress Bayou and Jefferson, Tex., could be availed of for this purpose. Lieutenant Fuller makes the fall of water from Fulton, Ark., to the head of the raft 0.20 to the mile. (I believe it to be somewhat greater, though I am not prepared to prove it.) From Springbank to Couchatta Bluff the distance by river is thirty-three miles. This will give a fall of 6.60 in this distance to be overcome by a dam extending from the west bank of Red River to the west bank of Black Bayou and the bluff forming the western limits of this basin. Should this dam be built four feet above flood-level, leaving at the river 30,000 feet superfice, no danger need be apprehended of the dam being flooded. This section, with the locks or waste-weirs that will be required at Black Bayou, will give a discharging section of one-third more than that of the river at Shreveport, where all the waters from above are confined to a single channel, a section of which is 23,000 feet long, being more than sufficient to contain within the banks the flood-water of 1874, which was greater in volume than that of any flood since 1849. A dam at the place named would be nearly 5½ miles in extent from bluff to bluff, and should have an average height from ground surface of 10½ feet, crossing Caddo Prairie and some other points that are above the mean swamp-level.

"These Caddo Prairie lands were in former days cultivated successfully, but for long years have been abandoned on account of constant liability to overflow. The basin formed here would of course prevent them from being cultivated in future. The number of acres which would thus be rendered permanently useless is less than four thousand; no other lands would be affected.

"The area covered by this basin is something more than 113 square miles, or 3,150,259,100 square feet, and will retain an average depth of water of five feet above mean low water, giving 15,751,296,000 cubic feet of water to be retained to feed the river at its lowest stages. The water discharged through the channel of the river at the 'Packery,' one mile below Shreveport, during low water does not exceed 3,000 feet of cross-section, with a current less than 2 miles per hour. The additional supply from the basin described of 2,000, making the section of discharge 5,000 feet, we shall have thus nearly four feet of water in the channel, that will last about 28 days coming from the basin.

"There is yet another basin which could be made to supply ¼ more water than the one just described, and which would serve to extend the time during which this additional quantity of water might be kept in the channel, say 35 days longer; giving in all 63 days of fair low-water navigation." Our low-water season usually commences in July, about the 15th, and continues until somewhere near the middle of November. The crops are usually disposed of before the commencement of low water in the river, and the supplies have been returned to the planters, who are again preparing another crop that cannot be made available until about October 1st, and then only a small part of it, (for the whole of the cotton-crop is seldom ready for market before the 25th of December,) consequently the supply of water in the river will not last long enough to serve in moving the crop as it is gathered, for the water from the basins becomes exhausted in September.

"The area covered by the second basin before named would be something more than 160 square miles, embracing within its limits Ferry Lake, Caddo Lake, Jim's Bayou, Clear Lake, and all the swamp-lands lying east of these, to the west bank of Red River, from Cowhide Bayou down to Gold Point on the eastern limit, and to the Gate-Posts above Albany on its western limit.

"A dam with locks and waste-weirs near Albany, running northeast and ending opposite Gold Point, would be about two and a half miles in extent. As one of the objects of this basin would be for the improvement of the navigation through to Jefferson by Cypress Bayou, the best way to accomplish this and make the navigation permanent would be to put locks at Albany and dredge through Ferry Lake and Cypress Bayou, the entire fall from Jefferson to Albany not being great enough to make this impracticable.

"This, however, would not improve the navigation from Albany to the foot of Twelve-mile Bayou, and probably the fall of water between these two points being too great to be readily retained by locks, and the character of the soil composing the banks, of such a nature as would render the construction of these locks altogether too expensive ; a channel cut from the extreme northeast arm of Soda Lake and entering the river two miles below Willow Chute and about the same distance above the proposed dam of Mr. Leavenworth, would probably be more effective than to depend upon Twelve-mile Bayou as the channel for navigation, as is now the case. I believe that a lock having a lift of 6 feet, will do.

"With the limited time commerce would be benefited by these expensive works, it may be a matter of doubt whether the almost certain destruction of the planting interest on the west side of the river from Dooley's Bayou down to the position occupied by this dam near Gold Point, will not be in excess of the benefits accruing from it. The formation of this reservoir would have for its purpose the improvement of the navigation through to Jefferson. But I am of the opinion that this consideration is of slight moment when it is understood that navigation to that place is but spasmodic and altogether uncertain, and for the greater time, when most wanted, not practicable.

"Bayou Bodceau, and the lake of that name, is sometimes mentioned as a convertible basin to relieve the floods of Red River. This lake can in no way be so utilized, as it has no connection of importance except through Loggy Bayou, 110 miles below Shreveport, and at this point the river has within its banks a section sufficient to discharge the waters of the ordinary annual floods; hence it can be of no value whatever in this connection.

"Lake Bisteneau, the recipient of the waters of Dorcheat Bayou and other smaller ones principally flowing into it from the east, is a lake of considerable extent and of commercial importance, affording, at ordinary stages of water, fair navigation to Minden, about eight miles above its head on the Dorcheat.

"Lake Bisteneau, unlike many of the other lakes, does not connect with any other series until it reaches the waters of Bodceau and other bayous near its foot in the bottom-lands of Red River, when it discharges through Loggy Bayou and Couchatta Bayou into this stream.

"The character of the lands bordering the lake and forming extensive bottoms, liable to overflow yearly, is of a superior quality, and crops can be and often are made after the floods have receded, which is seldom later than May, and often in the month of April.

"A project for converting this section into a reservoir would be of no benefit whatever, in my opinion; for, in the first place, it has not sufficient dimensions to be useful; next, its connection with the river-bottom from Swan Lake down to Bayou Couchatta is such that the work would be enormously expensive; and, finally, by this process much valuable bottom-lands in its borders would be rendered valueless. I conclude, therefore, that it will be best to leave Lake Bisteneau to take care of itself.

"Cross Lake, having its outlet through Cross Bayou at Shreveport, during medium and higher stages of water, is filled through Bluid Bayou and Bowman's Chute, and some lesser bayous, from Twelve-mile Bayou.

"According to Lieutenant Fuller, this lake, at mean low water, is rather more than 20 feet lower than Soda Lake. The distance from the gate-posts to Bluid Bayou is about 21 miles by water-course. It does not, during flood-seasons, damage any valuable lands, except, perhaps, a few hundred acres lying between Twelve-mile Bayou and its eastern margin."

Mr. Melvin does not deem it at all practicable to utilize the natural basin, in which lies the Bayou Pierre, for several reasons, good and sufficient in my view, and which will be made to appear further along. One important effect may be accomplished by the formation of reservoirs above Shreveport, viz, the forcing the whole volume of water to find its way out through the main river from Carolina Bluffs to Shreveport. This part of the river has been gradually filling up since the formation of the raft above. The larger volume of water that will thus be made to pass through will increase the scouring process, and thereby its section of discharge, and will, at no very distant day, be found sufficient to carry off all the water which the floods may supply.

The question arises from this: Will it not be better to confine the waters by a system of levees on both banks of the river, that will effect the double purpose of reclaiming more than 150,000 acres of magnificent farming-lands, while at the same time improving navigation?

The State of Louisiana has a system of levees that possibly would be sufficient if under proper direction, and there was the necessary means within the State to perfect it in this river.

A line of levee built extends from the higher banks on east side of the river near the Hurricane Bluffs to Murray's Bayou, eight miles below Mrs. Cain's, opposite the city of Shreveport. This line closes every outlet through the east bank of river, except Mack's Bayou, and that I believe is to be closed during the current year.

The number closed already is seventeen, among the most important of which are Willow Chute, Williams' Bayou, Benoit's Bayou, and Cain's Bayou.

Willow Chute and Williams' Bayou conducted the waters of the river into Lake Bodceau near its foot, thence out through Red Chute Bayou to the foot of Lake Bisteneau, and through Loggy and Couchatta Bayous into Red River again. All the other bayous enter Red Chute Bayou, and through it again strike the river.

We come now to a very important system of levees, both in the interests of navigation and the very valuable planting-interests existing and to be created by it, embracing the entire basin lying west of the river, and extending west of Bayou Pierre to the hills forming the west boundary of the basin, and extending from the bluffs one mile below Shreveport, to the Bayou Wincey, a distance of 148 miles by river from Shreveport, embracing an area of more than 400,000 acres of the most fertile lands in this or in any other State.

It is said that for this class of lands 760 pounds of lint-cotton to the acre is not an unusual crop. But the liability to overflows prevents, in a great degree, planters from risking their means in the attempt to cultivate here. There should be good levees built from the bluff below Shreveport down, closing Bayou Pierre and all the old channels of Red River left by the cut-offs (there being three of them) down to Shreve cut-off, and thence down to Tone's Bayou.

This turbulent and altogether useless bayou depletes the river, during mean low water, of five-sevenths of its feed, drawing it back to Bayou

Pierre, and thence over the tough mixture of blue clay, muscle-shells, and gravel, that is found to extend from Gravel Point to above the Red Banks, and having no well-defined channel, but spreading over the whole bottom. With all its accessions of water this Bayou Pierre is not navigable its entire length at any time, and only about three months in the year is it navigable as high as Gravel Point, distant from Grand Bayou only three miles.

There have been numerous attempts made to effect a partial stoppage of Tone's Bayou, so that during low-water seasons the water would in the main be free to follow the river. Success has never attended any of these efforts, and any future attempt to partially close it must be one of doubtful results.

It should be permanently closed with a strong earth levee, having wings, sufficient to prevent any possible chance of the action of the water passing around it. I am informed that the Secretary of War authorizes the statement that an appropriation will be asked of Congress especially for the purpose of permanently closing this bayou. The State has at one time closed all the outlets hereabout of importance, except Grand Bayou. Bayou La Chute, one mile above the mouth of Loggy Bayou, is open. The State levee some years since broke, and has never been rebuilt. One-half mile below Loggy Bayou is another levee that caved into the river in 1873. Within this half mile there are two other bayous putting out, having good levees across them yet. From this point to Shreveport the levees will not average more than 5 feet in height. Forty-three miles of levee will here be required, sixteen and a half of which had at one time been built by the State. Below this not much is needed, the river being wide and deep enough to contain the flood-waters. Nothing has been said of the lands lying east of the river, though there are many valuable plantations on that side above Loggy Bayou. They are less than one-fifth in extent and value compared to those on the west side of the river.

As it would hardly be possible to carry on the work of leveeing both sides at the same time, it is obvious where the work should be first entered upon.

Time and assistance must be given to the river to scour its bed to a greater depth, and for its banks to cave. For this purpose, all the growing timber of every description that is standing within 60 feet of the crest of the banks should be cut away; roots and stumps loosened; in short, everything done to facilitate the caving and scouring process. A dredge-boat should be kept at the work of removing the obstructions in the bed of the river, such as wrecks of steamers and barges, sunken logs, &c., &c.

For this purpose the United States steam snag-boat Aid is well adapted, and it would entail no great expense to the Government, whilst it would be of incalculable benefit to navigation and commerce, by assisting the river to acquire rapidly the requisite capacity of discharge within its own banks.

The character of the soil composing these bank is such that, upon examination of them, any engineer would concede the correctness of this conclusion.

Mr. Melvin does not favor a system of reservoirs for reclamation, he says, for "the reason that instead of reclaiming, they would destroy their availability for agriculture, and thus detract from instead of adding to the value of the district through which the river passes."

The main object of these reservoirs being the better facility for navigation, and the prevention from overflows by the too sudden precipitation of the flood-waters upon the lands below, this purpose would the more readily be effected by leveeing both banks of the river where required, and gradually closing the outlets. By a complete system of levees commencing from Springbank on the east bank, and at Blanton's Bluff on the west bank of the river, closing every outlet on both sides, these lakes and swamps will be soon almost made dry. The only water entering them will be the drain from the high bluffs and lands surrounding the basin.

On the east of the river the only outlet required for this drainage will be Dutch John's Slough, putting into the river at Couchatta Bluffs. Posten Bayou will afford ample water-channel to Dutch John Lake and into the river.

On the west side of the basin Peace's Bayou and Black Bayou will prove ample to carry all the water drawn from the high lands on that side into Clear Lake and Shift-tail Lake, thence through Soda Lake and Twelve-Mile Bayou into Red River.

It will need, to effect this, levees on the east side of the river, extending through three townships, requiring perhaps 24 miles of levee, that will probably average 8 feet in height. On the west bank the levees would aggregate, say, 2,600,000 cubic yards, at a cost of 30 cents per yard, which would be $780,000. As a compensation for this outlay, we should have the improved and improving navigation of the river through this section, just cleared of raft, and heretofore useless; and for the second consideration 174,000 acres of the best cotton-lands in the world will be in a condition to be cultivated; one-half for immediate use, and the other half would gradually assume the same condition. It is a moderate estimate to say that this will enable us to produce 70,000 bales of cotton more than can now be produced, with a corresponding increase in the other products of the soil annually.

"The section of the river one mile below the city of Shreveport has a capacity of high-water discharge of 23,000 feet superfice nearly." The high water of 1874 left the bank on the east 1.20 feet above flood level. On the west it skirts along high bluffs. Though this channel all the waters of the river have been collected that above this point were distributed through various outlets; those of the eastern basin being all returned at and above Couchatta Bluffs; those of the western basin through Twelve-Mile Bayou and Cross Lake, on the northwest boundary of Shreveport; thus we need not fear being flooded at this point.

Below Shreveport on the west the river is depleted by Bayou Pierre, Sand-Beach Bayou, Tone's Bayou, and Bayou La Chute. On the eastern side of the river we have still open Mack's Bayou, branch of Murray's Bayou, and Braddock's and Mulberry Bayous, all of considerable extent, besides eleven other bayous, among which will be found Lay's Bayou above Lotier Point. As this bayou returns a portion of its waters to the river below the Scopini, it should be closed with the eleven mentioned.

With all these bayous taking the waters from the main river and conducting them through the more direct and shorter routes to re-enter the river through Loggy Bayou from the east, and Bayou Wincey through the west bank, twelve miles below Tone's Bayou, we have a section of discharge of nearly 3,700 feet superfice within its banks. Through Tone's Bayou we have a section of discharge about 5,600 feet, with a greatly accelerated current. Above Tone's Bayou we have a section of discharge in the river of about 9,000 feet. We shall then have lost, before arriving at Tone's Bayou, 14,000 feet of high-water section, and after passing Tone's we have lost 19,300 feet. This quantity then passes over the basins east and west of the main river The means used to recover and confine this to the river must be gradually applied.

Below the mouth of Bayou Cotile the State in time past had built a continuous line of levee down to Bayou Rapides, and from thence, commencing at the south bank of the bayou running up some miles, a continuous line down below the line between Rapides and Avoyelles, about six miles. A great part of these levees remains intact; but many serious breaks and crevasses exist, and so render the whole of the plantations from the town of Alexandria down (with but few exceptions here and there) entirely useless for planting.

I am informed by Mr. Melvin that in 1871, he, in his capacity as assistant State engineer for the Red River district, made thorough examination and estimates of the number of cubic yards and the character of each separate work of repair and construction, and that the cubic yards in number aggregated 763,000.

These repairs have been neglected so long that no doubt a greater amount of work will now be needed to be done. Owing to the high floods of last season in the Mississippi, and its crevasses, the Red River Valley lands were submerged from the mouth of the river to within fifty miles of Alexandria. Levees on the east side of the river are but little required, only here and there for particular plantations, from its mouth to Grand Ecore, whilst on the west they are not needed for a greater distance than thirty-five or forty miles on the river below Alexandria. Six to nine miles below this place, the levee, which was already in a precarious condition, has gone into the river for the distance of one-half mile since the recession of the waters. At Wilson's plantation, some thirty miles below Alexandria, the high water of last season broke through, doing much damage, owing to the very wretched state of the levee at that point. Upon the Atchafalaya River and the Bayou La Glaise even the very indifferent levees thereabout saved much very valuable land from the Mississippi overflow of the Lower Red River Valley. Here I would offer the suggestion, in view of the possibility of the General Government taking the conduct of the levees in charge, the necessity of prescribing stringent regulations providing against the habit, universal and most pernicious, of turning hogs upon the levees.

In my opinion, the key to the question of reclaiming the alluvial lands of this valley is to be found in the fact that, during the high flood of this year, the banks of the river, along its narrows between Tone's Bayou and Loggy Bayou were not inundated, save in some very low places. But on both sides of the river, the waters coming from the rear caused what damage was sustained; (fortunately the water subsided in time so that good crops were made.) Can this remarkable fact be accounted for by reason of the removal of the great raft-obstructions above? A correct solution of this query will, in my opinion, go far to solve the problem of reclamation in this valley. If the answer be in the affirmative, then the greater quantity of water heretofore dispersed through many outlets has now recovered its ordinary river-channel, with increased volume and velocity, and the scouring process becomes correspondingly increased; and thus already has the river in that region reduced the level of both its bed and surface to the degree requisite for its ready discharge through its own banks.

I believe that the hitherto controverted question of the effect of levees upon rivers has been conclusively settled in favor of the system. Where there are few outlets to raise the level of beds in sedimentary streams, the effect of volume gives increased velocity, and the combined effect deepens the bed and enlarges the surface.

It is a well-ascertained fact that the Mississippi River becomes deeper as it approaches the sea, and the amount of sedimentary deposit washed through defies close estimate, though we have some approximate of it by the obstructive bars outside of its mouth.

G. W. R. Bayley, civil engineer and member of the commission of engineers for levees in Louisiana, kindly furnished me with some opinions, which I deem worthy of record here:

"Colonel Charles M. Fauntleroy, &c.:

"DEAR SIR: As requested by you, I submit the following brief statement of my general views respecting what should be done for the improvement of the Red River Valley country in Louisiana.

"I would apply the levee system to Red River, and thereby facilitate and expedite the washing out and enlargement of the channel between Grand Ecore and Shreveport, and between Shreveport and the head of the raft, by retaining all the water possible in the main river. The removal of obstructions, logs, snags, rafts of drift-timber, &c., to the free flow of the water in the main river where contracted and elevated, both bed and surface, by deposits caused by the old raft below Shreveport and the new raft above, would be necessary to favor the required enlargement of the main river. Levees should be located far enough back from the river-bank to allow for enlargement; and outlets which divert water from the main channel should be closed, from time to time, and so rapidly as the enlargement of the main river will permit of its being done. I would build levees of ample width of crown and base, and not less than two feet above the highest known water-mark.

"The greater the quantity of water thus retained in the channel, the greater the velocity and the more rapid the scour; and the greater the quantity the less the slopes of bed and surface required for its discharge.

"Where the rafts were, the bed and surface and banks of the river are many feet higher than they were before the raft-formation, when all the water was confined to one channel, as between Cotile and Alexandria, and below, opposite Grand Ecore and Shreveport, and above the upper limits of the raft. Where the greatest quantity of water is confined to one channel, the slopes are least. The rafts, acting as dams, caused lateral overflow, the elevation of the river-banks, and the filling up of the river-bed by deposits and sunken logs. The effect of outlets, however caused, is to raise the bed and surface of sedimentary rivers. I would reverse the process on Red River, and particularly through the old and new raft-regions. In time, the levels of bed and surface would be reduced, and the dangers of overflow much lessened thereby.

"The lakes between Grand Ecore and Shreveport owe their origin to the elevation of the bed and banks of the main river caused by rafts. The head of the raft was near Natchitoches, when Louisiana was first settled, and the beds of portions of the lakes above Shreveport were above overflow and in cultivation within the memory of men yet living. The removal of the raft and the maintenance of a judicious levee-system is, in my opinion, the best and indeed the only remedy.

"Reverse the process by which mischief was done.

"It is possible, as you say, to convert the lakes above Shreveport into an immense reservoir, and to utilize the water so retained to prolong navigation below Shreveport during the low-water periods. This is practicable, but would be expensive.

"At present the valley-lands above Shreveport are of little value and but little cultivated. Their submergence to make the reservoir would therefore entail but little loss. I think that such a reservoir would be of very little, if any, practical use to reduce the danger of overflow below. After it became filled—and it would fill long before the floods pass, generally—it would be, of course, useless, and the breaking of such a dam, from any cause, would be a terrible calamity.

"Below Shreveport you could not make reservoirs without overflowing, by back-water, the cultivated and cultivable lands on the river-banks.

"I think that the best policy would be to try to facilitate the drainage of all these lakes, and to favor the discharge of water from them by excavating, by means of dredging-machinery, draining canals up into them from their lower ends, where they empty into Red River, just above Shreveport, Grand Ecore, Loggy Bayou, Couchatta, &c.

"In substance, then, my plan of improvement for the Red River Valley, in Louisiana, would be a levee system, with a gradual closure of all outlets for the main river, and thereby a cutting off the water-supply which makes the lakes, in great part, and the drainage of the lakes themselves at their lower ends, and their reclamation by means of deep canals carried into them at the level of the river below them."

I concur generally with the foregoing, and would be glad to see the levees built and maintained by the General Government under an organized levee department, comprised entirely of officers of the Engineer Corps, United States Army, within the nominal purview of the Engineer-in-chief.

It is absolutely certain that in the bankrupt condition of the people, and of the State of Louisiana, nothing worth while will or can be done to remedy the widespread existing disastrous crevasses, or as a remedy for future occurrences of similar character. If the General Government does not come to the rescue, the richest portion of this fertile country will have to be abandoned.

I regret the impossibility of obtaining any reliable information regarding the high-water marks of flood seasons between the years of 1849 and 1874. There are special facts not heretofore stated that primarily affect the navigability of the Red River that perhaps had best be noted here. I shall, however, mention the one which I regard of the greatest importance. It is as to the condition of Latier's Bend, twenty miles below Shreveport. The neck of Latier's point is now about 250 feet across; the distance around it is 6½ miles. The difference in water-level at this neck, as measured at various times, gives an average of 2.30. That part of the point passing from the upper side of the neck is encumbered with numerous wrecks of steamers, dangerous snags, and logs.

The action of the water at the neck of the point is rapidly cutting through, and doubtless will, in a year or two at most, divert the water by this cut-off there made. The effect of this will be to cause still greater difficulty in navigating this part of the river, unless means are promptly applied; for when the water has cut through the upper strata of the deposit, a channel of not more than 8 or 10 feet deep will have been made down to the older formation that at one time formed the bed of a lake, and which is so hard and tough, that the water in its passage over it will be powerless to effect a deeper cut; here, then, dredging will be requisite to effect a channel of sufficient depth and width for the water to pass readily at all stages.

Very respectfully, your obedient servant,

CHAS. M. FAUNTLEROY,
Secretary to the Commission.

G. K. WARREN, *Major Engineers, &c.,*
President of Commission.

APPENDIX B.

REPORT OF SURVEY AND BORINGS MADE AT THE PROPOSED SITE OF THE LAKE BORGNE OUTLET,

BY C. G. FORSHEY, ASSISTANT ENGINEER, UNDER ORDERS OF THE COMMISSION.

Among the many propositions for controlling the floods of the Mississippi River, for the protection of the cultivator of its alluvial lands, attention has been prominently turned to outlets or weirs, for the discharge of the surplus waters during the flood season.

Only two localities present themselves for such weirs, with any feasible means of guarding and disposing of the waters thus extravasated, without defeating the object of the levees; that object being the safe defense of the cultivator against river-floods.

These localities are the Bonnet Carre and the English Turn, and call for more thorough examination.

Both were treated in the great delta survey of 1851 and 1860, by Humphreys and Abbot, whose opinions favored such experiments under certain conditions prescribed by them.

The consideration of the Bonnet Carre, where the river approaches near Lake Pontchartrain with a very high levee on the left bank, showed, however, some momentous consequences of an outlet there, namely, the obstruction of Lake Pontchartrain as a navigable lake, by deposits from the river, and the destruction of the Great Northern Railroad; both of which seemed inevitable, and stood as weighty objections to that locality.

The English Turn (two miles below) brings the river in like nearness to Lake Borgne, and without involving consequences so grave as obstacles to an outlet for the river. Lake Borgne has but minor value as a navigable water; and, with shores opening directly to the Gulf, could not have its level materially elevated by receiving a discharge of Mississippi waters.

The distance from the river to Lake Borgne at Story and Repose plantations, is only 5.3 miles. (See map A.)

The bend of the river is somewhat convex, and slowly encroaching upon the land, with a high-water level above the land, varying from 5 to 6 feet along the banks nearest to the lake.

The bayou Bienvenue, of historic note, bounds above, and bayou Duprez limits below, the area over which the waters must be guided, in case of a weir being established here. The Mexican Gulf Canal has been cut from near the river-bank to bayou Duprez, and, utilizing its channel, the canal passes with it into the lake, at about four miles south of the mouth of bayou Bienvenue. Both these channels must be avoided by the works which will be required to control these waters and guide them to the open lake; and, even then, it is probable that both would soon be destroyed as navigable channels.

TOPOGRAPHY OF THE GROUNDS.

I have caused an exact survey to be made of the lines selected for the probable location of the levees of protection, starting 8,000 feet apart on the levee-front, the lower line 82 feet below the line of Story and Repose plantations.

This line bears about N. 65° E., and reaches the lake 1,583 feet above the mouth of Bayou Duprez.

Its length from levee to lake is about 28,200 feet = 5.322 miles. The upper line makes an angle of 120° with the river, bearing N. 35° E., and steers clear of, and reaches the lake just below the mouth of Bayou Bienvenue. Its length from the river to the lake is 34,400 feet = 6.5 miles.

Within this area of 12.5 square miles the space of open plantation-land, chiefly on the Story estate, is 750 acres = 1.2 square miles.

The area of swamp-land, covered with trees, generally small maple and ash with large cypress, is 4.74 square miles = 3,033 acres.

All the prairie is liable to daily tidal inundations, while the forest is but little higher, in the main, and is frequently, much of it daily, under water.

The lower boundary-line, starting from the river, now at low water, rises ten feet to the batture bank, (nearly one hundred feet wide from there to the levee.) This rises two and a half feet above the batture, and two inches above high-water mark of 1874, the highest known flood in this portion of the river.

The line then descends 4 feet to the base of the levee on the land side, and thence with the land surface nearly 4 additional feet in the first station of 700 feet. It then rises, after crossing this low ground, to an elevation of only 4.5 feet below the datum, and thence the ground declines, with slight undulations, for about 4,000 feet farther, or a mile from the levee, to the general level of the forest swamp. This is only 1.5 feet above the lake level at mean tide, or 11.5 feet below the high water of the Mississippi River.

This level is maintained, with very gentle undulations of only half a foot, to the end of a long forest projection that reaches within a mile of the lake itself.

Near the lake the ground rises 1 foot to the shore, where it has a natural ridge or levee of an additional foot, beyond which it falls directly to the level of the Gulf, just 13 feet below the high-water mark of 1874, as taken on the levee November 5, 1874.*

The upper boundary-line has a batture about 200 feet, 3.5 feet below high-water mark, a levee 4.5 feet above batture, and the line descends on land side to 5.5 feet.

In 1,000 feet it descends to 8 feet, and in 4,000 feet it reaches, at the end of the plantation, a depression of 12 feet, to the forest swamp level. The forest, like that on the lower line, is of small saplings, increasing in size with some large cypress, back to 12,127 feet. Thence the prairie marsh maintains nearly the same level of 12 feet below datum to within 500 feet of the lake. Thence it rises 1 foot to the very shore, which is bounded by a natural bank 1 foot high, and drops to 13 feet, the lake and gulf level.

The lake along this entire front has a depth of 10 feet within 1,500 feet of the shore-line.

Near the shore it deepens 1 for every 150 feet, and the bottom is hard, compact black or blue clay.

Above and below our area of discharge are considerable bayou channels—Bienvenue and Duprez, with channels of 20 feet and 10 feet depth, and 100 and 300 width; but from their mouths out into the lake

* Day calm and clear, without extra tides, but relative state of tides at 14 inches in lake and river not well ascertained.

there is no defined channel, (except as cut for the canal at Duprez's mouth,) and only a mud-bar of about 4 feet of water. Into Duprez vessels of 8-feet draught, with lumber and oysters, enter and pass up the channel and through the Mexican Gulf Canal, near the river-bank, half a mile below our lower line.

Thus the whole area is without topographic vicissitude. The forests would have to be razed and entirely removed, or burned, to give free flow to the waters from the river to the lake. It will be seen from the profiles herewith (see Chart B) that the outlet could not be depended upon for more than 5 feet discharge at high water, nor for more than 4 feet during the dangerous flood-season.

This would furnish a jutage of 32,000 square feet, and practical discharge of not more than 4 feet per second. The discharge then would amount to 128,000 cubic feet per second.

In like manner the lake front being leveed by an elevation of 1.5 feet above the swamp-level, reduces the discharging depth by as much, and leaves a practical cross-section 16,000 by 2 = 32,000 square feet, with a fall of 9.5 feet in $\frac{56 + 68}{4}$ = 31,000 feet = mean distance to the lake.

Such discharge, over a very rough bottom at best, would probably equal 4 feet per second, but could not be relied upon for more than 5 feet, and this rate would deliver 150,000 feet per second.

Should this opening be made, the revetting required to protect it from abrasion and cutting a channel should be confined to the jaws and river above and below them, and should not cross the channel-front nearer than about 1,000 feet back, until the surface-front should be carried away back to that distance. There is much doubt whether that would be effected by the current. But without it the discharge would not render the amount of service expected.

Beyond that distance, I should have no expectation of abrasion or disturbance of the surface-soil.

In the forest portion of the weir, even after the smoothest practicable clearing, I would expect accumulations of drift-wood, tow-heads, and rafts to form, and be half buried in the sand, thus encouraging the closure of the weir.

These must be annually removed, if practicable. And even with the exercise of all human effort, I doubt our capacity to prevent the destruction of the Lake Borgne outlet.

The levees will be so little diverged as to make the delivery at the lake about double the width at the river. It would be 16,000 feet wide and 2 feet deep in delivery = 32,000 × 5 = 160,000 cubic feet.

It is probable that such delivery would best accomplish its purposes and have least risk of self-closure.

I respectfully recommend the weir of this form.

GEOLOGY OF DEPTHS AND TOPOGRAPHY OF SURFACE.

The general slope of the lands fronting on the river is rapid back toward the lake, reaching near the swamp-level at about 3,000 or 4,000 feet from the river-bank. In like manner with the habitudes of the river throughout its alluvial beds, it has here graded its banks back to the swamp by dropping its heaviest and coarsest material first, and by bearing farther from the channel the lighter and alluminous particles. Thus, when the overflow was arrested by the levees, the process of the swamp elevation and extension of the higher alluvion back toward the lake was cut off, leaving the graded slopes a permanence forever.

PROCESS OF GEOLOGICAL FORMATION.

Our borings at the river penetrate the level of the Gulf at about ten feet from the surface.

The deposit below this was made in the sea, as was all the alluvial material below the Gulf level.

In the process of filling the Gulf the river has, doubtless, preserved a fluctuating channel beneath the sea-water. Hence, any shaft sunk into the alluvion, for example between the river and lake, at the proposed outlet, may pass through all the variety of material thrown down *in the channel*, and along the channel-banks.

These materials vary from coarse sand, associated with logs and fragments of wood, to fine sand, various clayey matters, chiefly aluminous, iron oxides, and decayed vegetation. Each of these may form a bed for itself, but more generally they are mixed two or more together, excepting quicksands and blue clay. These are often found pure, and in greatest depths.

BORINGS TO DETERMINE THE STRATIFICATION BETWEEN LAKE BORGNE AND THE MISSISSIPPI RIVER AT "ENGLISH TURN."

Apparatus.—The augur used for penetrating the ground and bringing up samples of the matter beneath, is a common one and a quarter-inch boring-augur, with screw-shaft of one foot length and handle-shafting of one inch gas-pipe in five-foot sections. This penetrates through 1½-inch gas-piping, driven down by a small pile-hammer worked by hand, lifting and dropping it upon an anvil or heading fitted on and in the head of the pipe.

Experience has shown that in driving these five-feet sections of piping the matter penetrated rises in the tube, and that the driving readily reports the moment when this ceases. The auger is then introduced, and by a few revolutions fills the whorls of the screw with the mud, clay, or sand in the tube.

Generally it is withdrawn at each foot of descent, often passing two or three feet below the tube's extremity, and samples of the borings are bottled and labeled and preserved for inspection.

The tube is then driven with greater ease as far as the auger has preceded it. Most of the penetrations are without difficulties except that all the deep borings show increased difficulty in driving, owing of course to friction against the ground.

Quicksands are not penetrable by driving, but the force-pump is attached to the auger-shafting, the inner tube conducting water down to the quicksand and forcing sand and water up the sides between the two tubes; and this is easily driven, if promptly plied, down the cavity thus made, following to the bottom of our quicksand stratum.

Samples of this are kept in like manner as other materials.

In two instances only were impassable obstructions found.

In boring No. 3, on the river-front, we found at eighty feet an obstacle stubbornly resisting the tubing, and battering its lower end in such manner as to indicate some hard rock, which, when pulverized, left a whitish matter on the battered end of the tube.

I believe it to have been a granite bowlder, or other very hard rock, probably pertaining to the drift-beds* supposed to pass beneath the Gulf.

* The diluvial beds or the stratum of pebbles, siliceous rocks, in the bluff formation at Vicksburgh, Grand Gulf, Natchez, Tunica, Bayou Sara, and even Baton Rouge, show the dip southward to be very gentle; and whether at that geological age the Gulf held its present level or not, there is good reason to believe that some of its material was borne forward and dropped into the depths, by the melting ice of the glacial sea. It is no matter of surprise that our shaft should encounter such obstacles.

Another obstacle in another boring arrested the auger and tubing. But we believe that this was compact indurated sand. Our haste forbade delay in favor of mere scientific inquiry. The area for the proposed weir (see plan) was thus sounded for its stratification in fourteen localities, as shown, four in front, four at 1½ miles back, three midway, thence to the lake, and three on the lake-front.

The minutes of these borings were carefully recorded by Capt. Jenks Brown, and his book of record is transmitted for examination in proof of the care and detail of his work.

The samples taken at every five feet of depth are preserved in glass jars, closed and labeled on the spot.

The time allowed for this work was insufficient by a month; and the necessity of work at night, in these nearly inaccessible marshes, amid serpents and mosquitoes, must explain many deficiencies. The depths obtained for the first two lines is one hundred feet, and for the others about seventy feet, mean.

The following are general remarks deduced from the study of the samples obtained from the borings:*

---

*A complete analysis of the specimens obtained from the borings will be made, but could not be prepared in time for this report.

A selection from these specimens was sent in boxes by Professor Forshey to Prof. S. F. Baird, of the Smithsonian Institution, for identification and classification. The latter referred them to Prof. A. Verrill, of New Haven. By him part were sent to Professor Dawson and part to Professor Carpenter, of Montreal. Answers to these applications for scientific assistance were not received by Professor Forshey in time to be embodied in the report submitted by him to the commission. These gentlemen, however, very kindly and promptly complied with the requests made upon them, and the information on being received by Professor Forshey was sent by him to the commission, and is here embodied as a note to this report, at the place indicated therein by him.

G. K. WARREN,
President of Commission.

Extract from a letter from Prof. Philip B. Carpenter, Ph. D., to Prof. C. G. Forshey.

Principal Dawson writes that "the sand in your box is purely siliceous. There are no *Foraminefera* in it, but there is very little material. There is one piece ot a *Bryozoon*, probably *Membranipora;* species unknown to me."

Professor Verrill writes: "The fragments of *Echinids* apparently belong to two different genera, one a *Spatangoid*, and the other is perhaps *Mellita pentapora*."

List of Mollusca from boriny No. 6, 64 feet deep, in Mississippi delta; compared by Professor Carpenter, Montreal.

Marked species:

(1.) *Nassa Hotessieri*, D'Orb., 1 + fragment, adult.
(2.) *Olivella nitidula*, Dillw., 1 sp., *jun.*
(3.) *Olivella? fulgens*, Riv., 1 sp., very young.
(4.) *Pleurotomid.* Small fragment, not enough to recognize even the genus.
Lucina? Carribœorum, D'Orb., 3 valves.
Anania. Fragment.
Pecten. Fragment.
Lithophagus. Fragment.
Cardium? muricatum. Fragment.
Tellenids. Various fragments, genus and species uncertain.
(3*a*.) *Corbula, larribœa*, D'Orb., 2 valves.
(3*b*.) *Spirula lateralis*, Say., 3 valves + fragments.

All the above are believed to be now living in the Florida seas.

There are, besides, two fragments of *Bulanid;* one fragment? *Membranipora;* several fragments *Spatangoid* and? *Mellita pentapora;* all in siliceous sand.

At various points, for example, in boring No. 7 we found white sand, indicative of pure marine source. This was without shells. At several other places our auger brought up fragments of marine shells, sometimes whole ones, mostly young, all of recent genera and species, evidently at the then bottom of the Gulf.

They were so frail and light as to prove their residence in some cove, or protected locality on the sea-bottom. The material in which they were found was manifestly alluvial, cast down through salt-waters, ultimately smothering and destroying them.

The inference is encouraged that the Gulf, beneath the alluvion, is not deeper here than 100 to 200 feet.

Other reasons for the same conclusion, in the Gulf shore depths, may be found both west and east of the delta, at near this distance.

An approximate estimate of Gulf depth at this point of the river may be had by inspection of the soundings made by the Coast Survey along the Gulf borders, say in the Vermillion Bay, west of the delta, and in the Mississippi Sound, east of the delta. Prolong the Gulf shore curve from west of Vermillion to east of Bay Saint Louis, it will pass through New Orleans, and ten miles north of this point.

The ten-fathom line would not be distant from this point.

Wherever the river-bed has occupied the ground sounded, we should expect a depth of 100 feet or more for the alluvial beds.

Elsewhere the depths may be (and probably are) less than a hundred feet from the bottom of the bay that projected up to Manchac and beyond, prior to this alluvial deposit.

Accordingly in several of these shafts we pierced the sea-shore or sea-bottom materials, both in recent sea-shells and sands, and at times muck lying immediately upon the bottom sands. This I supposed to have been sea-weed cumulated in masses in the bottom of interior bays.

Mud of soft black or bluish kind is found, of considerable depths, in some of these borings, resembling the mud-lump borings nearer the river's mouth. The irruptions of carburetted hydrogen gas from the shafts were marked by violence, throwing mud and shells in quantities, and for several minutes, from the tube, from sixty or seventy feet of depth. This gas burned freely, with reddish flame; and, from one of the shafts, continued several days. This is a general phenomenon of the craters of mud-lumps.

Please find a sample of the shells and mud thrown up from sixty-five feet depth in Shaft No. 11, box marked (P.,) also a sample from boring No. 10, at sixty to seventy feet depth, marked (Q.)

This resemblance of some localities in our borings to the mud-lumps is not unlikely, *a priori*, when we reflect that the Mississippi has been encroaching upon the Gulf from far above this locality, and with precisely similar materials has been reclaiming it from the sea. As the phenomena of the mud-lump, its shiny mud, its salt springs, and its gaseous eruptions, now exhibit themselves along the bars of the river as they push out in front of the present passes, so in remote times, when the mouths were discharging into Lake Borgne, and filling the gulf beneath it, the bars pushed forward as at present, suppressing the springs that discharge themselves from the diluvium, and choking their discharge, and causing the upheavals called mud-lumps, and the volumes of gas constantly generating from the decomposition of masses of vegetable matter.

The shafts sunk in New Orleans a few years since furnished such quantities of gas as to promise a permanent supply for illuminating the city.

The jets have gradually subsided, as should have been expected.

All these facts point to the extent of the source, and justify the impression that it is generated in the bottom of the river-alluvion, and probably from the accumulations of sea-weed and sunken marsh grasses, in the interior and shallow bays. The trembling prairies may have furnished much that was carried to these depths, as the Mississippi sediment actually found above it was precipitated upon those prairies.

These considerations are submitted from but a cursory examination of the material brought up from the depths.

Many of the most striking features have been presented in the very last of the borings.

A further examination of the series of samples would doubtless develop much of scientific interest. But time is wanting.

The boxes containing the parcels have just come from the field, and have not been opened or inspected, except as seen occasionally during the work. They await the orders of the board.

I respectfully ask for time, at least another month, for the study and report of these "voices from the delta depths."

One result of the boring may be taken as fully established. The area proposed for this outlet presents no risks whatever of the formation ot a river-channel to the Gulf by means of the proposed outlet.

THE CROSS-SECTIONS OF THE RIVER.

The soundings made across the river-channel above, in front of, and below our proposed weir are made at a distance of 6,500 feet apart.

These exhibit a contraction in channel-capacity unusual in these comparatively stable portions of the river-bed; the largest of these shows a mean section of the Mississippi, the lower sections indicating a more tenacious material in the bed.

The concave bank selected for the proposed weir is gradually, but very slowly, yielding to abrasion, the encroachment having driven back the levee only one remove at the lowest end, according to tradition, within the levee history.

These sections show a depth of only a few feet below our borings in front of them; these borings on the front line show no evidence of the base of alluvial deposits. Borings No. 2 and 3 lie above and below this middle section; they are the lower 82 feet and the upper 100 feet deep, starting only 7 feet above the river-level as sounded. The river would appear here, at least, as carrying its own channel in alluvial deposits. For form, depth, and location, please refer to Chart B, herewith.

ESTIMATES OF COST OF LEVEE-PROTECTION FOR THE LAKE BORGNE OUTLET.

It must be borne in mind that the public highway, on the Mississippi River, is along the river-banks at the land-side base of the levees.

In making an opening for outlet of the river's flood-waters, it will be necessary to cut off this highway entirely. And as there is no way to flank the outlet, nor to preserve its bottom for a public road, even during season of water too low to escape through the weir, the public opposition of the inhabitants will manifest itself in demands for damages. Nor is it improbable they will be able to make the damage apparent, at least the inhabitants within twenty miles below the weir.

No roads in Louisiana are half so much traveled as the two, running one up and the other down the river from the city.

While it is impossible to put this damage into the limits of an estimate in dollars, it must be held in view as one of the pecuniary obstacles.

The next item is more easily approximated, namely:

The levee-protection of the weir.

Above and below the proposed weir, the country must be protected from inundation by guard-levees, properly built and protected against breach or abrasion.

Two methods have been estimated upon, as already submitted to the board, and now recomputed from accurate data, and the results submitted herewith:

Ordinary earth-work levee.

I have assumed for this levee a wide crown in consequence of its importance, say twenty feet, have taken slopes at three and three to one, and then computed the prismoid.

The upper levee, reaching the lake a short distance below Bayou Bienvenue, has a length of 3,440 feet, to which I add a return of like dimensions, up the river-bank 1,000 feet.

The lower levee has a length of 28,200 feet, to which I add a like return on the river front of 1,000 feet.

An examination by our borings of the surface stratum shows the vegetable and spongy matter to be about five feet in depth, a material that will not be reliable for more than two feet of solid embankment.

Hence it will be necessary to add to the height of our levee three feet to cover actual sinking throughout all the marine-marsh distance traversed.

Of this marsh, we find 24,000 feet length on the upper, and 6,000 feet length on the lower line.

The following are the cubic contents:

	Cubic yards.
Upper levee	643, 158. 88
Lower levee	527, 240. 18
Guard-levees	21, 260. 00
Sinkage	275, 000. 00
Total earth-work	1, 466, 659. 00
Probable cost at 50 cts. for earth-work	$733, 329 00

The cost of clearing the forest portion of the area, 5,053 acres, smooth to the ground, wood cut to pieces of ten feet, at, say, $10 per acre, $30,530.

Value of lands to be purchased.

One entire plantation, Story's, with improvements, sugar-mill, machinery, and buildings, &c., Story's cultivable land, 750 acres, at $100	$75, 000 00	
Forest-swamp, 3,529 acres, at $5	17, 645 00	
Marine marsh, 3,857 acres, at $1	3, 857 00	
Improvements of all kinds	25, 000 00	
		$121, 502 00
Ervine's plantation-land, 10 acres, at $100	1, 000 00	
Forest-swamp land, 524 acres, at $5	2, 620 00	
Marine-marsh land, 330 acres, at $1	330 00	
		3, 950 00
Total value of lands to be purchased		125, 452 00

Revetment for outlet floor and walls.

The investigations of this survey warrant the conviction that there will be no abrasion of the general floor beyond the immediate vicinity of the front.

For the better delivery into the weir, with the depth of the estimate, some abrasion of the floor in front would be desirable.

Any revetment, therefore, for the floor should be brought not nearer than 1,000 feet from the river's bank.

Both guard-levees, however, and the walls or jaws of the weir, should be well guarded by such protection of piles, timbers, and fascines, as should entirely prevent abrasion.

For this purpose let piles be driven at 6-feet intervals, and timbers let into them horizontally, securing fascines of cypress-brush, compactly covering the surface on front of the levees, and to a distance of 40 feet from base. Let this defense be stronger and wider for 200 feet length around the angles, and extend thence for 800 feet ± down the entrance on each side.

At this distance, let the piling and fascine revetment extend across the weir, with piles at 10 feet apart, sunk 5 feet in the ground, and timbers secured to them, holding firmly and smoothly a fascine floor of cypress-brush. Let this fascining extend back 800 feet, limited by the height of the ground. At a descent of 10 feet below datum (high-water mark) the revetment would be useless, because of the toughness of the ground.

But the protection of the levees from driftwood and abrasion of violent currents should be extended the whole length of the lake, requiring a line of piles and timber defenses in front, on both sides.

All timbers and lumber to be of cypress.

A very rude estimate, based upon these requirements, exhibits the following:

Flooring piles, at 30 cents per foot	$130,000
Lumber, $40 per M	80,000
Fascines, 10 per square yard	71,000
Revetting mouth of weir	9,000
Defensive work to lake	43,000
Total revetment	333,000

Second levee estimate—Levee with partition.

Give a crown of four feet, at three feet above high-water mark, and prescribe the slopes at 1 to 1.

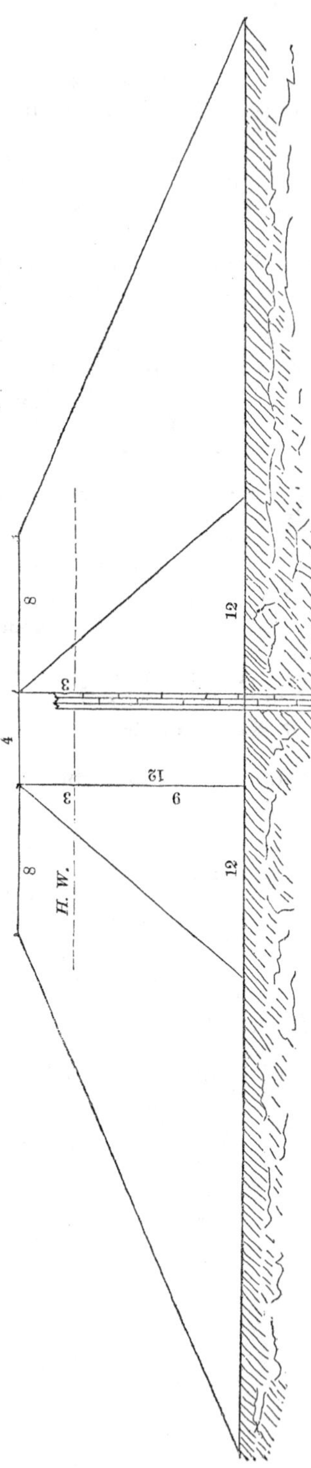

The earth-work of this levee would be reduced to 378,138 yards, after allowance for sinkage of 73,333 yards.

The lumber would amount to 2,791,906 feet, with posts 2 by 12 inches, and planking 2 inches thick, doubled to break joints—the posts to be six feet apart.

The fence rising above high-water mark must be covered three feet by the crown of the levee, and be sunk about three feet in the natural ground, cutting off all roots in the forest portion of the line. In the marsh portion, the fence to be sunk five feet below the surface, the mean depth of the muck and roots of the grasses.

Summary of costs.

Levee, 347,850 yards, at 50 cents	$173,925
Lumber, 2,792 M feet, at $50	139,600
Total amount for levee	313,525
For clearing	30,530
For property	125,452
For channel revetting	333,000
Total cost with Forshey levee	802,507

Cost of earthen levees.

1,446,659 yards, at 50 cents		733,329
Other items as above, viz:		
Clearing	$30,530	
Property	125,452	
Channel revetting	333,000	
		488,982
		1,222,311

The above estimates are rendered as nearly as practicable to the true cost, but with diffidence as to their certainty.

CONCLUSION.

Having, as herein shown, completed the work upon the Lake Borgne outlet survey as thoroughly as the limited time allowed would permit, this report of all the operations is most respectfully submitted.

C. G. FORSHEY,
Assistant Engineer,

NEW ORLEANS, LA.,
November 30, 1874.

APPENDIX C.

STATISTICS OF COTTON, SUGAR, AND CORN CROPS IN THE ALLUVIAL BASIN OF THE MISSISSIPPI RIVER SINCE 1840.

BY MR. A. D. BANKS.

VICKSBURG, MISS.,
November 1, 1874.

In accordance with the resolution of your board, adopted at its session in New York City, July, 1874, I have the honor to submit the following memoranda and statistics.

Very respectfully,

A. D. BANKS.

Maj. Gen. G. K. WARREN,
President, &c.

The object apparently contemplated in the resolution of Congress, creating your commission, is to examine into the expediency of protecting from inundation, and bringing into safe cultivation, a region of country, covering an area of over thirty-two thousand square miles, or twenty millions four hundred and eighty thousand acres.* This soil is of unsurpassed fertility, and has no equal either in extent or in productive capacity in any other alluvial formation in the world.

This vast territory has been subdivided, by the distinguished United States engineers who have examined it, into four sections:

First, the country below Red River belonging to the Louisiana sugar and rice region.

Second, the area lying between the Red and Arkansas Rivers, bounded on the west and north by the highlands of Louisiana and Arkansas. This region embraces the four front north parishes of Louisiana, Concordia, Tensas, Madison, and Carroll, with Chicot and Desha Counties in Arkansas.

Third, the "Yazoo basin," bounded on the east by the Yazoo, Tallahatchie, and Coldwater Rivers, and on the south and north by the bluffs of Mississippi and Tennessee.

Fourth, that portion extending from Cape Girardeau on the north to Helena on the south, and from the Mississippi on the east to Crowley's Ridges on the west, and known as the "Saint Francis basin."

Nearly the whole of this vast space is annually at the mercy of the Mississippi River, and all who plant there, have to do so at the risk of inundation.

Once reclaim, by a permanent system of protection, the prolific lands of the Mississippi Valley, and in ten years, it is believed, the cotton export from the United States would be doubled. On this alluvial soil, the labor of the cotton States can be intrenched, and it can successfully contend with all Christian and Pagan attempts to compete with this country in the production of cotton.

These bottoms are capable of making from 1,500 to 2,500 pounds of seed-cotton per acre, and, in the climatic conditions necessary for the growth of this great staple, have no equal in the world. The soil is the accretion of centuries, and is of great depth and surpassing fertility.

---

* Report of Generals Humphreys and Abbot.

FIRST LOUISIANA SECTION.

Parishes.	Improved acres.	Cash value of plantations.	Sugar, hogsheads.	Molasses, gallons.	Rice, pounds
1850.					
Ascension	28, 346	$7, 121, 695	13, 434	554, 975	....
Assumption	31, 361	6, 000, 325	17, 160	930, 186	....
Avoyelles	33, 898	1, 409, 239	4, 481	291, 350	12, 200
East Baton Rouge	37, 535	2, 458, 886	7, 074	407, 358	....
West Baton Rouge	25, 775	2, 291, 125	7, 920	518, 870	....
Iberville	40, 050	5, 128, 400	23, 208	1, 310, 750	....
Jefferson	22, 430	1, 821, 928	8, 897	430, 580	....
Lafourche	40, 268	2, 479, 324	10, 055	345, 126	....
Orleans	4, 844	579, 200	1, 495	52, 055	....
Plaquemines	39, 774	5, 669, 150	16, 835	589, 130	....
Point Coupee	43, 010	2, 547, 777	8, 560	321, 546	....
Saint Bernard	11, 435	1, 211, 043	4, 367	173, 000	....
Saint Charles	20, 596	2, 362, 000	10, 206	531, 300	....
Saint James	41, 905	3, 096, 155	21, 670	926, 438	....
Saint John the Baptist	22, 285	2, 367, 300	11, 935	638, 230	....
Saint Landry	87, 584	2, 184, 748	5, 951	317, 970	....
Saint Martin's	35, 971	1, 635, 971	4, 188	237, 160	....
Saint Mary's	43, 051	4, 710, 920	24, 765	897, 660	....
Terrebonne	18, 706	2, 397, 939	9, 171	435, 290	....
1860.					
Ascension	42, 666	6, 253, 790	16, 087	881, 297	....
Assumption	57, 881	7, 013, 350	17, 707	1, 230, 584	50, 800
Avoyelles	58, 078	5, 175, 358	4, 445	284, 424	739
East Baton Rouge	55, 220	2, 588, 300	5, 447	412, 680	....
West Baton Rouge	39, 044	3, 650, 210	10, 176	724, 570	....
Iberville	62, 523	12, 661, 190	33, 828	2, 149 820	....
Jefferson	24, 148	2, 682, 080	9, 467	702, 300	....
Lafourche	40, 555	4, 104, 100	14, 736	1, 001, 210	381, 550
Orleans	5, 749	1, 301, 000	2, 050	134, 000	....
Plaquemines	28, 975	2, 791, 700	12, 607	819, 600	4, 635, 500
Point Coupee	82, 932	8, 815, 520	12, 187	1, 342, 195	3, 000
Saint Bernard*	....	....	....	....	....
Saint Charles	29, 969	3, 261, 900	7, 067	543, 500	821, 385
Saint James	45, 166	3, 557, 050	13, 736	1, 193, 160	11, 772
Saint John the Baptist	32, 481	2, 592, 800	4, 981	462, 250	134, 600
Saint Landry	93, 292	5, 026, 118	3, 437	339, 610	59, 640
Saint Martin's	42, 870	4, 850, 021	7, 499	524, 329	....
Saint Mary's	78, 389	9, 737, 100	30, 731	43, 336	22, 049
Terrebonne	38, 816	7, 166, 390	17, 022	1, 210, 603	131, 016
1870.					
Ascension	40, 691	1, 475, 633	6, 423	308, 587	15, 926
Assumption	39, 895	1, 953, 395	9, 558	499, 135	17, 229
Avoyelles	38, 525	1, 525, 955	325	25, 600	78, 385
East Baton Rouge	50, 355	1, 719, 591	833	59, 497	....
West Baton Rouge	21, 628	1, 046, 255	806	50, 740	....
Iberville	32, 812	1, 334, 675	4, 907	323, 600	....
Jefferson	17, 806	1, 333, 700	2, 196	136, 200	269, 620
Lafourche	32, 820	1, 998, 950	7, 128	366, 685	1, 691, 410
Orleans	4, 603	859, 012	751	17, 910	198
Plaquemines	36, 777	3, 808, 300	7, 723	421, 562	8, 639, 026
Point Coupee	38, 166	1, 611, 037	1, 548	113, 210	....
Saint Bernard	7, 648	438, 700	686	42, 580	190, 480
Saint Charles	15, 330	920, 800	3, 914	247, 120	2, 238, 200
Saint James	26, 513	2, 097, 131	6, 265	347, 722	934, 915
Saint John the Baptist	19, 880	1, 621, 127	4, 962	346, 100	632, 670
Saint Landry	80, 452	2, 258, 502	1, 988	118, 110	33, 375
Saint Martin's	33, 776	1, 621, 150	1, 494	75, 740	....
Saint Mary's	43, 564	4, 710, 540	6, 591	341, 445	69, 327
Terrebonne	36, 693	2, 742, 325	6, 537	366, 282	233, 000

* No returns.

SECOND SECTION, LOUISIANA AND ARKANSAS

Counties or parishes.	Improved acres.	Cash value of plantations.	Cotton, bales.	Corn, bushels.
1850.				
Concordia	87, 406	$12, 335, 729	63, 970	423, 478
Tensas	117, 355	15, 452. 763	141, 493	579, 650
Madison	104, 383	11, 640, 660	44, 870	899, 050
Carroll	118, 116	15, 068, 712	84, 165	556, 581
Chicot	29, 886	1, 403, 204	12, 192	222, 595
Desha	9, 207	415, 053	2, 672	95, 355
1860.				
Concordia	87, 406	12, 335, 729	63, 970	423, 478
Tensas	117, 355	15, 452, 763	141, 493	579, 650
Madison	104, 383	11, 640, 660	44, 870	899, 050
Carroll	118, 116	15, 068, 712	84, 165	556, 581
Chicot	66, 423	4, 399, 554	40, 948	329, 941
Desha	42, 264	4, 198, 240	12, 261	239, 923
1870.				
Concordia	87, 275	3, 168, 500	15, 809	321, 365
Tensas,	77, 724	3, 223, 840	25, 371	94, 500
Madison	42, 284	1, 757, 403	17, 189	170, 477
Carroll	4, 448	2, 376, 630	20, 384	142, 525
Chicot	34, 181	1, 484, 065	10, 187	85, 462
Desha	33, 202	976, 504	8, 166	44, 797

THIRD SECTION, MISSISSIPPI AND TENNESSEE.

Counties or parishes.	Improved acres.	Cash value of plantations.	Cotton, bales.	Corn, bushels.
1850.				
Bolivar	16, 973	$808, 005	4, 723	107, 075
Issequena	27, 031	1, 072, 088	8, 461	143, 130
Washington	59, 126	3, 593, 705	26, 178	424, 600
Tunica	6, 015	282, 767	717	94, 735
Coahoma	11, 478	419, 059	2, 430	134, 815
Sunflower	5, 966	215, 099	1, 900	33, 390
Tallahatchee	27, 372	514, 589	4, 977	190, 930
Holmes*	89, 395	1, 447, 136	8, 461	543, 155
De Soto*	116, 044	2, 072, 394	20, 278	741, 519
Panola*	73, 713	1, 312, 725	8, 918	451, 909
Yazoo*	107, 298	1, 977, 731	22, 052	556, 505
1860.				
Bolivar	85, 188	8, 759, 270	33, 452	401, 966
Coahoma	39, 139	5, 100, 595	13, 325	235, 380
De Soto*	174, 952	6, 578, 547	40, 113	834, 165
Holmes*	136, 992	6, 074, 192	41, 840	845, 724
Issequena	56, 596	6, 576, 505	41, 170	398, 500
Panola	102, 986	3, 682, 361	24, 311	533, 340
Sunflower, (no return)	....	....	....	....
Tallahatchee	54, 907	3, 337, 592	15, 894	373, 150
Carroll*	164, 239	8, 276, 506	42, 880	1, 140, 174
Tunica	29, 341	4, 217, 575	13, 025	18, 055
Washington	....	....	80, 000	1, 500, 000
Yazoo*	179, 288	10, 287, 227	64, 075	956, 220
1870.				
Bolivar	39, 629	1, 449, 525	15, 571	182, 728
Coahoma	28, 959	2, 002, 295	11, 456	151, 985
De Soto*	191, 692	4, 670, 763	24, 118	741, 363
Holmes*	93, 691	1, 725, 089	19, 027	352, 623
Issequena	35, 286	1, 723, 230	15, 821	82, 825
Panola	103, 567	3, 030, 587	15, 764	390, 767
Sunflower	30, 264	1, 227, 452	7, 028	155, 672
Tallahatchee	38, 420	1, 130, 222	6, 760	203, 425
Carroll*	115, 479	1, 833, 972	14, 135	433, 245
Tunica	14, 141	889, 115	6, 424	82, 155
Washington	70, 119	6, 002, 270	35, 902	248, 991
Yazoo*	111, 232	2, 890, 611	26, 047	290, 448

* A portion of these counties thus marked is upland.

FOURTH SECTION, SAINT FRANCIS BASIN, ARKANSAS AND MISSOURI.

Counties or parishes.	Improved acres.	Cash value of plantations.	Cotton, bales.	Corn, bushels.
1850.*				
Phillips †	26, 427	$1, 086, 775	5, 165	281, 889
Mississippi	8, 111	344, 556	455	200, 500
Crittenden	8, 475	506, 050	698	163, 970
Scott	....	....	....	....
Pemiscott	....	....	....	....
Dunklin	....	....	....	....
New Madrid	....	....	....	....
Mississippi	....	....	....	....
1860.*				
Phillips †	83, 737	8, 037, 268	26, 993	578, 137
Mississippi	17, 584	1, 741, 201	9, 275	359, 697
Crittenden	19, 897	2, 408, 415	4, 675	211, 700

FOURTH SECTION, SAINT FRANCIS BASIN—Continued.

Counties.	Improved acres.	Cash value of plantations.	Cotton, bales.	Corn, bushels.
Scott	21, 999	626, 323	....	328, 940
Pemiscott	11, 910	578, 915	....	197, 500
Dunklin	15, 822	614, 457	....	319, 055
New Madrid	40, 791	1, 688, 142	....	802, 306
Mississippi	33, 624	1, 381, 300	....	543, 095
1870.*				
Phillips †	49, 947	194, 365	18, 002	293, 849
Mississippi	12, 573	477, 166	3, 587	120, 700
Crittenden	18, 242	443, 335	1, 841	76, 340
Scott	32, 542	1, 081, 580	....	428, 587
Pemiscott	8, 919	193, 985	....	210, 145
Dunklin	20, 997	413, 985	....	256, 620
New Madrid	35, 385	581, 230	....	717, 495
Mississippi	21, 109	406, 725	....	491, 990

* Census of these years. † A portion of this country is upland.

In 1840, the five front counties north of the mouth of the Yazoo River made thirty-nine thousand bales of cotton. In 1850, the same counties made forty-two thousand bales, showing but little improvement over the production of 1840. After the cession to the State of Mississippi of swamp-lands in aid of a levee system, and after the construction of these levees in 1860, the production of these counties reached 156,000 bales, and an amount of corn more than enough for the extravagant consumption of their people. This increase of cotton in the front counties was accompanied by a corresponding addition in the cotton-product of the other eight counties in the rear, as evidenced in the following:

Comparative statement of the product of cotton in these counties in the State of Mississippi.

NUMBER OF BALES PRODUCED.

Names of counties.	Per census report of 1850.	Per census report of 1860.	Per census report of 1870.
Bolivar	4, 723	33, 452	15, 571
Coahoma	2, 430	13, 325	11, 456
De Soto	20, 278	40, 113	24, 118
Holmes	12, 635	41, 840	19, 027
Issequena	8, 461	41, 170	15, 821
Panola	8, 918	24, 311	15, 764
Sunflower	1, 900	No returns.	7, 028
Tallahatchee	4, 977	15, 894	6, 760
Tunica	717	13, 025	6, 424
Washington	26, 178	No returns.	35, 902
Yazoo	22, 052	64, 075	26, 047

Prepared from census report by

EDWARD YOUNG,
Chief of Bureau of Statistics.

DECEMBER 16, 1874.

The cotton-supply is a problem engaging the attention of the civilized world. Six millions of bales are annually required to furnish Europe and America alone. The average weekly consumption of Europe, according to Mr. Edmund Ashworth, vice-president of the Cotton-Supply Association, is over four millions of bales a year.

The following table presents a fair average estimate of the present production of the cotton-growing territory of the world:*

	Bales.
East Indies	1,500,000
Egypt	250,000
Turkey, Levant, &c	120,000
Brazil, Peru, and West Indies	700,000
United States	3,750,000
All other sources	50,000

* Report of British Cotton-Supply Association.

During the war, and the famine prices which the failure of the American cotton-supply produced, British energy and enterprise were greatly stimulated to open new fields of production, and to rid its manufacturers of their dependence upon this country for its raw material.

The English government has greatly encouraged the cultivation of cotton all over its colonies, and in other countries has stimulated great interest in this matter. France, Greece, Turkey, Morocco, Egypt, Portugal, Japan, and even Russia, have been each appealed to; and all are aiding, by exemption from taxation, by land-grants, and bounties, the growth of cotton in their dominions. The results of these exertions are seen in these figures: Hayti, between 1860 and 1862, had increased her cotton-export threefold. Malta produced in 1862 four times as much as in 1860. Smyrna contributed in 1862 sixty thousand bales; in 1860, only ten thousand. In 1864, Manchester was receiving its cotton-supply from thirty-nine sources; among these additional sources of supply were China, with 210,000 bales, Turkey with 38,000, and Japan with 21,000, while the Indian cotton rose from 455,000, in 1860, to 1,500,000 bales in 1866.*

In 1861 Lord Dalhousie inaugurated the railway system for India, projecting 4,600 miles of railroad, to be constructed at an expense of $440,000,000.

The government engaged to pay the interest on all sums invested in these India roads, in the belief that with these works of internal improvement all obstacles to a full supply of cheap cotton will be removed. It is not out of place to remark in this connection that if England can afford to take such risks to wrest from America its monopoly of the cotton-plant, surely our Government should make some expenditure to preserve it.

In 1860, cotton constituted three-fourths of the value of our exports; last year, (1873,) under one-half.

The monthly report, No. 6, of the Bureau of Statistics contains a comparative statement of the imports and exports for the year ending December 31, 1872 and 1873.

Importations for 1872	$677,144,579
Importations for 1873	624,997,362
Difference in favor of 1872	52,147,217
Exports for 1872, domestic	$534,438,789
Exports for 1872, foreign	25,086,083
	569,524,872
Exports for 1873, domestic	$603,366,531
Exports for 1873, foreign	24,968,204
	631,334,735
Difference in favor of 1873	61,809,863

In 1873, the export of raw cotton amounted to $219,738,746 against $197,656,806 in 1872.

It has been truly said that the importance of a large production of cotton as the chief export of the country in adjusting the balances of trade and exchanges, and especially in its bearing upon the future position of the public debt so largely held abroad, cannot be overstated. In this connection the following statistics show the ebb and flow of this export-trade with Great Britain for a series of years, as compared with the cotton-export of other countries.

* Report of the British Cotton-Supply Association in 1868.

Cotton imports into the United Kingdom.

Sources.	Bales.											
	1860.	1861.	1862.	1863.	1864.	1865.	1866.	1867.	1868.	1869.	1870.	1871.
Africa, South and West	....	1, 097	1, 607	613	1, 669	6, 628	6, 118	7, 764	7, 620	19, 332	13, 136	9, 909
Australia	....	9	3	64	240	662	1, 431	1, 524	4, 406	Not known.	Not known.	Not known.
Peru	2, 515	2, 667	1, 289	13, 275	27, 059	70, 338	49, 081	63, 601	58, 911	62, 228	48, 423	80, 997
West Indies, &c	7, 259	7, 188	11, 436	8, 610	32, 586	61, 159	62, 745	64, 593	41, 770	43, 042	112, 100	Not known.
Egypt	110, 009	97, 759	135, 420	205, 788	257, 102	333, 575	167, 451	181, 173	188, 689	185, 670	219, 920	264, 880
Brazil	103, 084	99, 224	133, 807	137, 142	212, 192	340, 261	407, 646	437, 208	636, 897	514, 200	402, 760	500, 466
India	562, 738	986, 290	1, 071, 768	1, 229, 989	1, 399, 514	1, 266, 513	1, 847, 759	1, 508, 754	1, 451, 979	1, 496, 426	1, 063, 540	1, 235, 940
United States	2, 580, 980	1, 841, 643	72, 369	132, 028	197, 776	460, 606	1, 162, 745	1, 225, 686	1, 269, 060	1, 039, 641	1, 664, 010	2, 233, 984

In 1860 the receipts of cotton from the United States into Great Britain were 1,115,890,608 pounds. From all other countries, 275,048,144 pounds. In 1872 the receipts of cotton from the United States into Great Britain, 625,600,080 pounds; from all other countries, 783,237,592 pounds. It is estimated that an efficient levee system would bring into safe cultivation in the course of a few years seven million of acres of the finest cotton-lands in the world, capable of producing one bale to the acre.*

Scarcely secondary in importance to the growth of cotton is the sugar-crop of Louisiana, produced almost entirely in the alluvion of that State.

At one time the cane-sugar grown in Louisiana equaled about three-fourths of the sugar consumed in the United States. Were its past production restored, which cannot be done without protecting it from the ravages of the river, the amount would even now equal nearly one-half of the sugar consumed in this country.

To give an idea of the decay of this great interest, we present the number of hogsheads produed in 1860 and 1866, with the number of plantations in the same years. (Report of the New Orleans Chamber of Commerce in 1867.)

	1861.	1866.
Crop	449,000 hhds.	39,000 hhds.
Number of plantations	1,291	347

The total amount of sugar consumed in the United States is about 450,000 tons. Louisiana in 1861 produced nearly one-half of this amount, thereby saving an export of gold for foreign sugar of about $25,000,000.

Last year the importation of molasses amounted to nearly 40,000,000 gallons, which, at 40 cents per gallon, would amount to $16,000,000 of additional gold-drain from the country.

Twenty-five hundred thousand acres, it is believed, if proper protection should be afforded, could be used for sugar-growing in Louisiana. (Report of Generals Humphreys and Abbot.)

APPENDIX D.

FLOOD-NOTES ON TRIBUTARY RIVERS.

Ohio River—Wabash River—Cumberland River—Tennessee River—Upper Mississippi River—Missouri River—Arkansas River—Red River—Yazoo River.

As the three floods of 1862, 1865, and 1867 will no doubt often be studied and discussed hereafter, I have thought it advisable to append a brief abstract of the most important facts collected respecting them for each of the main tributaries, beginning near the sources and proceeding in regular geographical order toward the mouths. The records for the Yazoo River also include the flood of 1874; which, in general, is treated in Appendix B.

* Generals Humphreys and Abbot.

OHIO RIVER.

Pittsburgh.—The ice broke up on February 3, 1867, causing the river to rise and immediately to fall 8 feet. The next freshet began to rise rapidly on February 14. By February 15, it stood 22 feet by the Allegheny pier-mark and began falling. The largest freshet of the year attained its height 22.3 feet by the Allegheny pier-mark, on March 13, and then rapidly fell. It was 10 feet below high water of 1832, and 8 feet below that of 1865, which was highest on March 18, and chiefly due to an Allegheny freshet.

Rochester, (26 miles below Pittsburgh.)—The freshet of February 15, 1867, was higher by 6 inches than that of March 12, 1867, being 28 5 feet in the channel. It was 13.5 feet below high water of 1832, 10.5 feet below that of 1852, and 7.5 feet below that of March 18, 1865, which was precisely equal to the 1860 and 1861 freshets.

Marietta, (171 miles below Pittsburgh.)—River began rising slowly on February 9, 1867; attained highest point, 35 feet above low water, on February 17–18; fell slowly; began rising on March 9, and culminated on March 13–14, at a point 28 feet above low water; then slowly receded. Downfall in February, 1.8 inches; in March, 5.3 inches.

Parkersburgh, (183 miles below Pittsburgh.)—River began rising on February 13, 1867; was highest, 36 feet above low water, on February 17–18; fell slowly. Its high-water mark was 2.5 feet below that of 1865.

Cincinnati, (466 miles below Pittsburgh.)—The *duration* of the flood of 1867 was unprecedented. For 32 consecutive days (February 16 to March 19) the mean channel depth was 51.3 feet, the greatest depth being 55.8 feet on February 22, and 57.3 feet on March 14–15, and the least depth being 44.6 feet on March 2–3. The March rise was 0.6 foot below high water of 1865, and 1.3 feet below that of 1862. Immense local rains during flood of 1867.

Louisville, (618 miles below Pittsburgh.)—The rise of February 22, 1867, was 8 feet, and that of March 15, 2.8 feet below the high water of 1832. The March rise was a little below the high water of 1847. For five months snows and rains had been excessive, the downfall being estimated at three times the usual amount.

Wabash River.—In 1867 there was only one important rise, which occurred in February. At Eugene, Ind., (350 miles above mouth,) by exact marks the high water of 1858 was the highest on record, being 28 feet above low water. It was 1 foot above the high water of 1828 and 1844, 4 feet above that of 1851, and 2 feet above that of 1867. In latter years the river remained bank-full from the latter part of February until the middle of May; snows during winter and rains in March being excessive. In 1862 the high water occurred in February, and was very destructive. During the 34 years between 1833 and 1866, six crops have been lost from overflow. At Terre Haute the high water of 1867 was 1.3 feet below the high water of 1858, the highest on record, culminating on February 21 with river 25.3 feet above low water. The rise began on February 9. At Vincennes the river was out of its banks from February 19 to March 2, inclusive, being highest on February 22–23, when it was 0.5 foot higher than ever known before, (25 feet above low water.) Snows and rains had prevailed during the winter.

Caseyville, Ky.—In 1867 the river began rising on February 1, and reached highest point on March 1, being then 0.5 foot above high water of 1832, and 4.1 feet above high water of 1847. The second rise culminated about March 16, and was 0.4 foot below the first, the fall between the two rises being about three feet; downfall during the winter was without precedent.

Cumberland River.—At Carthage the high water of 1867 was 7 feet below that of 1826, 4 feet below 1847, and 1 foot below 1862; and was 40 feet above low water. The rise began on February 25, culminated on March 9–12, subsided 8 feet, but again swelled until March 25 or 26, when it finally fell. At Nashville the flood was 0.8 foot below the high water of 1847 on March 13. On Harpeth Shoals, 30 miles below, where extreme low water gives a depth of only 13 inches, this flood stood 64 feet. The rise there began on February 28, the water standing 19 feet. It culminated on March 13. After March 16 the river fell very rapidly, with no second swell. It was over banks (above about 55 on shoals) from March 8 to March 16, inclusive, indicating a flood of unusually long duration. At Eddyville the flood was 1.2 feet above high water of 1847 on March 18, the highest floods previously on record there.

Tennessee River.—The flood of 1867 far exceeded all precedents for the past 90 years. It consisted of one great rise due to furious rain-storms which covered its entire valley, particularly the mountain region. At Kingsport, on the Holston, rain fell nearly continuously from February 28 to March 7. At noon of March 7, the river attained its highest point, being 30 feet above low water and 4 feet above any other flood. In 20 hours it fell 10 feet. At Strawberry Plains the freshet rose 52 feet above low water and 11 feet above any other flood. At Knoxville the river rose 12 feet above high-water mark of 1847, and was over 50 feet deep. Near Harrison, the Tennessee rose 15 feet above any known water-mark. At Chattanooga the rise began on March 4, overflowed banks on March 8, and attained height on March 11, being 53 feet above low water and 15.5 feet above the high water of 1847, the highest on record. The river fell with equal rapidity to usual level. Rains were incessant for four days before highest water. At Bridgeport, Ala., the flood reached its maximum, 11.5 feet above all former marks, late on March 12. At Bellefonte, Ala., rise began on March 5, and was highest on March 13, when it was 9.1 feet above high water of 1847. At Decatur the freshet culminated on March 16, being six or seven feet above any other flood; it remained stationary for two days. At Florence, Ala., the freshet began on March 1, culminated on March 15 falling very slowly for three days. It stood 6 feet above all other floods. At Eastport it stood 7 feet above any known flood. At Johnsonville the flood culminated on March 22, being 3.8 feet above all previous water-marks, and 44.8 feet above ordinary low water; by April 1 it had returned within banks. At Paducah the rise culminated on March 21. The destruction of property and life occasioned by this flood was beyond parallel in the history of the Tennessee Valley.

Metropolis, (40 miles above Cairo.)—The February rise of 1867 was 1.5 feet below high water of 1847. The river remained nearly stationary until March 9, when it began to swell; it culminated on March 20 at a point above all previous water-marks, being 3 feet above high water of 1865, and 4.4 feet above that of 1847. The fall was rapid.

Mound City, (6 miles above Cairo.)—The flood of 1867 rose 0.9 foot above high water of 1862.

UPPER MISSISSIPPI RIVER.

Fort Ripley.—No rain fell between November 26, 1866, and April 13, 1867; no spring rise in 1867.

Winona.—There were not 12 hours of rain between January 6 and April 13, 1867; no early spring rise, the river being frozen in March.

The highest points reached between October 4, 1866, and April 22, 1867, were on December 24, when the river was 6.6 feet above low water, and on April 22, 1867, when it was 9.4 above low water and rising. The total range here is about 14 feet.

Rock Island.—The highest recorded mark is that of March, 1870, which was 16.7 feet above low water of 1864. The high water of 1862 was 1 foot and that of 1867 was 2.35 feet below high water of 1870.

Illinois River.—At La Salle, 18.5 inches of rain fell between February 1 and June 3, 1867. A freshet, rising within 1 foot of top of levees, culminated on February 17, 1867, being 26 feet above the low stand of February 3; the river remained high, but oscillating, until June 3, (date of letter,) the lowest point being about 7 feet above low water, on May 19.

MISSOURI RIVER.

Fort Randall.—The river remained frozen until April 9, 1867, being at low-water mark, or about 5 feet deep. It began rising on April 12, and on April 17–19 it was bank-full, but it fell at once to usual summer level. The freshet did no damage. No local rains fell for the five months ending April 16.

Niobrara.—In March, 1867, about 2.5 feet of snow fell; and on April 17, about 3 inches of rain. On April 1, the river was at usual summer level, but a sudden and excessive (10 feet) freshet in the Niobrara raised it rapidly. Combined with the rise above, this freshet raised the Missouri, on April 18, to a point 1.5 feet below the high water of 1858, and 2 feet below the high water of 1866, the highest recorded flood.

Omaha.—Ice broke up on April 7, 1867, the river being very low. The melting snows caused it to rise rapidly until, on April 23, it stood 18.8 feet above extreme low-water mark, (1863.) It was 1.9 feet above high water of 1866, and 0.1 foot above that of 1844. By April 30 it had receded within banks, a fall of about 7 feet. The levees were completely overflowed.

South Platte River.—At Fort Sedgwick much snow fell in March, 1867. The mean temperature was very cold; and the river there, about half a mile wide and 2 feet deep at low water, was frozen solid. The ice broke up on April 8, with a little freshet.

Saint Joseph.—The ice broke up on February 13, 1867, causing a little rise of 5 feet, due to melting snow and ice-gorges. The highest stand in February or March was 12 feet within banks.

Leavenworth.—The Missouri was very low during March, 1867. Quite a freshet occurred between April 10 and May 9, the river being at these dates 5.5 feet above low-water mark. At its height, on April 27 and 28, it stood 18.6 feet above low water, and 0.7 foot above the mark of April, 1866. No damage was done by freshets locally.

ARKANSAS RIVER.

Fort Smith.—The high water of June, 1866, was 3.8 feet above that of 1862, and 2 feet above that of 1867.

Little Rock.—There were heavy rains and snows in March, 1867, which, however, flooded the White, Little Red, Washita, and Saline Rivers, heading near the Arkansas, more than they did that river itself. Before the storms occurred the latter river was about 3 feet above low water; in two days after the rains began the river commenced to rise so rapidly that in about three days it rose 25 feet, to its highest point, which was 6 feet below high water of 1833, and 1.1 feet below that of

August, 1866. The river rapidly subsided, doing little damage above the influence of back-water from the Mississippi.

Pine Bluffs.—In 1867, the river did not reach the top of its banks by some feet. The flood of 1833 is the greatest recorded. Next to it is that of 1844, which was occasioned by a general freshet in all the tributaries. The river began rising late in March; on May 8 and May 20 it reached the mark of 1833; about July 1 it retired within banks; on August 10 it attained low-water level. The construction of levees on the Lower Arkansas, since 1844, has affected the relative heights of later floods.

Heckatoo Plantation, (15 miles above South Bend.) In 1862 there was no great flood in Arkansas River itself. In 1867 the waters rose 0.3 foot above high water of 1866, which reached a higher point than any other flood since 1844. There were several crevasses near and below this plantation in 1867.

South Bend.—The date of highest water in 1867 was June 7. About four miles of gaps in Arkansas River levees in vicinity. A moderate flood in Arkansas River at date of high water in 1862.

RED RIVER.

Cut-off Landing, (nearly west of Lewisville, Ark.)—There was an over. flow in May and June, 1867, damaging about three-fourths of crops- The highest water was about 0.3 foot above high water in June, 1865, and April, 1866.

Shreveport to Alexandria.—On June 22, 1867, the river was falling fast. The flood had caused very considerable damage in this region.

YAZOO RIVER.

As the Yazoo Pass near Delta exerts a great influence on the floods of this stream when open, the following notes as to the various levees which have been made to close it are of value:

The first levee, near present location, gave way in 1856.(?) It was rebuilt, and again washed away by the flood of 1858. It was again rebuilt in the autumn of 1859, and stood until cut as a military necessity by the Navy, in March, 1863. It was closed again in 1871, and has stood until the present time, although now threatened by the rapid caving of the bank of the Mississippi in the vicinity.

At Red Cross, on the Tallahatchie, 50 miles above Greenwood, the high water of 1874 was 1.3 feet below that of 1867.

At a point on the Yalobusha, 25 miles above Greenwood, the water in 1874 rose 0.5 foot above the mark of 1867.

Greenwood.—The highest recorded flood was that of 1874; it was here due entirely to rain, unaided by crevasse-water from the Mississippi, which usually exerts a great influence upon the flood-level. The following figures give a comparison between floods of different years; the extreme range of the river being 39 feet:

High water, July, 1844, was 12 inches below high water of 1874.
High water, March, 1849, was 14 inches below high water of 1874.
High water, March, 1850, was 13 inches below high water of 1874.
High water, April, 1851, was 14 inches below high water of 1874.
High water, August, 1858, was 20 inches below high water of 1874.
High water, June, 1862, was 7 inches below high water of 1874.
High water, March, 1865, was 8 inches below high water of 1874.
High water, March, 1867, was 2 inches below high water of 1874.

High water, March, 1871, was 38 inches below high water of 1874.
Water-surface, April 18, 1874, was 18 inches below high water of 1874.
Water-surface, April 22, 1874, was 0 inches below high water of 1874.
Water-surface, May 9, 1874, was 58 inches below high water of 1874.
Water-surface, May 23, 1874, was 146 inches below high water of 1874.

Honey Island.—The highest stage in 1874 occurred on April 24, when the water was 2 feet below high water of 1867. Below this place the influence of crevasse-water began to be felt.

Yazoo City.—The following is a record of the flood of 1874 at this locality:

Water-surface on April 15 was 5.3 feet below high water of 1867; water-surface on April 22 was 3.8 feet below high water of 1867; water-surface on April 24 was 3.6 feet below high water of 1867. Highest point on April 26 was 3.4 feet below high water of 1867. Water began to fall on April 28. Water-surface on May 15 was 4.6 feet below high water of 1867.

APPENDIX E.

GAUGE-RECORDS.

FLOOD OF 1874.

On the Lower Mississippi.—Saint Louis, Cairo, Memphis, Helena, Lake Providence, Vicksburg, Natchez, Red River Landing, Baton Rouge, Carrollton, New Orleans.

Lake Ponchartrain.—New Canal, at Magnolia street, New Orleans.

On the Ohio.—Cincinnati: Louisville above the falls; Louisville below falls.

On the Cumberland.—Nashville.

On the Tennessee.—Florence.

On the Upper Mississippi.—Rock Island.

On the Missouri.—Fort Leavenworth.

On the White.—Jacksonport.

On the Arkansas.—Little Rock.

On the Washita.—Camden.

On the Black.—Trinity.

On the Red.—Shreveport, Alexandria.

SAINT LOUIS, MISSOURI.

Authority, Corps of Engineers, United States Army.—High water of 1844 reads 41.39 feet; Saint Louis directrix reads 33.81 feet.

Date.	December.		January.		February.		March.		April.		May.		June.	
	Gauge.	Wind.	Gauge.	Wind.	Gauge.	Wind.	Gauge.	Wind.	Gauge.	Wind.	Gauge.	Wind.	Gauge.	Wind.
1	3.9	S.	5.8	S.	11.2	N. E.	9.8	S.	17.1	W.	15.2	S.	12.3	N. E.
2	3.9	S. S. E.	5.7	S. E.	10.8	W.	9.7	S. S. E.	17.8	N. W.	14.6	S. E.	11.9	S.
3	4.3	W.	6.0	S.	10.2	W. N. W.	9.6	S.	17.6	S. W.	14.4	E.	11.7	W.
4	4.8	S. W.	5.6	N. W.	9.9	N. W.	9.6	N. E.	17.2	E.	14.9	N. W.	11.4	S. E.
5	6.0	E. N. E.	5.8	N.	9.4	E.	10.3	S. E.	16.7	W.	15.3	N.	11.2	S. W.
6	6.5	E.	5.9	N. W.	9.2	W.	12.1	S.	16.0	N.	16.2	N.	11.0	S.
7	7.0	S. E.	5.6	N. W.	8.8	S. E.	13.2	N. W.	15.3	N. E.	16.3	S. E.	11.0	S.
8	5.4	S. W.	5.5	S. W.	8.4	....	15.5	N. W.	14.7	N.	15.5	S.	11.0	S.
9	4.8	N.	5.5	W.	8.0	N. W.	15.9	S. E.	14.3	N.	14.7	S.	10.9	S.
10	5.9	S. E.	5.5	N. W.	7.8	S.	16.3	N.	14.1	W.	14.0	S.	12.9	S. E.
11	7.7	S.	5.0	N. W.	7.5	S.	16.4	N.	13.9	W.	13.6	S.	15.1	W.
12	7.7	W.	5.0	N. E.	7.4	S.	16.1	N. W.	13.8	S. E.	13.9	N.	16.2	N.
13	10.9	W.	4.9	N. W.	7.6	N. W.	15.8	N.	13.9	S.	14.7	E.	16.4	S. E.
14	14.0	S. W.	4.8	N. W.	8.9	S. E.	15.6	S. E.	13.8	N. W.	14.3	S.	16.5	S. E.
15	15.3	S. E.	4.2	N. W.	10.5	N. W.	15.4	S. E.	13.3	N. E.	14.4	N. W.	16.8	S. W.
16	15.3	S. S. E.	3.9	S. E.	10.6	N.	15.2	S. E.	12.8	N.	15.2	N. W.	17.3	W.
17	14.6	N. W.	3.7	S. E.	10.5	N. E.	15.0	S.	12.4	N.	16.1	N.	17.6	S.
18	13.6	W.	3.5	S. E.	10.5	S. E.	14.5	S.	12.3	E.	15.7	N.	17.8	S. E.
19	12.6	W.	3.4	N.	10.3	S.	14.3	W.	12.4	N. E.	14.9	S.	18.4	S. E.
20	12.6	N. W.	3.9	S. E.	10.2	N. E.	14.0	S. E.	13.2	W.	14.2	N. W.	18.4	S. E.
21	10.6	S. E.	4.4	S. E.	10.2	N.	13.9	S. S. W.	15.6	N. E.	13.7	N. E.	18.2	S.
22	9.4	E. N. E.	5.6	S.	10.4	....	13.8	N. W.	16.9	N.	13.4	S.	17.9	S. E.
23	8.4	S. W.	7.6	S. E.	10.9	N. W.	13.8	N.	17.8	N.	13.3	N. W.	17.5	S. E.
24	7.5	W. N. W.	13.2	S.	10.9	N. E.	14.4	S. E.	17.9	E.	13.2	S. W.	17.2	S. W.
25	7.0	S. W.	13.9	S. W.	10.8	N. W.	15.4	S.	17.6	N.	12.9	N. W.	16.4	S. W.
26	6.7	W. N. W.	14.3	W.	10.7	S.	15.9	N.	16.9	E.	12.7	S.	16.0	S. W.
27	6.7	W.	13.2	S.	10.4	S. E.	16.2	N. W.	16.2	N.	12.5	S. E.	15.3	S.
28	6.6	S.	12.6	W.	10.2	S. E.	16.4	N.	16.1	N.	12.6	S. E.	14.8	S. W.
29	6.5	W. N. W.	12.3	S.	....	....	16.4	N.	16.0	S.	13.2	S. E.	14.8	N.
30	6.0	S.	11.9	N. W.	....	....	16.1	E.	15.7	S. W.	13.2	S. W.	14.3	N.
31	6.0	S.	11.4	N. E.	....	....	16.0	N.	....	....	12.9	N. N. W.	....	....

CAIRO, ILLINOIS.

Authority, Corps of Engineers, United States Army.—B. M. of Cairo City Company reads 9.16 feet; to reduce to delta survey-gauge, subtract 9.16 feet.

Date.	December.		January.		February.		March.		April.		May.		June.	
	Gauge.	Wind.	Gauge.	Wind.	Gauge.	Wind.	Gauge.	Wind.	Gauge.	Wind.	Gauge.	Wind.	Gauge.	Wind.
1	14. 1	S.	17. 4	S.	32. 9	E.	41. 0	N.	39. 4	N.	46. 0	S.	14. 6	N. E.
2	15. 6	S.	15. 9	S. W.	33. 0	N.	40. 9	S. E.	38. 4	S.	45. 5	S. W.	14. 4	N. E.
3	16. 8	W.	14. 7	S. W.	32. 8	N.	40. 8	S.	37. 5	N. W.	45. 3	S. W.	13. 9	S. W.
4	18. 1	S.	13. 7	N. W.	32. 3	N.	40. 8	N. E.	36. 8	N. E.	45. 1	N.	13. 4	S. W.
5	18. 9	E.	12. 8	N. E.	31. 4	N. E.	40. 7	E.	35. 8	S.	45. 0	N.	12. 8	S. W.
6	19. 2	E.	12. 5	N. E.	30. 5	N. E.	41. 1	S.	34. 7	E.	45. 0	N. W.	12. 3	S.
7	20. 6	N. E.	11. 9	N. E.	29. 3	N. W.	41. 9	N. W.	33. 5	N. E.	45. 0	E.	11. 8	W.
8	21. 6	S.	12. 4	S. W.	27. 7	E.	42. 5	N.	33. 4	N. E.	45. 0	S.	11. 4	S.
9	24. 1	N. E.	14. 5	N. W.	26. 1	S. E.	43. 2	N. E.	34. 7	N. E.	44. 8	S.	11. 0	S.
10	25. 3	N. E.	17. 7	S. W.	24. 5	S. E.	43. 8	S.	35. 4	N. E.	44. 3	S.	10. 9	S.
11	26. 2	S.	21. 5	N.	22. 9	S. E.	44. 0	N.	36. 5	S.	43. 5	S.	10. 8	S.
12	26. 9	S.	24. 5	N. E.	21. 6	S.	43. 6	W.	37. 4	E.	42. 3	S.	11. 1	N.
13	27. 7	N. W.	27. 9	N. E.	20. 8	N.	43. 1	N.	37. 9	S.	40. 6	N. E.	13. 4	N. E.
14	29. 0	S. W.	29. 5	N.	21. 3	S. E.	42. 2	S. E.	38. 6	S.	38. 5	N.	14. 8	S. E.
15	30. 1	S. E.	30. 4	N.	21. 5	S.	41. 1	E.	39. 7	N. E.	36. 2	N.	15. 6	S. E.
16	32. 0	S. E.	30. 8	E.	22. 0	N. E.	39. 8	S. E.	41. 1	N. E.	33. 4	W.	16. 1	S. W.
17	33. 2	S. W.	31. 0	S. E.	23. 9	N. E.	38. 5	S.	42. 0	N. E.	30. 3	S.	16. 3	S. W.
18	33. 5	S. E.	30. 8	S.	25. 8	N. E.	37. 1	S.	42. 9	E.	27. 7	N. E.	16. 6	N. E.
19	33. 3	N.	30. 3	S.	27. 0	S	36. 9	N.	43. 6	E.	25. 8	S. E.	17. 3	N. E.
20	33. 0	N.	29. 3	E.	28. 0	N.	36. 9	N. E.	44. 4	S.	24. 2	S. W.	17. 7	N. E.
21	32. 7	E.	27. 6	S.	29. 8	S. W.	36. 5	N. E.	45. 1	N. E.	22. 6	N. E.	18. 0	N. E.
22	32. 5	N. E.	25. 7	N. W.	32. 3	N. E.	36. 3	N.	45. 6	N. E.	21. 1	N. E.	18. 3	N. E.
23	32. 1	N.	24. 0	N. W.	34. 3	N. W.	36. 3	N. E.	46. 2	N.	19. 8	S.	18. 2	S.
24	31. 5	N. W.	23. 3	N.	36. 6	N. E.	36. 5	N. E.	46. 8	N. E.	18. 8	S. W.	17. 8	S. E.
25	30. 6	N.	23. 3	S.	38. 5	W.	36. 8	S.	47. 2	N. E.	18. 0	S. W.	17. 3	S.
26	29. 5	S. W.	25. 3	S.	39. 9	S. E.	37. 4	S.	47. 4	N.	17. 1	E.	16. 8	S. W.
27	28. 3	N. W.	27. 6	S.	40. 7	N. E.	38. 2	N. E.	47. 4	S.	16. 5	E.	16. 2	S. W.
28	25. 8	S. W.	29. 4	N. W.	41. 0	E.	39. 1	N. E.	47. 1	N.	15. 8	E.	15. 5	S.
29	23. 2	N. W.	30. 7	S.	....	....	39. 6	N. E.	46. 7	N.	15. 3	S.	14. 9	N. E.
30	20. 9	N. E.	31. 7	S.	....	....	39. 8	N. E.	46. 4	S.	14. 8	S.	14. 3	N. E.
31	19. 0	S.	32. 4	N. E.	....	....	39. 5	N.	....	....	14. 6	S.	....	....

MEMPHIS, TENNESSEE.

Authority, Corps of Engineers, United States Army.—To reduce to delta survey-gauge add 1.02 feet.

Date.	December.		January.		February.		March.		April.		May.		June.	
	Gauge.	Wind.	Gauge.	Wind.	Gauge.	Wind.	Gauge.	Wind.	Gauge.	Wind.	Gauge.	Wind.	Gauge.	Wind.
1	8.4	S. W.	17.2	S. W.	24.1	N. W.	30.7	N. W.	32.3	N.	34.0	S.	12.8	N. E.
2	9.3	S. W.	16.1	W.	24.8	N. W.	31.4	S.	32.3	N. E.	34.0	S. E.	12.2	N. E.
3	9.9	W.	14.4	S. W.	25.5	N. W.	31.7	S.	32.2	S. W.	34.0	S. W.	11.8	S. W.
4	10.4	N.	12.5	W.	25.8	N.	32.0	N. W.	32.2	N. W.	33.9	N. W.	11.4	S. W.
5	10.9	N. W.	10.7	N.	25.7	N.	32.2	N. E.	32.0	N. W.	33.9	N. W.	11.1	S. E.
6	11.8	N. E.	9.6	N. W.	25.5	N. W.	32.5	S. E.	31.8	N. E.	33.9	S. W.	10.9	S. E.
7	12.6	N. E.	8.5	W.	25.0	W.	32.8	N. W.	31.4	N. E.	33.8	S. W.	10.7	S. E.
8	13.6	S. E.	8.1	N. W.	24.4	N.	33.0	N. W.	31.0	N. E.	33.8		10.4	S. W.
9	14.5	S.	7.7	N. W.	23.8	N. W.	33.2	S. E.	30.7	N. E.	33.7		10.1	S. W.
10	15.7		7.7	W.	22.8	S. W.	33.2	N. E.	30.4	S. W.	33.7		9.7	S.
11	17.0		8.8	N. E.	21.2	S.	33.3	N. E.	30.3	S. W.	33.6		9.3	S. W.
12	18.1	S.	11.6	N. W.	19.5	S. W.	33.3	N. W.	30.5	S. W.	33.5	S. W.	8.9	N. W.
13	19.3	N. W.	13.8	N. W.	18.1	S. W.	33.3	N. W.	30.7	S. W.	33.4		8.5	N. W.
14	19.3	N. W.	16.4	N.	16.8	S.	33.4	N. E.	30.9	S. W.	33.3	S. W.	8.7	
15	20.6		19.2	N.	15.5	S. E.	33.4	N. E.	31.3	N. E.	33.1		9.1	
16	21.6	S. E.	21.1	N. W.	14.7	N. E.	33.4		31.9	N. W.	32.8	N. W.	10.5	
17	22.9	S. W.	21.9	S. E.	14.9	N.	33.2	S. W.	32.4	N. W.	32.5	S. W.	11.6	
18	24.0	S. W.	22.6	S.	15.1	N. W.	33.1	S. W.	32.8	N. E.	31.9	N. E.	12.5	
19	25.6	N. W.	23.2	S. E.	15.8	S. E.	33.0	S. W.	33.1	S. W.	30.5	N. W.	12.7	
20	26.2	N. W.	23.7	S. E.	16.6	S. E.	32.9	N. E.	33.4	S. W.	28.1	S. W.	12.8	
21	26.8	N. W.	23.4	S.	18.1	S. E.	32.8	N. E.	33.6	E.	25.4	S. E.	13.0	
22	26.7	N. W.	23.1	S. E.	20.0	N. E.	32.6	N. W.	33.7	S. E.	22.6	S. W.	13.3	S. E.
23	26.1	S. W.	21.8	S. E.	22.6	N. W.	32.4	N. E.	33.7	N. W.	20.8	S. W.	13.6	S. E.
24	25.5	S. W.	20.3	S.	24.5	N. E.	32.1	N.	33.8	N. E.	19.1	S. W.	13.9	S. W.
25	24.6	S.	18.7	S. E.	26.4	N. W.	31.8	S. E.	33.8	N. W.	17.7	S. W.	13.8	S. W.
26	24.3	S.	17.5	S.	27.8	N. E.	31.6	S. E.	33.8	S. W.	16.7	S.	13.6	S. W.
27	24.0	N. W.	16.4	S. W.	29.1	N. W.	31.5	N. E.	33.9	S. W.	15.7	S. E.	13.2	S. W.
28	22.2	N. W.	17.4	N. W.	30.3	E.	31.6	N. W.	33.9	N.	14.7	N. W.		
29	21.1	N. W.	19.6	S.			31.8	N. W.	33.9	S.	14.0	N. W.		
30	19.9	S. E.	21.4	S. W.			31.9	N. E.	34.0	S. W.	13.5			
31	18.8	N. W.	22.9	S.			32.1	N. E.			13.1			

HELENA, ARKANSAS.

Authority, Corps of Engineers, United States Army.—To reduce to delta survey-gauge add 2.59 feet.

Date.	December.		January.		February.		March.		April.		May.		June.	
	Gauge.	Wind.	Gauge.	Wind.	Gauge.	Wind.	Gauge.	Wind.	Gauge.	Wind.	Gauge.	Wind.	Gauge.	Wind.
1	10.1	S.	25.0	S.	28.4	....	35.5	N.	40.2	N. W.	41.0	S. W.	21.8	N. E.
2	11.0	S.	22.7	S.	29.3	N.	36.2	S.	40.2	W.	41.2	S. W.	20.9	N. E.
3	11.6	S. E.	20.6	S.	30.1	N. E.	36.8	S.	40.2	S. E.	41.3	S.	20.0	N. E.
4	12.0	S. E.	18.5	N. W.	30.8	N.	37.3	N.	40.1	S. W.	41.5	W.	19.4	S. E.
5	13.3	N. E.	16.5	N.	31.1	N. E.	37.5	N. E.	40.0	S.	41.7	N.	19.6	S. E.
6	14.5	N. E.	14.8	N.	31.3	S. W.	38.2	S. E.	39.9	S.	42.1	W.	18.5	S.
7	15.9	N.	13.7	N. W.	31.3	N.	38.5	N. E.	39.9	N. E.	42.5	W.	17.4	S. W.
8	16.9	S. E.	12.5	S.	31.0	N.	38.7	N. E.	39.7	N. E.	43.0	S.	16.3	S. W.
9	17.8	N. W.	11.6	S. W.	30.6	N. E.	38.8	S.	39.5	N. E.	43.3	S.	15.3	W.
10	19.2	S.	11.3	S.	29.7	S.	39.0	S.	39.2	N.	43.5	S. E.	14.5	S. W.
11	20.9	S.	11.3	N. E.	28.6	S.	39.2	N. E.	38.9	S.	43.6	S. E.	13.7	S. W.
12	22.3	S.	12.5	N. E.	27.3	S.	39.3	N. E.	38.7	S. E.	43.5	S.	13.1	N. E.
13	23.6	N. W.	14.4	N.	26.3	S.	39.4	N. E.	38.6	S. E.	43.3	S. E.	12.6	N. E.
14	24.5	N. E.	17.8	N.	24.3	N. E.	39.5	N. E.	38.6	S.	43.2	....	12.3	S. E.
15	25.3	S.	21.5	N. E.	22.3	S.	39.7	N. E.	38.8	S.	43.0	S. E.	12.4	S.
16	26.3	S.	24.3	N. E.	21.4	N. E.	39.8	N. E.	39.0	S.	42.8	N. E.	13.4	S. E.
17	27.3	S.	26.3	S. E.	20.9	N. E.	39.9	S.	39.2	N. E.	42.6	S. E.	14.6	N. E.
18	28.3	S.	27.3	S. E.	20.5	N. E.	39.9	S.	39.4	N. E.	42.3	N. E.	15.7	N. E.
19	29.4	N.	28.1	S.	21.0	S. E.	40.1	S.	39.6	S. E.	41.9	S. E.	16.5	N. E.
20	30.3	N.	28.5	....	22.0	S.	40.2	N. E.	39.9	S. W.	41.2	S.	16.8	N. E.
21	30.9	N. E.	28.8	S.	23.5	S. W.	40.2	N. E.	40.0	N. E.	39.7	N. E.	17.1	N. W.
22	31.3	N. E.	28.8	S.	25.0	S.	40.2	N. E.	40.2	S. W.	38.2	N. E.	17.4	S. E.
23	31.3	N. E.	28.3	N. E.	26.6	N. W.	40.2	E.	40.4	N.	36.6	S. W.	17.9	S. E.
24	31.3	N.	27.5	N.	28.5	N. E.	40.2	N. E.	40.5	N.	34.7	S. W.	18.3	S. E.
25	31.3	N. W.	26.3	E.	30.3	N. W.	40.1	S. E.	40.5	N. W.	33.2	S. W.	18.5	S. E.
26	31.3	S. W.	25.0	S.	31.8	S. E.	40.1	S. W.	40.6	N. E.	31.3	S. E.	18.6	W.
27	31.1	N. W.	24.0	S.	33.4	S. E.	40.1	S. E.	40.6	S. W.	29.6	N. E.	18.3	W.
28	30.4	S. W.	23.6	N. W.	34.6	N. E.	40.0	N. E.	40.7	N. W.	28.0	S. W.	17.8	W.
29	29.6	S. W.	24.4	S.	....	....	40.1	N. E.	40.8	N.	26.5	....	17.3	E.
30	28.5	N. E.	25.8	S.	....	....	40.1	N. E.	40.9	S.	24.9	N. E.	16.7	N. E.
31	26.9	S. E.	27.3	N. E.	....	....	40.2	S. W.	....	....	23.2	N. E.	....	....

LAKE PROVIDENCE, LOUISIANA.

Authority, Corps of Engineers, United States Army.

Date.	December.		January.		February.		March.		April.		May.		June.	
	Gauge.	Wind.	Gauge.	Wind.	Gauge.	Wind.	Gauge.	Wind.	Gauge.	Wind.	Gauge.	Wind.	Gauge.	Wind.
1	5.4	N. E.	30.6	S. E.	27.7	N. W.	33.8	N. W.	37.1	N. W.	37.1	S. E.	33.5	E.
2	6.5	S.	29.8	S.	28.6	N. W.	34.4	S. W.	37.1	N. W.	37.1	S. E.	32.6	W.
3	7.6	S.	28.7	S.	29.4	N. E.	34.7	S. E.	37.1	N. E.	37.1	S. W.	31.6	N. W.
4	8.5	N. W.	27.3	N. W.	30.1	N. E.	35.0	N.	37.0	S. E.	37.0	N. W.	30.5	N. W.
5	9.2	E.	25.6	N.	30.7	E.	35.4	S. E.	37.0	S.	37.0	N. W.	29.3	S.
6	9.8	E.	23.9	N.	31.2	W.	35.6	N. E.	37.0	N.	37.0	N. E.	28.0	S.
7	11.3	N. E.	22.0	N. W.	31.6	N.	35.9	N.	36.9	N. E.	36.9	N. E.	26.6	S. W.
8	13.3	S.	20.0	S. E.	31.8	N. E.	36.2	N. W.	36.9	N. E.	36.9	N. E.	25.2	S. W.
9	15.2	S.	18.5	S.	32.0	N. E.	36.4	S. E.	36.9	N. W.	36.9	N. E.	23.9	S.
10	16.5	S.	17.0	S.	32.0	N. E.	36.6	S.	36.8	N. E.	38.8	S. E.	22.2	S. W.
11	17.6	S.	15.9	S.	31.9	N. W.	36.8	N.	36.8	S. E.	36.8	S. E.	20.8	S.
12	19.3	S.	14.8	N. E.	31.7	S. W.	37.0	N. W.	36.8	S. W.	36.8	S. E.	19.4	N. E.
13	21.5	N. W.	14.2	N.	31.4	S. W.	37.1	N. E.	36.7	S. E.	36.8	S.	18.2	N. E.
14	23.3	N. E.	14.2	N. E.	30.8	N. E.	37.1	N. E.	36.7	S.	36.8	S.	16.9	N. E.
15	24.6	N. W.	15.3	N. E.	30.0	E.	37.2	N. E.	36.9	N. E.	36.8	S.	16.0	S. E.
16	25.8	N. W.	17.1	N.	29.0	N. W.	37.2	S. E.	36.8	S. E.	36.7	N. E.	15.0	S. E.
17	26.9	S. E.	19.7	S. E.	27.8	W.	37.3	S.	36.8	N.	36.7	E.	14.6	S. E.
18	27.8	S.	21.9	S. E.	26.7	N.	37.3	S. E.	36.8	N. E.	36.7	N. W.	14.5	S. E.
19	28.7	N. E.	23.7	S. E.	25.7	N. E.	37.3	S.	36.9	S. E.	36.6	N. E.	15.2	S.
20	29.6	N. E.	25.1	S.	24.9	S.	37.4	N. W.	36.9	S. W.	36.6	E.	16.6	N. W.
21	30.2	N. E.	26.1	S.	24.5	S.	37.4	S.	36.9	N. E.	36.6	S.	17.0	N. E.
22	30.9	N. W.	26.8	S.	24.9	S.	37.4	N. W.	37.0	S. E.	36.5	N. E.	17.5	N. E.
23	31.3	N. W.	27.5	N.	25.5	N.	37.4	N. E.	37.0	N. W.	36.4	W.	17.8	S. E.
24	31.5	N. E.	27.8	N.	26.6	N. E.	37.3	N. E.	37.0	N. E.	36.3	W.	18.1	S. E.
25	31.7	N. W.	27.7	N.	28.5	N.	37.3	S. E.	37.0	W.	36.2	W.	18.2	S.
26	31.7	S. W.	27.5	S. E.	30.0	E.	37.3	S. E.	37.0	N.	36.1	S. E.	18.4	S. W.
27	31.8	N. W.	27.2	S. E.	31.6	N. E.	37.2	N. E.	37.0	S.	35.9	S. E.	18.6	N. W.
28	31.7	S. E.	26.9	W.	32.8	S. W.	37.2	N. E.	37.1	N. W.	35.6	W.	18.6	S. W.
29	31.6	N.	26.5	N. E.	....	....	37.2	N. W.	37.1	N. W.	35.3	S.	18.5	N. W.
30	31.5	N. E.	26.5	S.	....	....	37.2	S. E.	37.1	S. E.	34.8	N. E.	18.2	N. W.
31	31.2	S. E.	26.8	N. E.	....	....	37.1	S. E.	....	....	34.2	N. E.	....	....

VICKSBURG, MISS.

Authority, Corps of Engineers, United States Army.—To reduce to delta survey-gauge, deduct 0.4 feet.

Date.	December.		January.		February.		March.		April.		May.		June.	
	Gauge.	Wind.	Gauge.	Wind.	Gauge.	Wind.	Gauge.	Wind.	Gauge.	Wind.	Gauge.	Wind.	Gauge.	Wind.
1	8.3	S.	34.9	S.	30.9	S.	36.6	S. W.	43.1	N. W.	45.7	S. W.	42.8	S. W.
2	9.0	E.	34.4	S.	31.5	S.	37.3	W.	43.1	N. W.	45.7	S. W.	42 3	S.
3	10.6	S. E.	33.6	S.	32.5	N. W.	37.9	S. W.	43.1	N. W.	45.7	S.	41.7	S. W.
4	11.7	S.	32.4	N. W.	33.2	N. W.	38.4	S.	43.1	S. W.	45.7	W.	41.0	S.
5	12.3	S.	31.2	N. E.	34.0	N. E.	38.8	S.	43.1	S.	45.7	N. W.	40.2	S. E.
6	13.0	S.	29.6	N.	34.5	N. W.	39.1	S.	43.1	N. W.	45.6	N. W.	39.2	N. E.
7	13.8	S.	28.0	N.	35.0	N. W.	39.5	N. W.	43.4	S. W.	45.5	N. W.	38.2	S.
8	15.0	S.	26.3	N.	35.4	N. W.	39.8	N. W.	43.7	N. W.	45.5	N. W.	36.9	S.
9	16.8	N. E.	24.5	N. W.	35.6	W.	40.0	W.	(*)	N. W.	45.4	S. E.	35.6	S.
10	18.3	S.	22.5	N. W.	35.8	W.	40.2	S. W.	43.8	N. W.	45.3	S. E.	34.0	S. W.
11	19.6	S.	21.0	S.	35.8	E.	40.5	S. W.	43.8	N.	45.3	W.	32.4	W.
12	21.0	S.	19.5	S.	35.7	S. E.	40 7	N. E.	43.8	N. W.	45.2	N. W.	30.8	N.
13	22.8	N. W.	18.4	S.	35.5	S.	40.9	N. W.	43.8	W.	45.2	N. E.	29.2	N. E.
14	24.7	N. W.	18.0	E.	35.2	N. W.	41.1	W.	43.8	N. W.	45.1	S. E.	27.7	S.
15	26.4	W.	18.0	S.	34.8	N. E.	41.4	E.	(*)	N. W.	45·1	S. W.	26.2	S.
16	28.0	W.	19.3	S. E.	34.0	S.	41.6	N. E.	44.3	N. E.	45.0	N. W.	24.9	S.
17	29.4	S.	21.3	S.	32.9	S. E.	41.8	S.	44.4	W.	45.0	N. W.	23.9	S.
18	30.3	S.	23.4	S.	31.9	W.	41.9	S.	44.4	N. E.	44.9	W.	23.1	E.
19	31.3	W.	25.5	S.	30.8	S.	42.0	S.	44.7	E.	44.8	W.	22.8	S.
20	32.3	N. W.	27.5	E.	29.7	E.	42.2	N.	44.8	N. W.	44.7	N. W.	22.9	N.
21	33.0	W.	28.9	E.	29.1	S. E.	42.3	S.	44.8	N. W.	44.6	N. W.	23.0	E.
22	33.7	W.	29.9	E.	29.0	S.	42.4	S.	45.0	S. E.	44.5	W.	23.1	S. E.
23	34.4	N. W.	30.7	W.	29.2	N. W.	42.5	S. E.	45.2	S. E.	44.4	N. E.	23.2	S.
24	34.8	N. W.	31.2	N. W.	29.9	W.	42.6	N. W.	45.2	N. E.	44.3	S. E.	23.2	S.
25	35.1	W.	31.5	N. W.	31.1	N. W.	42.7	N. W.	45.4	N. W.	44.2	S.	23.1	S.
26	35.3	S. W.	31.6	S. E.	32.6	N. E.	42.8	E.	45.4	N. W.	44.1	S.	23.0	S.
27	35.4	N.	31.4	E.	34.0	S. E.	42.8	N. W.	45.5	N. W.	44.0	S.	22.9	S.
28	35.5	W.	31.2	E.	35.4	S.	42.8	N. W.	45.5	S. E.	43.9	S.	22.8	S.
29	35.5	S.	30.9	N. W.	....	....	42.8	N. E.	45.6	N. W.	43.7	S. W.	22.7	S.
30	35.5	N. W.	30.6	W.	....	....	42.9	N. E.	45.6	N.	43.4	S. W.	22.4	S.
31	35.3	N. W.	30.6	W.	....	....	43.0	N. E.	....	....	43.1	S. W.	....	....

* No observation.

NATCHEZ, MISSISSIPPI.

[Authority, Corps of Engineers, United States Army.—To reduce to delta survey-gauge, add 5.46 feet.

Date.	December.		January.		February.		March.		April.		May.		June.	
	Gauge.	Wind.	Gauge.	Wind.	Gauge.	Wind.	Gauge.	Wind.	Gauge.	Wind.	Gauge.	Wind.	Gauge.	Wind.
1	6.6	S.	33.1	S. E.	29.0	S. E.	33.3	N.	41.7	N.	44.0	S. E.	42.4	S.
2	7.1	S.	32.8	S. E.	29.3	S. E.	34.1	S. E.	41.8	S. E.	44.0	S. E.	42.2	S.
3	7.8	S. E.	32.4	S. E.	29.8	S. E.	34.9	S. E.	41.8	E.	44.0	S. E.	42.0	S.
4	9.0	N.	31.3	S. E.	30.5	N. E.	35.5	S. E.	41.9	N.	43.9	N.	41.8	S.
5	10.3	N.	30.7	N.	31.1	E.	36.0	S. E.	42.0	S. E.	43.9	N.	41.4	S.
6	11.3	N.	29.7	N.	32.1	N. E.	36.4	S. E.	42.0	S. E.	43.9	S.	41.0	S.
7	12.0	S. E.	28.7	N.	32.6	N. E.	36.8	N.	42.2	N.	43.8	S.	40.2	S.
8	12.7	E.	27.4	E.	33.0	N. E.	37.2	N.	42.3	N. E.	43.8	S.	39.6	S.
9	13.8	S.	25.7	E.	33.3	N.	37.4	S. E.	42.9	S. E.	43.8	S. E.	38.8	S.
10	15.2	S. E.	24.2	S. E.	33.5	N.	37.5	S. E.	43.0	N. E.	43.7	S. E.	37.8	S.
11	16.5	S. E.	22.9	S. E.	33.6	S. E.	37.7	N.	43.2	S. E.	43.7	S. E.	36.5	S.
12	17.8	S.	20.7	S. E.	33.7	S. E.	38.0	N.	43.3	S. E.	43.6	S. E.	35.2	S.
13	19.0	N.	18.4	N.	33.7	S. E.	38.3	N.	43.4	S. E.	43.6	S. E.	33.8	S.
14	20.5	N.	18.0	N.	33.5	S.	38.5	N.	43.4	S. E.	43.6	S. E.	32.3	S.
15	22.3	S.	18.0	N.	33.3	S.	38.7	E.	43.5	S. E.	43.6	S. E.	30.9	S.
16	23.8	S.	18.0	N.	32.9	S.	39.1	S. E.	43.8	S. E.	43.5	N.	29.7	S.
17	25.2	S.	18.7	N.	32.4	S. E.	39.5	N.	44.0	S. E.	43.5	S. E.	28.5	S.
18	26.3	S.	18.7	E.	31.6	N.	39.6	S. E.	44.0	N. E.	43.4	S. E.	27.5	S.
19	27.4	N.	20.3	E.	30.6	S. E.	39.8	S. E.	44.3	N. E.	43.4	S. E.	26.7	S.
20	28.4	S.	22.1	S. E.	29.7	S. E.	39.9	S. E.	44.4	S. E.	43.3	S. E.	26.0	S.
21	29.2	N.	24.0	S. E.	29.0	S. E.	40.0	S. E.	44.3	S. E.	43.3	S. E.	25.8	S.
22	30.0	N.	25.0	S. E.	28.4	S. E.	40.3	S. E.	44.2	S. E.	43.2	S. E.	25.6	N.
23	30.8	N.	26.5	S.	28.1	N.	40.5	N. E.	44.2	N. E.	43.2	S. E.	25.5	S. E.
24	31.3	N.	27.5	N.	28.3	N.	40.8	N. E.	44.2	N. E.	43.1	S. E.	25.4	S.
25	31.9	N.	29.0	N.	28.8	N.	40.9	N.	44.2	S. E.	43.0	S. E.	25.2	S.
26	32.4	N.	29.3	S. E.	29.8	N.	41.0	S. E.	44.2	S. E.	43.0	S. E.	25.0	S.
27	32.6	N.	29.4	S. E.	30.3	E.	41.1	S. E.	44.1	S. E.	42.9	S. E.	24.7	S.
28	32.9	N.	29.4	E.	32.3	E.	41.2	S. E.	44.1	S. E.	42.8	S. E.	24.4	S.
29	33.0	E.	29.3	S. E.	....	....	41.2	N. E.	44.0	S. E.	42.7	S. E.	24.0	S.
30	33.1	N. E.	29.1	S. E.	....	....	41.5	S. E.	44.0	S. E.	42.7	S. E.	23.7	S.
31	33.1	S.	28.9	S. E.	....	....	41.5	S. E.	....	....	42.6	S.	....	....

RED RIVER LANDING, LOUISIANA.

Authority, Corps of Engineers, United States Army.

Date.	December.		January.		February.		March.		April.		May.		June.	
	Gauge.	Wind.	Gauge.	Wind.	Gauge.	Wind.	Gauge.	Wind.	Gauge.	Wind.	Gauge.	Wind.	Gauge.	Wind.
1	4.3	S.	29.8	N. E.	26.5	S. E.	30.0	S. E.	39.9	N.	43.2	N. E.	41.8	S.
2	5.0	S.	29.8	S.	26.7	E.	30.8	E.	40.1	N. W.	43.1	S. W.	41.6	S.
3	5.2	S.	29.6	S.	27.0	S.	31.5	S. W.	40.2	N. W.	43.1	S.	41.5	S. W.
4	5.4	N.	29.3	W.	27.4	......	32.0	S.	40.4	W.	43.1	N.	41.3	N. W.
5	6.3	N.	28.9	N. W.	27.9	S.	32.4	S.	40.7	S.	43.1	E.	41.1	N. W.
6	8.8	N. E.	28.3	N. W.	28.9	N.	32.8	S. E.	41.0	S.	43.1	E.	40.9	N. W.
7	9.7	S.	27.6	E.	29.3	N.	33.4	N. E.	41.3	E.	43.1	E.	......	......
8	10.2	S.	26.8	S.	29.6	N.	33.5	S. E.	41.6	S. E.	43.1	S.	......	......
9	10.9	S.	25.9	S.	29.9	E.	33.7	N. E.	42.1	N.	43.1	S.	......	......
10	12.0	E.	25.0	S.	30.2	S.	33.9	S.	42.4	N.	43.1	S. E.	......	......
11	13.3	E.	23.1	......	30.4	E.	34.1	S. W.	42.7	N.	43.1	S.	......	......
12	14.4	S. E.	21.5	S.	30.5	S.	34.3	S. W.	43.0	N. E.	43.1	S.	......	......
13	15.5	N.	20.2	......	30.6	S.	34.5	E.	43.2	S. E.	43.0	S.	......	......
14	16.8	N.	19.1	N.	30.6	N.	34.7	S. W.	43.4	S.	43.0	S.	......	......
15	18.2	E.	18.0	N.	30, 6	E.	35.0	......	43.5	S.	42.9	S.	......	......
16	19.9	E.	17.6	N.	30.4	......	35.5	S. W.	44.0	S.	42.9	N. E.	......	......
17	21.2	S.	17.6	E.	30.1	S.	36.0	......	43.8	N. E.	42.9	S.	......	......
18	22.4	S. E.	18.3	S.	29.7	N.	36.2	S. E.	43.6	S. E.	42.9	S.	......	......
19	23.5	S. E.	19.0	S.	29.1	S. E.	36.3	S. E.	43.8	S.	42.8	S. E.	......	......
20	24.4	N. E.	20.3	E.	28.4	S.	36.6	S.	43.7	S. E.	42.7	S.	......	......
21	25.2	N.	21.8	N. E.	27.9	N. W.	36.8	S.	43.6	S.	42.6	S. E.	......	......
22	25.8	E.	23.2	W.	27.4	E.	37.0	......	43.5	W.	42.6	S.	......	......
23	26.2	N.	24.5	S.	26.9	N.	37.4	N. E.	43.4	N.	42.5	S.	......	......
24	27.3	N.	25.5	N.	26.8	N.	37.7	E.	43.5	N. E.	42.4	S. E.	......	......
25	28.0	N.	26.1	N. E.	27.0	N.	37.9	S. E.	43.4	S.	42.3	S.	......	......
26	28.5	S.	26.6	S. E.	27.4	N. W.	38.1	......	43.4	......	42.3	......	......	......
27	28.8	N.	26.8	E.	28.2	W.	38.3	S. E.	43.3	S.	42.3	S.	......	......
28	29.1	S.	26.9	S.	29.0	S.	38.5	N. E.	43.2	S.	42.3	E.	......	......
29	29.4	E.	26.9	S.	......	......	38.8	N.	43.2	S.	42.2	S. E.	......	......
30	29.6	S.	26.8	E.	......	......	39.3	S.	43.2	S. E.	42.1	E.	......	......
31	29.7	S.	26.6	S. E.	......	......	39.5	S.	......	......	42 0	S. E.	......	......

BATON ROUGE, LOUISIANA.

Authority, Corps of Engineers, United States Army.—To reduce to delta survey-gauge, deduct 0.9 feet.

Date.	December.		January.		February.		March.		April.		May.		June.	
	Gauge.	Wind.	Gauge.	Wind.	Gauge.	Wind.	Gauge.	Wind.	Gauge.	Wind.	Gauge.	Wind.	Gauge.	Wind.
1	4.6	E.	25.0	E.	22.9	E.	25.2	E.	32.8	N.	32.9	S.	31.5	W.
2	5.3	E.	25.0	E.	22.9	E.	26.0	W.	33.0	N.	32.9	S.	31.4	W.
3	5.9	S.	24.9	E.	23.2	E.	26.5	E.	33.2	N.	32.9	S.	31.3	W.
4	6.3	N.	24.8	E.	23.4	E.	26.7	E.	33.4	N.	32.9	N.	31.2	N.
5	7.0	E.	24.6	N.	23.7	N.	27.3	E.	33.7	E.	32.8	N.	31.1	N.
6	7.5	E.	24.3	N. W.	25.0	N.	27.6	E.	33.9	E.	32.8	N.	31.0	W.
7	7.8	E.	23.5	N.	24.9	N.	27.9	N.	34.1	E.	32.7	S.	30.8	W.
8	8.3	E.	22.9	E.	25.1	N.	27.9	E.	34.4	E.	32.7	S.	30.6	W.
9	8.6	E.	22.1	E.	25.4	N.	28.0	E.	35.0	W.	32.7	S.	30.3	E.
10	9.3	E.	21.1	E.	25.6	N.	28.1	E.	35.2	W.	32.7	E.	30.0	E.
11	10.2	E.	20.1	E.	25.8	E.	28.4	N. W.	35.5	W.	32.7	E.	29.6	E.
12	11.1	E.	19.0	E.	26.0	E.	28.4	N.	35.7	E.	32.6	E.	29.1	E.
13	12.1	N.	17.9	E.	26.1	E.	28.5	E.	35.9	S.	32.6	E.	28.8	W.
14	12.9	N.	17.0	N. E.	26.1	N.	28.7	E.	36.0	S. E.	32.6	E.	28.3	W.
15	14.1	N.	16.1	N.	26.0	N.	29.1	S. E.	36.0	S. E.	32.5	N. W.	27.7	E.
16	15.4	N.	15.5	N.	25.9	E.	29.4	E.	36.2	E.	32.4	N.	27.2	E.
17	16.7	E.	15.4	N.	25.7	E.	29.7	E.	34.8	E.	32.3	N.	26.6	E.
18	17.8	E.	15.8	E.	25.5	E.	29.9	E.	34.3	E.	32.3	N.	26.1	W.
19	18.7	N.	16.4	E.	24.9	E.	30.0	E.	34.2	E.	32.3	E.	25.5	N. W.
20	19.6	N.	17.6	E.	24.4	E.	30.1	E.	33.9	W.	32.3	W.	24.9	W.
21	20.4	N. E.	18.9	E.	24.0	E.	30.4	E.	33.7	E.	32.2	W.	24.4	W.
22	21.3	N.	20.0	E.	23.4	E.	30.5	E.	33.6	S. W.	32.2	W.	24.0	W.
23	21.9	N.	21.0	N.	23.2	N.	30.7	E.	33.6	N.	32.0	W.	23.6	E.
24	22.4	N.	21.8	N.	22.9	N.	31.0	E.	33.6	E.	32.0	W.	23.3	W.
25	23.0	N.	22.4	N.	22.9	N.	31.2	E.	33.5	N.	31.9	N.	22.9	W.
26	23.5	E.	22.7	E.	23.2	E.	31.4	E.	33.3	N.	31.8	N.	22.5	S. W.
27	23.8	N.	23.0	E.	23.7	E.	31.6	E.	33.2	W.	31.8	E.	22.1	W.
28	24.0	N.	23.1	E.	24.4	S. E.	31.8	E.	33.1	N.	31.8	E.	21.7	W.
29	24.3	E.	23.0	E.			32.1	E.	33.0	N.	31.8	E.	21.3	W.
30	24.5	E.	22.9	E.			32.5	E.	33.0	E.	31.6	W.	20.9	N. W.
31	24.7	E.	22.9	E.			32.5	E.			31.6	W.		

CARROLLTON, LOUISIANA.

Authority, Corps of Engineers, United States Army.—Zero of this and of the delta survey-gauge arei dentical.

Date.	December.		January.		February.		March.		April.		May.		June.	
	Gauge.	Wind.	Gauge.	Wind.	Gauge.	Wind.	Gauge.	Wind.	Gauge.	Wind.	Gauge.	Wind.	Gauge.	Wind.
1	0.7	E.	10.1	E.	9.2	S.	10.3	S. W.	14.6	N. W.	13.5	S.	12.3	W.
2	1.0	E.	10.3	S. E.	9.3	E.	10.9	N.	14.6	N.	13.6	S.	12.3	S. W.
3	1.4	S. E.	10.4	S. E.	9.3	N. W.	11.3	S. E.	14.8	N.	13.5	S. S. W.	12.1	W.
4	1.5	S.	10.4	S.	9.6	N. E.	11.7	S. W.	14.8	W.	13.5	N. W.	12.1	S. W.
5	1.8	N. E.	10.3	N. W.	9.8	E.	11.9	S.	15.0	S. S. E.	13.3	N. W.	12.0	N. W.
6	1.9	E.	10.2	N. W.	10.4	W.	12.0	....	15.0	S. E.	13.3	N.	12.0	N. W.
7	2.2	S. E.	9.8	N. W.	10.5	N.	12.1	N.	15.1	S.	13.3	N. W.	11.9	S. W.
8	2.8	E.	9.4	....	10.8	N. W.	12.2	E.	15.3	S.	13.2	N. E.	11.8	S.
9	2.8	E.	9.0	W.	10.6	N. W.	12.0	E.	15.6	W.	13.2	S	11.8	S.
10	2.9	E.	8.5	....	10.7	E.	12.0	....	15.5	N. W.	13.3	E. S. E.	11.7	....
11	3.4	E.	8.0	S. E.	10.8	S. E.	12.2	W.	15.6	N. E.	13.3	S. E.	11.5	....
12	3.7	S. E.	7.5	S. E.	10.9	S. E.	12.2	N. E.	15.7	E.	13.3	N. W.	11.3	W. S. W.
13	4.1	N.	6.9	....	11.0	S. E.	12.3	N.	15.8	S. E.	13.4	E.	11.2	W. N. W.
14	4.2	N. E.	6.3	N.	11.0	N.	12.3	N. E.	15.9	S. E.	13.3	N. E.	10.9	E.
15	4.7	N. E.	5.8	N.	11.0	S. W.	12.6	S.	16.0	S. E.	13.2	W.	10.8	S. E.
16	5.2	N.	5.6	N. E.	11.0	S. W.	12.9	S.	16.1	N. E.	13.2	W.	10.6	N. N. W.
17	5.7	....	5.6	N. E.	11.0	N.	13.2	S. E.	15.4	N. E.	13.2	N.	10.3	S. E.
18	6.2	....	5.6	E.	10.8	S. E.	13.2	S. E.	15.1	S. E.	13.0	N.	10.1	S.
19	6.7	N.	6.0	E.	10.6	S. E.	13.2	S. E.	14.8	S.	12.9	N. E.	9.9	N.
20	7.2	N.	6.6	....	10.4	S. E.	13.2	S. E.	14.6	S. W.	12.9	W.	9.7	N.
21	7.7	N. E.	7.4	E. S. E.	10.2	S. E.	13.2	S. E.	14.3	N. E.	12.8	W.	9.5	E.
22	8.4	S. E.	8.0	S. E.	9.8	S. E.	13.2	S.	14.3	S. W.	12.7	N.	9.4	....
23	8.7	N.	8.3	N.	9.3	N.	13.3	E.	14.3	N. W.	12.7	E.	9.3	E.
24	9.0	N.	8.7	N.	9.1	N. E.	13.3	N.	14.3	N.	12.7	....	9.1	E.
25	9.4	N. W.	8.9	N. E.	9.1	N. W.	13.5	E.	14.1	N.	12.7	....	9.0	S.
26	9.4	....	9.0	N. E.	9.3	N. E.	13.7	N. W.	13.9	W.	12.7	E.	8.9	S. W.
27	9.5	N. W.	9.2	S.	9.6	E.	13.6	E. S. E.	13.8	S. W.	12.7	S.	8.7	S. W.
28	9.5	N. E.	9.3	N. W.	9.9	E.	13.7	E.	13.8	S. W.	12.6	E.	8.5	W.
29	9.6	W.	9.2	N.	....	....	13.9	S.	13.7	N.	12.6	E.	8.3	W.
30	9.8	N. N. E.	9.2	N. E.	....	....	14.1	N. E.	13.6	E.	12.5	E.	8.1	W.
31	10.0	N.	9.1	N. E.	....	....	14.3	S.	....	....	12.5	W.	....	....

NEW ORLEANS, LOUISIANA.

Authority, Signal Service, United States Army.—High water of 1871 reads 15.4 feet.

Date.	December.		January.		February.		March.		April.		May.		June.	
	Gauge.	Wind.	Gauge.	Wind.	Gauge.	Wind.	Gauge.	Wind.	Gauge.	Wind.	Gauge.	Wind.	Gauge.	Wind.
1	2.2		10.4		9.7		10.9		14.7		13.7		12.8	
2	2.7		10.4		9.7		11.2		14.7		13.9		12.8	
3	2.4		10.4		9.8		11.7		14.7		13.8		12.6	
4	2.3		10.7		10.0		12.0		14.9		13.8		12.5	
5	2.3		10.2		10.2		12.1		15.2		13.7		12.6	
6	2.7		10.3		10.8		12.3		15.0		13.7		12.4	
7	2.7		9.9		11.0		12.4		15.3		13.7		12.2	
8	3.2		9.4		11.1		12.7		15.5		13.7		12.1	
9	3.3		9.3		11.1		12.3		15.4		13.7		11.9	
10	3.7		8.8		11.2		12.4		15.4		13.7		11.9	
11	4.2		8.3		11.3		12.7		15.4		13.7		11.9	
12	4.7		7.9		11.4		12.7		15.4		13.5		11.7	
13	5.2		7.4		11.4		12.7		15.7		13.5		11.6	
14	5.1		6.7		11.2		12.7		15.8		13.5		11.4	
15	5.4		6.2		11.1		12.9		15.9		13.5		11.4	
16	6.0		6.1		11.1		13.3		15.9		13.5		11.1	
17	6.3		6.1		11.1		13.3		15.2		13.5		10.9	
18	6.7		6.1		11.0		13.3		15.2		13.4		10.7	
19	7.1		6.4		11.0		13.3		15.2		13.3		10.5	
20	7.7		7.1		10.9		13.7		14.7		13.2		10.2	
21	8.1		7.9		10.9		13.3		14.4		13.1		10.0	
22	8.7		8.7		10.4		13.3		14.7		12.9		9.9	
23	8.8		9.0		9.8		13.8		14.3		12.9		9.7	
24	9.1		9.4		10.0		13.8		14.4		12.9		9.6	
25	9.4		9.7		9.8		13.8		14.2		12.9		9.5	
26	9.8		9.7		9.8		14.0		13.9		12.8		9.4	
27	9.8		10.0		10.0		13.8		14.1		12.9		9.2	
28	10.0		9.8		10.4		13.9		14.1		12.8		9.1	
29	10.1		9.7				14.0		14.1		12.8		9.0	
30	10.2		9.4				14.1		13.7		12.8		8.9	
31	10.4		9.3				14.3				12.8			

LAKE PONTCHARTRAIN.—NEW CANAL AT MAGNOLIA STREET.

Authority, W. H. Bell, city surveyor.—Gauge reads downward, from XX below city datum-line.

Date.	December.		January.		February.		March.		April.		May.		June.	
	Gauge.	Wind.	Gauge.	Wind.	Gauge.	Wind.	Gauge.	Wind.	Gauge.	Wind.	Gauge.	Wind.	Gauge.	Wind.
1	5. 35		4. 95		4. 85		5. 00		4. 45		4. 30		4. 00	
2	4. 65		4. 90		4. 85		5. 00		4. 65		4. 25		4. 15	
3	4. 35		4. 95		4. 90		5. 00		5. 00		4. 15		4. 35	
4	4. 15		4. 90		5. 10		4. 95		5. 35		4. 00		4. 40	
5	4. 25		4. 55		4. 95		4. 85		5. 25		4. 50		4. 40	
6	4. 45		4. 75		4. 10		4. 50		5. 05		4. 70		4. 15	
7	4. 50		5. 40		4. 50		4. 30		4. 75		4. 75		4. 40	
8	4. 40		5. 95		4. 85		4. 50		4. 35		4. 45		4. 50	
9	4. 30		5. 85		5. 35		4. 50		4. 50		4. 30		4. 70	
10	4. 35		5. 80		5. 60		4. 60		5. 15		3. 90		4. 85	
11	4. 40		5. 65		5. 40		4. 65		5. 40		3. 80		4. 50	
12	4. 25		5. 40		4. 90		4. 25		5. 30		3. 70		4. 35	
13	4. 50		5. 15		4. 80		5. 10		4. 65		3. 90		4. 45	
14	5. 50		4. 95		4. 90		4. 90		4. 00		3. 95		4. 10	
15	5. 45		5. 20		4. 60		4. 15		3. 80		4. 00		4. 00	
16	4. 85		4. 50		4. 70		3. 85		4. 75		4. 35		3. 80	
17	4. 80		4. 30		4. 70		4. 00		3. 00		3. 95		3. 55	
18	4. 90		4. 25		4. 80		4. 05		3. 00		4. 05		3. 65	
19	4. 80		4. 20		4. 80		4. 30		2. 35		4. 05		3. 50	
20	4. 90		4. 35		4. 60		4. 40		2. 35		4. 00		3. 80	
21	4. 95		4. 50		4. 40		4. 65		2. 90		4. 30		3. 85	
22	4. 30		4. 70		4. 30		5. 00		3. 00		4. 35		3. 90	
23	4. 55		4. 65		4. 15		4. 90		2. 60		4. 35		3. 90	
24	4. 50		4. 70		4. 80		4. 30		2. 30		4. 35		4. 00	
25	4. 60		4. 70		4. 50		4. 15		2. 50		4. 45		4. 10	
26	5. 55		4. 70		4. 80		4. 00		3. 00		4. 65		4. 30	
27	5. 75		4. 80		5. 00		4. 25		3. 55		4. 60		4. 75	
28	5. 90		4. 70		4. 99		4. 45		3. 70		4. 15		4. 90	
29	5. 85		4. 85				4. 70		4. 15		3. 95		5. 05	
30	5. 80		4. 95				4. 55		4. 30		3. 80		5. 20	
31	5. 20		4. 95				4. 70				3. 95			

CINCINNATI, OHIO.

Authority, Signal Service United States Army.—Zero of gauge is at low-water mark, (20 inches above bottom;) high water of 1832 reads 62.5 feet.

Date.	December.		January.		February.		March.		April.		May.		June.	
	Gauge.	Wind.	Gauge.	Wind.	Gauge.	Wind.	Gauge.	Wind.	Gauge.	Wind.	Gauge.	Wind.	Gauge.	Wind.
1	25.4		12.9		28.3		37.1		19.4		46.0		8.8	
2	22.7		12.3		27.3		33.3		21.2		45.5		8.4	
3	20.5		11.7		26.0		29.2		23.0		44.1		8.1	
4	28.1		13.2		24.1		27.7		23.3		41.4		8.7	
5	26.2		18.6		22.2		26.1		22.6		38.0		8.5	
6	25.8		22.0		20.5		30.6		21.7		34.3		8.3	
7	28.0		29.2		18.9		30.0		19.2		31.2		7.9	
8	29.1		37.4		18.1		29.9		18.7		28.3		7.7	
9	30.1		43.3		17.9		31.1		21.3		25.8		7.4	
10	31.2		46.5		17.9		32.2		27.2		24.2		7.1	
11	29.9		47.9		17.4		31.8		27.1		22.4		6.7	
12	28.3		47.7		16.7		30.5		42.3		20.7		7.3	
13	37.7		45.8		16.1		28.1		43.8		19.2		7.6	
14	35.7		42.5		21.9		25.4		40.3		17.7		7.9	
15	36.7		37.4		22.9		22.7		36.2		16.2		7.8	
16	40.8		31.8		24.6		20.4		32.5		15.1		8.4	
17	43.8		26.5		28.3		18.5		32.2		14.1		7.7	
18	44.2		23.5		31.1		16.9		34.5		13.2		7.8	
19	43.1		22.4		32.2		16.1		36.3		12.2		8.7	
20	39.9		23.7		30.8		16.4		37.7		11.3		9.0	
21	35.4		22.4		32.3		19.9		36.9		10.7		9.7	
22	30.5		24.6		35.8		24.3		35.7		9.7		8.0	
23	26.3		28.8		40.2		27.5		34.0		9.6		7.3	
24	23.5		32.8		42.3		29.0		32.4		10.3		6.9	
25	21.7		34.5		43.7		28.4		31.3		10.0		6.3	
26	19.8		36.1		44.2		26.6		32.1		9.7		6.2	
27	18.3		35.8		43.0		24.0		37.3		9.8		7.2	
28	16.7		35.0		40.3		21.7		41.7		9.4		6.9	
29	15.3		33.5				20.0		43.8		9.5		6.5	
30	14.3		31.2				18.3		45.0		9.3		6.1	
31	13.7		29.6				17.7				9.1			

LOUISVILLE, KENTUCKY, (HEAD OF THE FALLS.)

Authority, Corps of Engineers, United States Army.—High water of 1832 reads 40.76 feet.

Date.	December.		January,		February.		March.		April.		May.		June.	
	Gauge.	Wind.	Gauge.	Wind.	Gauge.	Wind.	Gauge.	Wind.	Gauge.	Wind.	Gauge.	Wind.	Gauge.	Wind.
1	10.3	S.	6.5	S. W.	10.9	N.	17.5	E.	8.7	N.	20.7	S. W.	5.1	N. E.
2	9.8	S. E.	6.3	S. W.	10.5	N.	14.5	S.	8.5	W.	21.7	W.	4.9	N. E.
3	9.4	S.	6.2	S.	10.2	N.	12.0	S.	9.1	W.	22.0	N. E.	4.8	S.
4	10.4	W.	6.0	S.	9.9	N.	11.0	S. W.	9.5	N.	21.3	N. E.	4.8	S. W.
5	11.4	N.	6.4	N.	9.6	N.	10.5	S. W.	9.6	E.	19.1	N. W.	4.8	S. W.
6	10.8	N. W.	7.7	N.	9.1	N.	11.0	W.	9.4	N.	15.9	W.	4.7	S. W.
7	10.5	S. W.	9.0	N. W.	8.8	N.	12.0	N.	9.0	N.	12.9	N. E.	4.6	S.
8	10.9	N. E.	10.8	N. W.	8.5	N.	12.0	S.	8.9	N.	11.3	S. E.	4.5	S. W.
9	11.2	N. W.	13.0	N.	8.0	N.	11.3	E.	9.0	N.	10.6	S. W.	4.4	S. W.
10	11.5	N. E.	16.7	S. W.	8.0	N.	11.2	N.	9.6	S. W.	10.0	S.	4.3	S. W.
11	11.8	E.	20.2	N.	8.0	W.	11.3	W.	11.0	S.	9.6	E.	4.2	S. W.
12	11.3	N. E.	22.2	S. W.	8.0	S. W.	11.2	W.	13.7	N.	9.1	S. E.	4.4	N. W.
13	13.0	N. E.	22.2	S. W.	7.9	S.	11.0	N.	17.0	S.	8.9	N. E.	4.4	N. E.
14	15.4	S. W.	21.2	S. W.	8.6	N.	10.4	W.	19.0	S.	8.3	N.	4.2	E.
15	14.1	S. W.	18.8	N.	10.0	S. W.	9.9	E.	18.6	S.	8.0	E.	4.2	S.
16	13.5	S. W.	15.1	N. W.	9.9	S. W.	9.4	W.	16.6	N.	7.7	W.	4.3	S.
17	15.2	S. E.	11.6	N. W.	10.0	N.	8.6	E.	14.2	N. W.	7.1	E.	4.5	N. E.
18	17.1	S. E.	10.1	S.	10.5	N.	8.2	S.	12.6	N. W.	6.9	N. E.	4.4	E.
19	18.3	S. W.	9.4	S.	11.1	W.	8.1	S.	12.9	E.	6.5	E.	4.4	N. E.
20	17.8	S. W.	10.0	S.	11.2	W.	8.3	E.	14.7	S. W.	6.4	S. W.	4.3	N. E.
21	15.7	S. W.	10.1	S.	11.2	W.	8.9	W.	16.6	N. W.	6.0	N. E.	4.8	N. E.
22	12.8	S. W.	9.9	S.	13.1	W.	9.5	E.	16.2	N. W.	5.9	N. E.	5.0	S.
23	11.5	S. W.	10.1	N.	16.4	N.	9.5	E.	14.5	N. W.	5.8	S.	5.0	S. W.
24	10.0	S. W.	10.9	N.	20.8	N.	11.0	N.	12.5	N. W.	5.6	N. E.	4.7	W.
25	9.4	S. E.	11.4	N.	22.1	N.	11.3	E.	11.6	N. W.	5.5	N. W.	4.3	S. W.
26	9.0	S. E.	12.0	W.	22.4	W.	11.0	W.	11.2	W.	5.5	N. E.	4.1	W.
27	8.4	S. E.	12.5	W.	21.5	W.	10.4	E.	11.4	N. W.	5.3	N. E.	4.1	W.
28	8.0	S. W.	12.6	N.	20.0	E.	9.4	E.	12.8	W.	5.3	E.	4.6	S. W.
29	7.5	S. W.	12.5	W.	......	......	9.0	E.	16.1	W.	5.3	N. W.	4.3	N. W.
30	7.0	S. W.	11.6	W.	......	......	8.5	S.	19.0	S. W.	5.1	......	4.0	S. E.
31	6.9	S. W.	11.2	N.	......	......	8.5	S.	......	......	5.1	N. W.	......	......

LOUISVILLE, KENTUCKY, (FOOT OF THE FALLS.)

Authority, Corps of Engineers, United States Army.—High water of 1832 reads 67. 50 feet.

Date.	December.		January.		February.		March.		April.		May.		June.	
	Gauge.	Wind.	Gauge.	Wind.	Gauge.	Wind.	Gauge.	Wind.	Gauge.	Wind.	Gauge.	Wind.	Gauge.	Wind.
1	25. 0	S.	11. 0	S. W.	29. 4	N.	42. 8	E.	19. 5	N.	44. 8	S. W.	8. 1	N. E.
2	23. 7	S. E.	10. 6	S. W.	28. 0	N.	41. 4	S.	19. 0	W.	47. 0	W.	8. 0	N. E.
3	21. 5	S.	10. 0	S.	26. 5	N.	35. 4	S.	21. 0	W.	47. 4	N. E.	7. 8	S.
4	24. 4	W.	9. 8	S.	25. 0	N.	31. 5	S. W.	22. 5	N.	46. 5	N. E.	7. 7	S. W.
5	29. 2	N.	11. 0	N.	23. 2	N.	29. 0	S. W.	22. 4	E.	44. 3	N. W.	7. 7	S. W.
6	27. 6	N. W.	14. 3	N.	21. 1	N.	29. 5	W.	21. 5	N.	40. 9	W.	7. 5	S. W.
7	26. 0	S. W.	19. 1	N. W.	19. 5	N.	35. 0	N.	21. 2	N.	37. 3	N. E.	7. 4	S.
8	27. 0	N. E.	25. 8	N. W.	17. 5	N.	35. 0	S.	21. 0	N.	33. 3	S. E.	7. 3	S. W.
9	28. 0	S. W.	34. 5	N.	17. 0	N.	31. 0	E.	21. 2	N.	29. 7	S. W.	7. 0	S. W.
10	28. 9	N. E.	41. 0	S. W.	16. 5	N.	31. 0	N.	21. 5	N. W.	26. 5	S.	6. 8	S. W.
11	30. 0	E.	44. 9	S.	16. 3	W.	31. 0	W.	29. 8	S.	24. 0	E.	6. 6	S. W.
12	30. 0	S.	47. 0	S. W.	16. 0	S. W.	31. 0	W.	36. 8	N.	21. 9	S. E.	6. 8	N. W.
13	34. 9	N. E.	47. 4	S. W.	15. 4	S.	29. 5	N.	41. 3	S.	20. 0	N. E.	6. 6	N. E.
14	39. 4	S. W.	46. 5	S. W.	18. 3	N.	27. 5	W.	43. 7	S.	18. 1	N.	6. 5	E.
15	38. 0	S. W.	44. 0	N.	25. 0	S. W.	25. 0	E.	43. 9	S.	16. 3	E.	6. 5	S.
16	37. 5	S. W.	40. 0	N. W.	24. 0	S. W.	22. 5	W.	41. 6	N.	14. 7	E.	6. 7	S.
17	39. 0	S. E.	34. 5	N. W.	24. 1	N.	20. 0	E.	38. 6	N. W.	13. 4	E.	7. 0	N. E.
18	41. 6	S. E.	27. 0	S.	26. 0	N.	17. 9	S.	36. 5	N. W.	12. 2	N. E.	6. 9	E.
19	42. 8	S. W.	23. 1	S.	29. 0	W.	17. 3	S.	36. 7	E.	11. 7	E.	6. 8	N. E.
20	42. 0	S. W.	26. 0	S.	30. 0	W.	18. 9	E.	39. 3	S. W.	10. 9	S. W.	6. 7	N. E.
21	40. 4	S. W.	26. 0	S.	30. 0	W.	20. 9	W.	41. 5	S. W.	10. 3	N. E.	7. 2	N. E.
22	37. 6	S. W.	25. 0	S.	36. 1	W.	22. 5	E.	41. 1	N. W.	9. 7	N. E.	7. 8	S.
23	31. 0	S. W.	25. 5	N.	41. 0	N.	22. 5	E.	39. 0	N. W.	9. 4	S.	7. 8	S. W.
24	26. 6	S. W.	28. 0	N.	46. 0	N.	29. 4	N.	36. 6	N. W.	9. 3	N. E.	7. 4	W.
25	22. 8	S. E.	31. 9	N.	47. 4	N.	29. 8	E.	33. 5	N. W.	9. 1	N. W.	6. 9	S. W.
26	20. 0	S. E.	33. 8	W.	47. 6	W.	29. 0	W.	32. 0	W.	8. 8	N. E.	6. 6	W.
27	18. 0	S. E.	34. 5	W.	47. 0	W.	26. 9	E.	31. 9	N. W.	8. 3	N. E.	6. 6	W.
28	16. 2	S. W.	35. 5	N.	45. 4	....	24. 0	E.	35. 8	W.	8. 5	E.	6. 8	S. W.
29	14. 5	S. W.	35. 0	W.	....	....	21. 5	E.	40. 5	W.	8. 5	N. W.	6. 2	N. W.
30	13. 0	S. W.	33. 5	W.	....	....	19. 4	S.	43. 9	S. W.	8. 4	S. W.	6. 2	N. E.
31	11. 8	S. W.	31. 3	N.	....	....	18. 0	S.	....	....	8. 3	N. W.	....	....

NASHVILLE, TENNESSEE.

Authority, Corps of Engineers, United States Army.—Low water assumed to read zero.

Date.	December.		January.		February.		March.		April.		May.		June.	
	Gauge.	Wind.	Gauge.	Wind.	Gauge.	Wind.	Gauge.	Wind.	Gauge.	Wind.	Gauge.	Wind.	Gauge.	Wind.
1	15.0	S.	7.3	S.	21.6	S.	23.0	S.	12.0	N.	34.2	N.	3.0	W.
2	11.8	S.	7.1	S.	21.2	S.	20.0	S.	13.8	N.	33.7	E.	2.9	E.
3	10.0	S.	6.9	S.	20.5	N.	17.5	S.	14.0	S.	32.4	N. E.	2.8	N. E.
4	13.1	N. W.	8.8	S.	18.5	N.	17.0	N.	13.5	S.	31.4	N.	2.7	N.
5	17.5	N. E.	10.0	N.	15.5	S.	18.0	N.	13.0	S.	29.8	N.	2.7	S.
6	16.7	S. E.	15.0	N.	13.5	S.	19.0	S.	12.5	S.	29.3	N.	3.3	S.
7	19.1	N.	21.5	N.	12.5	N.	23.0	W.	18.1	N.	26.0	S.	3.2	E.
8	25.3	S.	27.0	N.	13.5	N.	22.9	W.	23.0	N.	25.5	N.	3.0	S.
9	26.7	N.	28.0	N.	14.2	N.	21.3	N.	35.1	N.	24.0	S.	2.9	S.
10	26.2	S. E.	30.0	S.	14.6	N.	20.0	S.	39.6	N.	21.8	S.	2.9	....
11	25.2	S.	31.8	N.	15.0	S.	18.0	N.	40.7	S.	18.4	S.	2.8	S. W.
12	23.9	S.	32.5	N.	14.8	S.	16.6	N.	41.8	N.	15.7	S.	2.7	N. W.
13	22.7	N. W.	30.5	N.	14.0	S.	15.5	N.	42.9	S. W.	13.2	S.	2.5	N.
14	20.4	N.	29.0	N.	12.9	N.	14.0	N.	43.8	S.	11.6	S.	2.4	S.
15	18.4	S.	27.0	N.	16.8	S.	11.5	N.	45.9	S.	10.2	W.	2.2	S.
16	16.0	N.	25.0	N.	18.5	N.	10.0	S.	48.6	S. E.	9.2	E.	2.6	S.
17	14.0	S.	21.5	N.	19.0	N.	9.5	S.	49.6	N.	8.4	S.	2.5	N.
18	11.9	S.	19.9	S	20.9	N.	9.0	S.	48.9	S.	7.6	N.	2.1	S.
19	11.5	N.	18.5	N.	21.4	N.	12.5	S.	49.0	S. E.	6.9	E.	1.9	S. E.
20	12.5	N.	15.0	S.	20.5	N.	23.0	N.	49.2	S.	6.5	N.	1.9	S.
21	12.0	N.	14.0	S.	19.0	S.	30.0	S.	48.9	N.	6.1	N.	1.9	S.
22	11.4	N. E.	12.9	S.	29.0	S.	34.0	N.	47.7	S. E.	5.7	E.	1.8	E.
23	11.0	N.	12.5	S.	36.4	N.	36.0	N.	46.5	N. W.	5.2	S.	1.8	S.
24	11.0	N.	13.0	S.	36.5	N. W.	37.2	N.	44.6	N.	4.9	S.	1.7	....
25	9.3	S.	15.5	S.	35.2	N.	37.9	S.	41.0	N.	4.6	S.	1.6	S.
26	8.9	S.	18.5	S.	34.0	N.	37.4	S.	38.0	S.	4.3	E.	1.4	S.
27	8.0	N. W.	20.0	S.	32.0	S.	36.0	S.	35.4	E.	4.0	S.	1.3	N.
28	8.0	W.	22.8	N.	30.0	N.	30.0	N.	34.4	S.	3.8	S.	1.3	E.
29	7.9	W.	23.2	S.	....	....	20.0	N.	34.4	N.	3.6	N.	1.2	S.
30	7.8	N.	22.5	....	....	....	15.0	S.	34.5	E.	3.4	S.	1.1	N. E.
31	7.5	S.	22.2	E.	....	....	11.0	S.	....	....	3.2	S.	....	....

FLORENCE, ALABAMA.

Authority, Corps of Engineers, United States Army.—High water of 1867 reads 31.08 feet.

Date.	December.		January.		February.		March.		April.		May.		June.	
	Gauge.	Wind.	Gauge.	Wind.	Gauge.	Wind.	Gauge.	Wind.	Gauge.	Wind.	Gauge.	Wind.	Gauge.	Wind.
1	5.2	E.	3.4	E.	9.1	E.	9.5	E.	9.5	N.	20.0	N.W.	2.9	N.E.
2	4.6	E.	3.2	E.	9.0	N.W.	11.4	E.	9.2	N.	20.0	S.	2.7	S.W.
3	3.8	S.E.	3.0	S.E.	8.4	N.	12.3	S.E.	8.5	N.	20.6	S.	2.6	S.
4	3.6	N.	3.0	S.E.	7.7	S.	12.3	N.	7.7	S.W.	20.3	N.	2.5	S.E.
5	4.3	N.	3.0	N.	7.0	N.E.	12.3	S.E.	7.0	S.E.	19.8	N.	2.4	S.E.
6	3.7	E.	3.8	N.	6.5	E.	12.2	S.E.	6.5	N.E.	19.2	S.W.	2.6	E.
7	4.7	E.	5.7	N.	6.3	N.W.	13.5	N.	6.4	S.E.	17.9	E.	2.8	S.W.
8	6.9	E.	7.6	E.	6.1	N.E.	12.6	N.	8.6	E.	16.7	S.E.	2.7	N.
9	6.8	E.	9.0	S.	5.9	N.	11.5	N.E.	14.7	E.	15.6	S.	2.7	S.W.
10	6.2	E.	10.9	S.	5.7	S.	10.7	S.E.	16.1	N.	14.5	S.E.	2.7	S.W.
11	6.2	S.E.	11.2	N.E.	5.4	S.W.	10.1	N.	17.7	N.	13.0	E.	2.7	S.W.
12	6.2	S.W.	10.5	N.E.	5.1	S.	9.4	W.	17.3	E.	11.0	S.	2.9	N.E.
13	6.1	W.	9.5	N.W.	4.9	S.W.	8.5	N.	16.7	S.E.	9.2		2.5	N.E.
14	6.0	N.	8.6	N.W.	5.7	N.	7.6	E.	17.6	S.E.	8.0	S.	2.4	S.
15	5.6	S.W.	8.2	N.	6.8	S.	6.8	E.	22.1	S.E.	7.1	N.	2.5	S.
16	5.0	S.E.	7.6	N.E.	7.0	N.E.	6.8	E.	25.7	S.E.	6.5	N.	3.0	S.
17	4.8	S.	7.0	E.	7.6	E.	7.2	E.	26.0	N.	6.0	N.E.	3.4	S.E.
18	4.7	S.	6.6	E.	9.1	E.	7.4	S.E.	25.2	E.	5.7	N.	3.7	E.
19	4.5	S.	6.1	S.E.	10.2	S.E.	8.0	S.	23.9	E.	5.3	N.E.	3.4	E.
20	4.3	N.	5.5	S.	10.2	S.E.	9.9	E.	23.3	S.W.	5.0	S.E.	2.9	E.
21	3.9	N.E.	4.9	S.	9.8	S.E.	12.9	E.	22.9	N.E.	4.7	E.	2.6	E.
22	3.6	E.	4.5	S.	9.2	S.E.	15.5	N.	22.5	S.E.	4.4	E.	2.3	E.
23	3.7	E.	4.3	N.W.	9.7	N.W.	17.9	N.	23.6	N.E.	4.2	S.	2.0	S.
24	4.6	N.E.	5.2	N.	8.8	N.	18.4	N.E.	24.2	N.E.	3.9	S.W.	1.7	S.
25	4.6	W.	5.8	N.E.	7.6	N.	17.9	E.	23.5	S.W.	3.7	S.W.	1.5	S.E.
26	4.7	W.	6.4	N.E.	7.1	N.E.	17.7	S.W.	22.3	N.	3.5	S.W.	1.3	W.
27	4.8	N.W.	7.2	S.	7.0	N.E.	17.0	S.	21.9	S.	3.4	E.	1.2	W.
28	4.8	N.W.	7.7	N.	7.7	E.	16.0	N.	20.9	N.	3.3	E.	1.1	S.W.
29	4.5	N.W.	8.1	N.			13.9	N.E.	20.3	N.	3.2	N.	1.0	S.W.
30	4.1	N.	8.0	S.			11.7	N.E.	20.0	N.	3.1	N.E.	0.9	S.W.
31	3.8	S.E.	8.5	N.E.			9.7	S.			3.0	N.E.		

ROCK ISLAND, ILLINOIS.

Authority, Corps of Engineers, United States Army.—High water of 1870 reads 16.7 feet.

Date.	December.		January.		February.		March.		April.		May.		June.	
	Gauge.	Wind.	Gauge.	Wind.	Gauge.	Wind.	Gauge.	Wind.	Gauge.	Wind.	Gauge.	Wind.	Gauge.	Wind.
1	0.9	E.	8.8	N. W.	7.4	N. E.	5.8	S. W.	5.1	S.	7.2	S. E.	5.9	N. E.
2	0.8	E.	7.9	S. E.	7.4	N.	5.8	S. W.	5.0	N. W.	7.2	E.	5.5	E.
3	1.3	E.	7.4	S.	7.6	N. W.	6.2	N. E.	5.0	N. E.	7.3	N. E.	5.5	N. W.
4	2.2	S. W.	7.0	N.	7.5	S. W.	7.1	E.	4.8	E.	7.4	N. E.	5.4	N. W.
5	2.6	N.	7.3	N. W.	7.3	E.	7.9	E.	4.7	N. W.	7.5	N.	5.4	S. W.
6	2.3	N. E.	8.2	N. W.	7.3	S. E.	7.9	E.	4.7	S. W.	7.6	E.	5.4	S. E.
7	1.9	S. E.	9.0	N.	7.2	S. W.	10.8	N. W.	4.7	N. W.	7.6	W.	5.5	N. W.
8	1.7	S.	10.2	S. W.	7.0	S. W.	11.4	N. W.	4.8	N. W.	7.9	S. W.	5.6	S.
9	1.5	N. W.	9.7	N.	7.0	W.	14.0	E.	4.7	N.	7.7	S. W.	5.9	S. W.
10	1.7	N. W.	9.1	S. E.	6.9	W.	14.9	N. E.	4.8	N. W.	7.8	S. W.	6.5	N. E.
11	2.3	W.	9.2	N.	7.0	E.	12.8	N. W.	4.8	N. E.	7.9	S. W.	6.9	S. W.
12	2.6	N. W.	8.8	N. E.	6.8	S.	12.3	N. W.	4.6	S. E.	7.9	S. W.	6.9	N. W.
13	2.6	N. W.	9.1	E.	6.9	W.	11.9	N.	4.4	S. E.	7.9	N. E.	6.5	S. E.
14	2.7	S. W.	8.9	N.	6.7	S. W.	12.1	S. E.	4.5	N. W.	8.0	S. W.	6.0	S. E.
15	2.9	S. E.	8.7	N.	6.7	W.	10.8	S. W.	4.7	N. W.	8.1	N. W.	5.7	S. W.
16	2.9	N. W.	8.5	S. W.	6.6	S. W.	8.7	E.	4.5	N. E.	8.1	N. W.	5.4	S. W.
17	2.9	N. W.	8.9	S.	7.7	N. E.	6.5	S. W.	4.5	N. E.	8.1	N.	5.2	W.
18	2.6	N. E.	8.7	S.	6.7	S. E.	5.3	N.	4.5	N. W.	8.1	N.	5.0	W.
19	2.8	S. W.	8.6	N.	6.6	S. W.	5.5	N.	4.6	E.	8.1	S. W.	4.8	S. W.
20	2.3	N.	8.3	S. E.	6.4	N. W.	6.0	S. W.	4.8	N. E.	7.9	N. E.	4.7	W.
21	5.6	S. W.	8.1	E.	6.4	N. E.	6.4	S. E.	5.0	N. W.	7.9	S. E.	4.7	S. W.
22	7.1	S.	8.3	N.	6.2	N. E.	6.9	N. W.	5.2	N. W.	7.6	S. W.	4.7	S. W.
23	5.8	N.	8.0	N.	6.2	N.	7.0	N.	5.5	N.	7.4	S.	4.7	S. W.
24	5.3	S. W.	8.1	W.	5.9	N.	7.1	N.	5.6	N. W.	7.3	N.	4.9	S. W.
25	4.7	S. W.	8.0	S. E.	5.9	N.	6.9	N. E.	5.9	S. W.	7.1	N. W.	5.0	S. W.
26	4.6	N. W.	8.1	S. W.	6.1	S. W.	6.7	N. W.	6.0	N. W.	6.8	S. W.	5.3	S. W.
27	5.0	N. W.	8.3	S. W.	5.8	S. W.	6.4	W.	6.2	N. E.	6.5	S. W.	5.4	S. W.
28	6.0	S. W.	8.1	N.	5.9	S. W.	6.1	N. W.	6.6	N. W.	6.5	S. W.	5.6	S.
29	6.7	N. W.	7.9	W.			5.3	N. W.	6.7	N. W.	6.3	S. W.	5.8	N. W.
30	8.9	S. W.	7.8	N. W.			5.2	N. W.	6.9	S. W.	6.1	N. W.	5.9	N.
31	7.9	W.	7.5	N. W.			5.1	N. E.			5.9	N. W.		

FORT LEAVENWORTH, KANSAS.

Authority, Corps of Engineers, United States Army.—High water of 1867 reads 22.06 feet.

Date.	December.		January.		February.		March.		April.		May.		June.	
	Gauge.	Wind.	Gauge.	Wind.	Gauge.	Wind.	Gauge.	Wind.	Gauge.	Wind.	Gauge.	Wind.	Gauge.	Wind.
1	5.3	S.	3.0	S.	9.4	N.	4.2		8.0		8.1	S.	7.8	
2	4.9	S.	2.8	S.	9.2	N. W.	4.1	S.	7.6	N.	8.1	S. E.	7.6	W.
3	4.5	N. W.	3.2	S.	9.0		4.0	N.	7.4	S. W.	8.0	S.	7.5	N. W.
4	3.7	S.	2.2	N. W.	8.7	W.	5.1	N. E.	7.2	N. E.	7.8	N. E.	7.4	S.
5	2.9	N. E.	2.9	S. W.	8.4	E.	5.7	S. E.	7.1	N. W.	7.6	N.	9.2	S. W.
6	2.5	N. E.	1.6		8.4	N. W.	6.0	N.	6.8	N. E.	7.3		11.4	N. E.
7	2.4		2.0	S.	7.9	N. W.	6.0	N. W.	6.5	N.	7.1	S.	12.5	S.
8	2.3	S.	2.5		7.9	N. W.	5.8	N. E.	6.3		6.9	S.	14.1	S.
9	2.2	N. E.	3.1	N. W.	7.8		5.8	S. E.	6.2	N. E.	6.8	S.	14.8	S. E.
10	1.8	E.	3.3	N. W.	7.5		5.9	N.	6.2	S.	7.0	S.	14.7	S. E.
11	2.2	N.	3.5	N. W.	7.5		6.0	N. E.	6.1	S.	7.4	N. W.	14.0	N. W.
12	2.5	N.	3.1	S. E.	7.5	S. W.	5.8	N. E.	6.0	S. E.	7.8		14.0	
13	2.0		3.1	N.	7.0	N.	5.9		6.0	S. E.	7.5	S. E.	13.9	S. E.
14	1.9		2.9	N.	6.9	S.	5.9	S. E.	5.9	N. W.	7.1	S. W.	15.3	
15	2.1	S. E.	2.3	N. E.	7.0	N. W.	5.7		5.8	N. E.	6.6	N. W.	15.3	W.
16	2.0	S.	3.7	S. E.	6.6		5.5	S. E.	5.8	N. E.	6.4		15.5	S. W.
17	2.1		3.5	S.	6.5	N. E.	5.5	S. W.	5.7	N. E.	6.4	N.	15.9	S. E.
18	2.3		4.0	S.	6.0	S. E.	5.6	N.	5.7		6.4	N. E.	15.9	S.
19	2.3	S.	4.1	N. W.	5.8	S. W.	7.3	N.	5.8	N. E.	6.2	S. E.	15.9	S.
20	2.3	N. W.	4.6	S. E.	5.4	N. E.	7.9	S.	5.8	N. W.	6.3	N.	15.8	S. E.
21	2.3	S.	4.3	N. W.	4.7	N.	8.3	N. E.	5.7	N.	6.6	N. E.	15.9	S. E.
22	2.1	S.	4.8	N. E.	5.4	N. W.	9.2	W.	6.0	N.	6.9	S. E.	15.4	S. E.
23	2.0	S.	5.9	N. W.	5.6	N. W.	9.7	N.	6.1	N. E.	6.8		14.4	S.
24	2.2	N. W.	6.7		5.0	N. E.	10.4	S.	9.0	S. E.	8.0	S. W.	13.9	S.
25	2.4	S.	6.6		5.0	N. W.	10.7	S.	9.5	N. W.	9.2	S. E.	13.5	S. W.
26	2.5	N. W.	6.5	S.	4.5	S.	10.3	N.	9.3	S. E.	9.1	S. E.	13.2	S. W.
27	2.6	N. W.	6.5	S.	4.4		9.7	N. E.	7.8		8.8	S.	13.0	S.
28	2.7	S.	6.6	N. W.	4.2		9.3		8.4	N.	8.6	S.	13.0	W.
29	2.7	N. W.	6.0	S. W.			8.9	N. E.	8.1	S.	8.3	S. E.	12.7	E.
30	2.5	S.	5.9	N. W.			8.5	E.	8.0	S.	8.1	S.	12.7	S. E.
31	2.6	S.	7.3	N. E.			8.3	N.			8.0	N.		

JACKSONPORT, ARKANSAS.

Authority, Corps of Engineers, United States Army.—High water of 1867 reads 32.83 feet.

Date.	December.		January.		February.		March.		April.		May.		June.	
	Gauge.	Wind.	Gauge.	Wind.	Gauge.	Wind.	Gauge.	Wind.	Gauge.	Wind.	Gauge.	Wind.	Gauge.	Wind.
1	0.0	S. W.	6.4	S. W.	15.1	N. W.	24.3	N. E.	16.5	N. W.	25.2	N. W.	6.4	S. E.
2	0.0	S. W.	5.9	S. W.	15.0	N. W.	23.5	N. E.	15.9	N. W.	24.4	S. W.	6.2	S. E.
3	1.1	S. W.	5.5	S. W.	13.1	N. W.	22.8	N. W.	16.5	N. W.	23.5	S. W.	6.3	S. E.
4	2.3	N. W.	4.8	N. W.	12.2	N. W.	22.3	N. W.	17.0	N. E.	23.0	S. W.	6.5	S. W.
5	11.9	N. W.	4.7	N. W.	11.3	N. E.	21.7	N. E.	17.2	N. E.	22.4	N. W.	6.3	S. W.
6	14.5	N. W.	4.4	S. W.	10.5	N. W.	23.2	S. W.	17.0	S. W.	21.7	N. E.	6.0	S. W.
7	13.3	N. W.	4.1	N. W.	10.1	N. W.	26.2	N. W.	16.6	N. W.	21.1	N. W.	5.5	S. E.
8	11.8	S. W.	3.7	N. E.	10.0	N. W.	27.6	N. W.	17.3	N. E.	20.3	N. W.	5.4	S. W.
9	12.2	S. W.	3.4	N. E.	9.5	N. W.	27.9	N. W.	23.0	N. W.	19.6	N. E.	5.0	S. E.
10	18.3	N. W.	3.2	N. E.	9.3	N. W.	27.6	S. W.	23.8	N. E.	18.8	N. E.	4.8	S. W.
11	22.0	S. W.	3.0	N. W.	9.0	N. E.	27.1	N. W.	25.2	N. E.	18.1	S. W.	4.5	S. W.
12	23.5	S. W.	2.8	N. W.	8.7	S. E.	26.5	N. W.	26.0	N. E.	17.7	S. W.	4.2	N. W.
13	23.6	N. W.	2.6	N. W.	8.4	N. E.	25.9	N. E.	26.3	N. E.	17.6	S. W.	4.0	N. W.
14	23.8	N. W.	2.5	N. E.	8.2	N. E.	25.3	N. E.	25.8	N. W.	18.1	S. W.	3.7	S. W.
15	23.7	N. W.	2.3	N. E.	8.4	N. E.	24.5	N. E.	25.0	N. E.	18.2	S. W.	3.6	S. E.
16	22.7	N. W.	2.2	N. E.	9.0	N. W.	24.3	N. E.	25.1	S. E.	18.2	N. E.	3.6	S. W.
17	21.4	N. W.	2.1	N. W.	9.3	N. W.	23.8	S. W.	25.9	N. W.	18.5	N. E.	4.0	S. W.
18	20.2	N. W.	2.0	S. W.	9.9	N. W.	23.1	S. W.	26.6	N. W.	17.7	N. W.	4.5	S. W.
19	18.2	N. W.	1.9	S. W.	10.3	N. E.	23.2	N. W.	26.9	S. W.	15.6	N. W.	4.4	S. W.
20	17.3	N. W.	1.9	S. W.	10.5	S. W.	23.4	N. E.	27.8	N. W.	14.3	S. W.	4.1	S. E.
21	15.7	N. E.	1.8	S. W.	12.2	S. E.	23.5	N. W.	29.3	N. E.	13.1	N. E.	3.9	S. W.
22	14.4	N. W.	2.1	S. W.	19.4	S. W.	23.5	N. W.	30.8	N. E.	11.9	N. E.	3.6	S. W.
23	13.1	N. W.	11.2	N. W.	24.0	N. W.	23.1	N. E.	31.1	N. W.	10.9	N. E.	3.3	S. W.
24	12.0	S. W.	15.0	N. W.	26.1	N. W.	24.4	N. E.	30.7	N. E.	10.1	S. W.	3.1	S. W.
25	11.0	N. W.	16.0	N. W.	26.8	N. W.	21.7	N. E.	30.0	N. E.	9.4	S. W.	2.9	S. E.
26	10.2	S. W.	15.3	N. E.	26.7	N. E.	20.9	N. E.	29.0	N. E.	8.9	S. W.	2.8	S. W.
27	9.2	N. W.	15.2	S. W.	26.2	N. E.	20.0	N. E.	28.0	N. W.	8.2	S. W.	2.7	S. W.
28	8.7	N. E.	15.8	S. W.	25.2	N. E.	19.2	N. W.	27.5	N. W.	7.8	S. W.	2.6	S. W.
29	8.0	N. E.	16.0	S. W.	....	....	18.6	N. W.	26.8	N. W.	7.4	S. W.	2.5	S. W.
30	7.4	N. E.	15.8	S. W.	....	....	17.8	N. E.	26.0	N. W.	7.0	S. W.	2.4	S. W.
31	6.9	S. W.	15.4	N. E.	....	....	17.2	S. W.	....	....	6.6	S. W.	....	....

LITTLE ROCK, ARKANSAS.

Authority, Corps of Engineers, United States Army.—High water of 1857 reads 31.00 feet.

Date.	December.		January.		February.		March.		April.		May.		June.	
	Gauge.	Wind.	Gauge.	Wind.	Gauge.	Wind.	Gauge.	Wind.	Gauge.	Wind.	Gauge.	Wind.	Gauge.	Wind.
1	1.4	S.	5.3	N. W.	11.0	W.	15.5	N.	7.8	N. W.	15.6	S. E.	5.2	N. W.
2	1.3	S. E.	4.8	E.	9.8	W.	13.9	S. E.	7.8	W.	14.0	S.	5.1	E.
3	1.5	S. E.	4.5	S. W.	9.0	S. W.	13.5	S. W.	7.7	W.	12.5	S. W.	5.0	E.
4	6.6	S. E.	4.3	W.	8.9	N. E.	13.8	S. W.	7.7	W.	11.5	S. W.	4.8	S. E.
5	12.0	N. E.	4.0	N. W.	9.5	S. E.	14.0	S. E.	9.0	S.	10.7	N. W.	4.6	S. E.
6	10.3	N.	3.9	W.	9.8	W.	14.5	S. E.	11.8	S. E.	9.6	S.	4.4	S. E.
7	9.2	E.	3.7	S. W.	9.6	S. W.	16.5	W.	11.7	N. E.	9.1	S.	4.2	W.
8	9.1	S.	3.5	S. W.	8.7	W.	17.1	S. E.	11.6	N. E.	8.6	W.	4.1	S. W.
9	9.8	N. W.	3.4	W.	9.0	S. E.	16.3	S.	12.4	N. E.	8.1	S. E.	3.9	S. W.
10	15.9	N. E.	3.2	S. W.	9.8	S.	15.0	W.	14.4	S. E.	7.9	S.	4.5	S. E.
11	17.5	E.	3.0	S. E.	9.2	S. E.	14.5	N.	16.5	S.	8.5	S.	4.7	E.
12	18.2	S. E.	2.9	E.	9.0	S. E.	13.6	W.	18.5	S.	10.3	S.	4.3	S. E.
13	18.9	W.	2.8	S. W.	8.5	W.	13.0	N. E.	20.5	S. E.	13.3	W.	4.0	N. E.
14	18.0	S. E.	2.7	W.	8.5	N. W.	11.5	N. W.	18.5	S.	14.5	W.	4.3	N. W.
15	17.5	S. W.	2.5	N. E.	8.0	W.	13.6	S. W.	17.5	W.	15.5	W.	4.9	W.
16	16.2	S.	2.4	E.	7.2	N. E.	14.5	S. E.	16.5	W.	15.2	S.	6.0	E.
17	15.0	W.	2.3	W.	7.0	S. W.	14.5	S. E.	17.0	N. W.	14.0	S. E.	7.1	S. E.
18	13.2	W.	2.2	E.	6.8	S. E.	14.4	S.	17.7	N. E.	13.2	N. W.	6.5	S. W.
19	12.0	W.	2.1	N. E.	6.6	S. E.	15.0	E.	18.0	S. E.	11.5	W.	5.9	W.
20	10.3	N. W.	2.0	E.	6.4	E.	15.6	N. E.	19.7	S. W.	10.0	E.	5.6	E.
21	9.5	N. W.	2.0	E.	6.4	E.	15.2	S. E.	21.5	S.	8.9	N. E.	5.9	E.
22	8.5	N. E.	3.6	S. E.	11.5	S. W.	14.2	N. E.	21.4	N. W.	8.0	S	6.3	S. E.
23	8.0	N. E.	7.8	N. E.	17.5	N. W.	13.5	N. E.	21.8	N. W.	7.5	S. W.	6.4	E.
24	7.3	S. E.	8.9	N. W.	18.5	N. W.	12.5	N.	22.9	E.	7.1	W.	6.0	W.
25	7.0	N. E.	11.5	N. E.	19.5	N. E.	11.5	S.	23.0	E.	6.8	W.	5.3	S.
26	6.5	E.	13.2	N. E.	20.0	S. E.	10.5	S. E.	22.1	S. E.	6.4	S. W.	5.0	S. E.
27	6.0	N. W.	13.6	W.	16.7	S. E.	9.7	S. E.	21.0	S. W.	6.2	W.	4.7	S. E.
28	6.0	W.	13.5	S. W.	16.0	N. E.	9.0	E.	20.2	W.	6.1	S. E.	4.5	S. W.
29	6.0	N. W.	13.3	S.	....	....	8.5	E.	19.0	S. E.	6.0	W.	4.3	W.
30	5.8	E.	13.0	W.	....	....	8.2	N. E.	17.5	S. E.	5.7	....	4.3	E.
31	5.6	S. E.	12.5	S. E.	....	....	7.9	W.	....	....	5.4	S.	....	....

CAMDEN, ARKANSAS.

Authority, Captain Benyaurd, Corps of Engineers.—Zero of gauge is at lowest recorded water, (1873.)

Date.	December.		January.		February.		March.		April.		May.		June.	
	Gauge.	Wind.	Gauge.	Wind.	Gauge.	Wind.	Gauge	Wind.	Gauge.	Wind.	Gauge.	Wind.	Gauge.	Wind.
1	27.7		11.9		29.5		30.6		25.4		25.9		5.4	
2	25.8		10.8		28.7		30.8		25.1		24.6		5.0	
3	23.0		9.8		27.5		30.8		24.8		22.8		4.6	
4	20.4		9.0		26.3		31.2		24.0		21.0		4.2	
5	20.7		8.4		24.8		31.7		22.9		19.6		3.9	
6	22.9		7.8		23.4		31.8		21.2		18.3		3.5	
7	24.9		7.2		21.9		31.2		19.3		16.8		3.3	
8	26.6		6.7		21.6		30.9		19.0		15.4		3.0	
9	27.7		6.3		22.0		30.9		23.0		14.2		2.8	
10	27.9		5.9		22.2		31.3		26.5		13.2		2.5	
11	28.0		5.6		21.8		31.8		29.2		12.5		2.3	
12	28.3		5.4		20.5		31.7		32.2		11.8		2.1	
13	29.2		5.9		18.6		31.5		33.2		14.3		2.0	
14	31.1		7.9		17.0		31.8		33.7		20.6		1.8	
15	32.6		10.8		15.8		31.9		34.3		24.4		1.8	
16	34.6		11.9		14.9		31.7		34.7		26.8		1.7	
17	32.4		11.5		14.2		31.2		35.2		31.2		1.6	
18	31.1		10.1		14.0		30.8		35.7		31.6		1.5	
19	29.6		8.9		14.8		30.9		35.9		30.4		1.4	
20	27.3		7.9		15.4		31.3		35.6		28.3		1.3	
21	25.8		7.2		15.6		31.6		35.2		25.8		1.3	
22	22.7		7.0		16.9		31.9		34.3		23.1		1.3	
23	21.5		10.4		22.0		31.9		33.6		19.7		1.3	
24	19.7		19.2		25.8		31.5		33.0		16.3		1.2	
25	18.6		23.9		28.9		31.1		32.3		13.4		1.3	
26	17.9		27.2		31.9		30.6		31.6		11.4		1.3	
27	17.2		30.5		33.1		29.6		30.8		10.0		1.2	
28	16.2		31.8		32.7		28.5		29.8		8.8		1.3	
29	15.2		31.4				27.6		28.6		7.7		1.1	
30	14.1		30.8				26.4		27.2		6.8		1.1	
31	13.0		30.2				25.5				6.0			

TRINITY, LOUISIANA.

Authority, Captain Benyaurd, Corps of Engineers.—Zero of gauge is at lowest known water, (1873.)

Date.	December.		January.		February.		March.		April.		May.		June.	
	Gauge.	Wind.	Gauge.	Wind.	Gauge.	Wind.	Gauge.	Wind.	Gauge.	Wind.	Gauge.	Wind.	Gauge.	Wind.
1	19.9		31.8		29.3		34.1		49.5		52.5		51.3	
2	21.0		32.0		29.3		34.3		49.8		52.6		51.2	
3	21.7		32.0		29.3		34.5		50.1		52.6		51.1	
4	22.4		32.3		29.3		34.8		50.3		52.6		51.0	
5	22.8		32.3		29.4		35.0		50.4		52.6		50.9	
6	23.1		32.4		30.0		35.3		50.5		52.6		50.7	
7	23.4		32.4		30.2		35.8		50.6		52.6		50.5	
8	23.6		32.3		30.5		36.1		50.8		52.5		50.3	
9	23.7		32.3		30.8		36.4		51.1		52.5		50.1	
10	23.9		32.1		31.0		36.7		51.2		52.5		49.9	
11	24.1		31.9		31.2		37.3		51.2		52.4		49.6	
12	24.3		31.6		31.5		37.7		51.3		52.4		49.3	
13	24.6		31.3		31.8		38.0		51.4		52.4		49.1	
14	24.8		31.0		32.0		38.3		51.4		52.3		48.7	
15	25.0		30.6		32.2		38.9		51.4		52.3		48.4	
16	25.4		30.2		32.4		39.5		51.6		52.3		48.0	
17	25.8		29.8		32.6		40.1		51.7		52.2		47.6	
18	26.3		29.5		32.8		40.6		51.7		52.1		47.3	
19	26.8		29.2		32.9		41.0		51.9		52.0		46.7	
20	27.2		29.0		33.0		41.6		52.0		52.0		46.2	
21	27.7		28.9		33.0		42.1		52.1		51.9		45.7	
22	28.2		28.9		33.2		42.9		52.2		51.8		45.2	
23	28.6		29.2		33.3		43.9		52.2		51.8		44.7	
24	29.0		29.3		33.3		44.8		52.3		51.7		44.3	
25	29.4		29.3		33.5		45.5		52.3		51.7		43.8	
26	29.8		29.3		33.6		46.2		52.4		51.6		43.3	
27	30.1		29.4		33.7		46.9		52.4		51.6		42.8	
28	30.6		29.5		33.9		47.5		52.4		51.6		42.3	
29	30.9		29.5				48.0		53.5		51.5		41.8	
30	31.3		29.4				48.6		52.5		51.5		41.2	
31	31.5		29.3				49.0				51.4			

SHREVEPORT, LOUISIANA.

Authority, Signal Service, United States Army.—High water of 1849 reads 33.0 feet.

Date.	December.		January.		February.		March.		April.		May.		June.	
	Gauge.	Wind.	Gauge.	Wind.	Gauge.	Wind.	Gauge.	Wind.	Gauge.	Wind.	Gauge.	Wind.	Gauge.	Wind.
1	12.4		21.9		16.7		22.8		27.6		30.3		24.1	
2	12.7		21.7		17.2		23.3		27.4		30.2		23.7	
3	13.2		21.4		17.5		23.4		27.2		30.1		23.3	
4	13.9				17.7		23.6		26.8		29.9		23.1	
5	14.3				18.1		23.7		26.4		29.7		22.3	
6	14.6				18.9		24.1		26.2		29.4		21.7	
7	14.7				19.5		24.3		25.9		29.2		21.2	
8	15.5				19.9		24.5		25.9		28.7		20.7	
9	15.6				20.4		24.6		25.9		27.7		20.0	
10	15.8				20.7		24.9		25.8		27.6		19.4	
11	16.0				20.9		24.8		25.6		27.1		18.7	
12	16.2				21.2		25.6		25.4		26.6		18.0	
13	16.7		17.6		21.5		25.8		25.4		26.1		17.7	
14	16.9		17.3		22.0		26.1		25.4		25.5		17.4	
15	17.2		16.8		22.3		26.3		25.4		24.9		17.1	
16	17.4		16.7		22.6		26.6		25.7		24.5		16.7	
17	17.8		16.3		22.7		26.7		26.0		24.0		16.7	
18	18.4		16.1		22.7		26.7		26.2		23.7		16.4	
19	19.0		15.7		22.7		26.7		26.6		23.5		16.2	
20	19.6		15.4		22.5		26.8		26.9		23.3		16.2	
21	20.1		15.1		22.5		27.1		27.3		23.2		16.2	
22	20.8		15.3		22.7		27.2		27.7		23.2		15.9	
23	21.3		15.3		22.7		27.3		28.3		23.7		15.7	
24	21.7		15.0		22.5		27.5		29.0		24.3		15.6	
25	22.1		14.7		22.3		27.6		29.4		24.7		15.5	
26	22.3		15.1		22.3		27.5		29.7		24.9		15.3	
27	22.5		15.2		22.6		27.5		30.0		25.0		15.2	
28	22.7		15.3		22.7		27.5		30.2		25.1		15.0	
29	22.4		15.5				27.6		30.3		24.9		14.6	
30	22.3		15.7				27.6		30.3		24.7		14.2	
31	22.2		16.2				27.6				24.4			

ALEXANDRIA, LOUISIANA.

Authority; Corps of Engineers, United States Army.—High water of 1866 reads 36.46 feet.

Date.	December.		January.		February.		March.		April.		May.		June.	
	Gauge.	Wind.	Gauge.	Wind.	Gauge.	Wind.	Gauge.	Wind.	Gauge.	Wind.	Gauge.	Wind.	Gauge.	Wind.
1	9.0	S.	16.9	S. E.	10.9	N.	22.0	E.	34.1	N.	34.2	S. E.	25.0	N. E.
2	9.6	S.	17.5	S. E.	10.9	N.	22.3	S.	34.3	N.	34.3	S. E.	24.9	N. E.
3	9.8	S.	17.6	S.	11.1	N.	22.5	S.	34.3	E.	34.4	S. E.	24.8	S.
4	9.9	N.	17.8	E.	11.3	N.	22.7	S.	34.4	S.	34.6	E.	24.7	W.
5	9.9	N.	18.0	N.	11.8	E.	23.0	S.	34.2	S.	34.7	N.	24.5	W.
6	9.9	N.	18.0	N.	12.7	N.	23.3	E.	34.0	S.	34.8	E.	24.1	N. E.
7	9.9	S.	18.0	N.	13.4	N.	23.8	N.	33.7	S. E.	34.8	E.	23.8	N.
8	10.1	S.	17.8	N.	13.7	N.	24.5	N.	33.3	S.	34.9	S.	23.3	N.
9	10.3	S.	17.6	E.	14.1	N.	25.0	N.	33.7	N.	34.9	S.	22.6	N.
10	10.4	S.	17.4	N.	14.2	N.	25.5	S.	33.8	N.	34.9	S.	22.2	N.
11	10.6	S.	17.1	E.	14.3	E.	26.0	N.	33.7	S.	34.8	E.	21.6	S.
12	10.8	S.	16.8	E.	14.4	E.	26.6	N. E.	33.5	S.	34.8	E.	20.9	N.
13	11.0	N.	16.2	N.	14.6	S.	26.9	N. E.	33.3	S.	34.7	E.	20.4	S.
14	11.0	N.	15.8	N.	14.8	N. E.	27.2	S.	33.0	S.	34.4	S.	19.7	S.
15	11.1	N.	15.4	N.	15.1	N. E.	27.5	N.	32.9	S.	34.2	S.	19.1	S.
16	11.2	N.	15.0	N.	15.8	....	28.3	E.	33.2	S.	33.8	N. E.	18.6	S.
17	11.4	S. E.	14.7	E.	16.3	S.	29.4	S.	33.4	N.	33.2	N. E.	18.0	S.
18	11.6	S. E.	14.4	S.	16.8	N.	30.0	S. E.	33.2	N.	32.5	N. E.	17.2	S.
19	11.8	N.	14.0	S.	17.1	S.	30.4	S. E.	33.5	S.	31.5	N. E.	16.8	E.
20	11.9	N.	13 5	S.	17.8	S.	30.5	E.	33.9	N.	30.3	E.	16.4	E.
21	12.0	N.	13.0	S.	18.2	S.	30.6	....	34.0	N.	29.0	E.	15.8	S.
22	12.5	N.	12.5	S.	18.5	S.	30.8	E.	33.9	S.	28.0	S.	15.4	S.
23	12.8	N.	12.3	N.	18.8	N.	31.3	N. E.	33.8	N.	27.1	S.	14.6	S.
24	13.2	N.	12.0	N.	19.2	N.	32.0	N. E.	33.9	N.	26.2	S.	14.1	S.
25	13.6	N.	11.9	N.	19.7	N.	32.6	S. W.	33.9	N.	25.7	S.	13.7	S.
26	14.0	N.	11.8	E.	20.2	N.	32.9	....	33.9	N. E.	25.1	S.	13.2	S.
27	14.4	N.	11.7	E.	20.8	E.	33.1	S.	33.8	S.	24.8	S.	12.9	S.
28	14.9	N-	11.6	N.	21.5	S.	33.3	S. E.	33.9	N.	24.5	S. E.	12.4	S.
29	15.4	N E.	11.4	N.	....	....	33.3	S. E.	34.0	N.	25.1	E.	12.0	S. W.
30	15.9	N.	11.2	N.	....	....	33.6	S. E.	34.1	S. E.	25.1	S.	11.6	S. W.
31	16.5	E.	11.0	N.	....	....	33.6	S.	....	....	25.0	S.	....	....

APPENDIX F.

Tables of relative heights of high waters, levees, and ground from Commerce, Mo., to the Louisiana line.

Distance in feet.	Elevation of ground.	Elevation of levee.	Remarks.
42,000	+ 5.0	+10.0	
500	− 5.0	....	Head of Big Lake.
25,000	+ 5.0	+ 9.0	South side of Big Lake.
17,000	+ 3.0	+ 6.0	Do.
3,000	− 2.0	+ 5.0	Do.
200	0.0	....	Do.
1,500	− 1.0	+ 3.0	Do.
200	− 1.0	....	Do.
3,000	− 1.0	+ 3.0	Do.
100	− 1.0	....	Do.
2,000	− 1.0	+ 2.5	Do.
500	− 1.0	....	Do.
1,000	− 1.0	+ 2.5	Do.
500	− 1.0	....	Do.
1,500	− 1.0	+ 2.5	Do.
600	− 1.5	+ 2.5	Do.
2,000	− 1.0	+ 2.0	Do.
500	0.0	....	Do.
1,000	− 1.0	+ 2.0	Do.
1,500	− 0.5	+ 1.5	Do.
1,000	− 1.0	....	Do.
1,500	− 0.5	+ 2.0	Do.
1,000	− 1.5	....	Do.
7,000	− 2.0	+ 1.5	Do.
9,000	− 3.5	....	Opposite Cairo.
1,800	− 1.5	+ 1.0	
22,000	+ 1.5	+ 3.0	
9,000	− 5.0	....	Opposite Island No. 1.
6,000	+ 1.5	....	
5,000	− 1.0	....	Above Hunter's Land'g.
1,500	+ 0.5	....	
2,000	− 3.0	....	Above Hunter's Land'g.
6,500	+ 7.0	....	Hunter's Landing.
1,700	− 2.0	....	Opposite Island 4.
4,000	− 0.5	+ 1.5	(Interior line.)
500	− 0.5	....	Below Lucas Bend.
58,500	0.0	+ 1.5	
15,000	− 2.0	....	Above Island 6.
400	− 8.0	....	
15,000	+ 1.0	....	Above Island 8.
21,000	− 1.0	....	Interior line.
100	−25.0	....	Bayou Saint James.
3,000	− 0.5	+ 1.5	
200	−12.0	....	Dry Bayou.
10,500	− 3.0	....	Opposite Island 8.
1,500	− 3.0	+ 1.0	
1,000	− 3.0	....	Opposite Island 8.
500	− 3.0	+ 1.0	
1,000	− 3.0	....	Opposite Island 8.
600	− 3.0	+ 1.0	
5,800	− 3.0	....	Interior line to New
7,900	− 8.0	....	Madrid north and west
5,000	− 3.0	....	of Hubbard Lake.
15,800	− 3.0	....	
10,500	− 8.0	....	
100	−25.0	....	Saint John's Bayou.
52,800	+ 5.0	....	New Madrid to Point
20,000	− 1.0	....	Pleasant.
4,000	− 2.5	....	Interior.
100	−15.0	....	Point Pleasant to Ca-
82,000	+ 0.5	....	ruthersville.
14,000	− 2.0	....	West of Big Lake and
2,500	− 4.0	....	Bayou west of Gayoso.
8,000	− 3.0	....	
5,000	− 3.0	+ 1.5	
2,500	+ 1.5	....	Caruthersville.
4,000	− 2.5	+ 2.0	
800	− 4.0	....	Opposite Linwood Bar.
4,000	− 3.0	+ 2.0	
200	− 3.0	....	Opposite Linwood Bar.
3,000	− 3.0	+ 2.0	

Distance in feet.	Elevation of ground.	Elevation of levee.	Remarks.
2,000	− 3.0	....	Opposite Linwood Bar.
5,000	− 3.0	+ 2.0	
400	− 3.0	....	
12,500	− 3.0	+ 2.0	
100	− 2.5	....	Opposite Island 16.
6,000	− 2.5	+ 1.5	
50	− 2.5	....	Opposite Island 16.
3,000	− 2.5	+ 1.5	
150	− 2.5	....	Opposite Island 16.
4,000	− 2.0	+ 2.0	
200	− 2.0	....	Opposite Island 16.
3,800	− 1.5	+ 1.5	
100	− 2.0	....	Head of Island 18.
4,000	− 2.0	+ 1.5	
500	− 2.0	....	Opposite Island 18.
3,500	− 2.5	+ 1.0	
600	− 2.5	....	
2,000	− 2.5	+ 1.0	Opposite Island 18.
500	− 2.5	....	
2,000	− 2.5	+ 1.5	
600	− 2.5	....	
1,500	− 2.0	+ 1.0	
200	−15.0	....	Half-Moon Bayou.
5,000	− 1.5	+ 1.5	Cottonwood Point.
5,000	− 4.0	......	Below Cottonwood Point
100	−15.0	....	Pemiscot Bayou.
12,000	− 6.0	....	
5,500	− 2.5	+ 1.5	
6,000	− 2.5	....	Head of Island 21.
3,000	− 2.5	+ 1.5	
4,000	− 2.5	+ 1.5	
22,000	− 3.0	....	Opposite Island 21.
2,000	− 2.5	+ 1.0	
1,000	− 3.0	....	
5,000	− 2.5	+ 0.5	
1,000	− 3.0	....	
7,000	− 2.5	+ 0.5	
100	−15.0	....	
3,000	− 2.5	+ 0.5	
21,500	− 4.0	....	Above Island 25.
11,500	− 4.0	+ 1.0	
300	− 5.0	....	
2,000	− 4.0	+ 1.0	
250	− 5.0	....	
13,000	− 4.0	+ 1.5	
13,000	− 6.0	....	Opposite Island, 26.
2,000	− 5.5	+ 1.0	
120	− 7.0	....	
3,000	− 5.0	+ 1.0	
300	− 5.0	....	
4,000	− 3.0	+ 1.5	
200	− 6.0	....	
9,000	− 2.0	+ 1.0	
100	−20.0	....	Mill Bayou.
18,500	− 2.0	+ 1.5	
2,700	− 4.0	....	Below Mill Bayou.
18,000	− 3.0	+ 1.5	
2,000	− 2.0	....	Opposite Island 30.
2,500	− 3.0	+ 2.0	
600	− 3.0	....	
21,000	− 2.5	+ 1.0	Osceola.
21,000	− 3.0	+ 2.0	
18,500	− 4.0	....	Across neck, opposite
3,000	− 4.0	+ 1.0	Flower Island.
300	− 5.0	....	
3,000	− 4.0	+ 1.0	
200	− 5.0	....	
6,000	− 3.5	+ 1.5	Nodina Plaçe.
1,400	− 3.0	....	
4,000	+ 1.5	....	Across neck below Isl-
7,800	− 3.0	....	and 34.

Tables of relative heights of high waters, levees, and ground, &c.—Continued.

Distance in feet.	Elevation of ground.	Elevation of levee.	Remarks.
3,500	− 3.0	+ 1.0	
5,000	− 3.0	....	Opposite Island 35.
3,300	− 3.0	+ 1.0	
7,000	− 3.0	....	Opposite Island 35.
8,000	− 3.0	+ 1.0	
14,300	− 3.0	....	Opposite Island 35.
12,000	− 4.0	+ 1.0	
27,000	− 4.0	+ 1.0	Pecan Point.
2,500	+ 1.5	....	
5,500	− 4.5	....	Opposite Dean's Island.
8,000	− 4.0	+ 1.0	
1,500	− 3.0	....	Opposite Dean's Island.
4,500	− 3.0	+ 1.5	
200	− 5.0	....	Opposite Dean's Island.
6,000	− 3.0	+ 2.0	
400	− 5.0	....	
20,000	+ 4.0	....	Shanesville, opposite Island 37.
200	− 4.0	....	Do.
2,000	− 5.0	+ 1.0	
2,500	− 4.5	....	Opposite Island 37.
45,000	− 4.0	+ 2.0	
150	−20.0	....	Old River Bayou.
4,500	− 3.0	+ 2.0	Pacific Place.
100	− 3.0	....	
2,000	− 3.5	+ 1.5	
15,000	− 4.0	....	Opposite Brandywine Bend.
7,700	− 3.0	+ 1.5	
5,000	− 4.0	....	Opposite Brandywine Bend.
4,500	− 3.0	+ 1.0	
2,500	− 2.5	....	Opposite Brandywine Bend.
100	−15.0	....	Slough.
6,000	− 2.5	....	
5,000	− 2.5	+ 3.0	Bradley's.
21,000	− 3.0	....	Opposite Island 40.
16,000	− 2.5	+ 1.0	
17,000	− 2.5	− 1.0	
100	−10.0	....	Fogleman's Bayou.
3,000	− 1.5	+ 1.0	
100	−15.0	....	Bayou.
1,500	− 1.5	+ 1.0	Mound City.
100	−15.0	....	Bayou.
7,000	− 1.0	+ 1.0	
16,000	− 4.0	....	Above Hopefield.
21,000	− 4.5	+ 0.5	
50	−10.0	....	Opposite Vice-President Island.
2.500	− 4.0	+ 1.0	
100	−12.0	....	Opposite Vice-President Island.
2,000	− 4.0	+ 1.0	
100	− 5.0	....	Opposite Vice-President Island.
2,000	− 4.5	+ 1.0	
200	− 5.0	....	Opposite Vice-President Island.
9,000	− 3.5	+ 1.0	
1,000	− 3.0	....	Opposite lower end of President Island.
1,500	− 3.0	+ 0.5	
5,500	− 4.0	....	Opposite lower end of President Island.
2,500	− 4.0	+ 0.5	
70	−12.0	....	Merriweather's.
3,500	− 2.5	+ 0.5	

Distance in feet.	Elevation of ground.	Elevation of levee.	Remarks.
4,500	+ 0.5	....	
8,000	− 3.0	+ 0.5	
150	− 4.0	....	
7,500	− 2.5	+ 0.5	
5,000	− 2.5	....	Scanlin's.
3,000	− 2.5	+ 0.5	
4,500	− 2.5	....	Below Scanlin's.
1,600	− 2.5	+ 0.5	
3,000	− 2.5	....	Below Scanlin's.
1,350	− 2.0	+ 1.0	
13,000	0.0	+ 2.5	H. Burgett.
5,000	− 2.0	+ 0.5	
100	− 5.0	....	
3,000	− 2.5	+ 0.5	
2,000	− 3.0	+ 3.0	
200	− 2.5	....	
2,000	− 2.5	+ 2.5	Opposite Cat Island.
200	− 3.0	....	
7,000	− 2.5	+ 1.0	Opposite Cat Island.
2,500	− 2.0	....	
1,500	− 2.5	+ 0.5	
1,500	− 2.5	....	
2,500	− 2.5	+ 0.5	
5,000	− 2.5	....	
150	− 6.0	....	
100	−20.0	....	Lost River Bayou.
15,600	− 2.5	+ 2.5	
300	− 4.0	....	
6,200	− 2.5	+ 2.5	
9,000	− 2.5	....	
5,800	− 2.5	+ 3.5	
9,800	− 1.5	....	(Interior.)
7,800	−10.0	....	Opposite Blue's Point.
2,500	+ 1.5	....	
3,500	− 1.5	....	
7,000	− 0.5	....	Above Bledsoe's.
100	−20.0	....	Bayou at Bledsoe's.
1,500	− 3.0	+ 0.5	
7,000	− 2.5	....	Council Bend.
70	−13.0	....	
14,000	− 2.5	....	
3,000	− 2.5	+ 2.0	Hamlin's.
400	− 4.0	....	
2,600	− 2.5	+ 1.5	
300	− 4.0	....	
2,700	− 2.5	+ 2.0	
300	− 4.0	....	
2,500	− 2.0	+ 2.0	Opposite Commerce Cut-off.
13,000	− 2.5	+ 1.0	Walnut Bend.
200	− 3.0	....	
4,700	− 2.5	+ 1.0	Walnut Bend.
150	− 3.0	....	
9,000	− 2.5	+ 1.0	Walnut Bend.
200	− 3.0	....	
4,500	− 2.5	+ 1.0	Askew's.
10,000	− 3.5	+ 1.0	
15,000	− 4.5	....	Above Saint Francis Island.

MOUTH OF SAINT FRANCIS RIVER.

Distance in feet.	Elevation of ground.	Elevation of levee.	Remarks.
8,000	− 3.0	+ 1.0	Helena.
63,500	− 3.0	+ 1.0	
1,200	− 8.0	....	Fort Penny.
31,300	− 5.0	+ 1.5	
150	−35.0	....	Old Town Bayou.
30,850	− 3.0	+ 1.5	
70	− 7.0	....	6 miles below Old Town Bayou.
800	− 4.0	+ 1.5	
200	− 8.0	....	6 miles below Old Town Bayou.
11,300	− 5.0	+ 1.0	
1,700	− 5.0	....	Foot of Island 63.

Distance in feet.	Elevation of ground.	Elevation of levee.	Remarks.
2,300	− 4.0	+ 1.0	McGuire's.
7,000	− 6.0	....	Below Island 63.
35,000	− 5.0	+ 1.5	Dixie.
17,500	− 5.0	....	Opposite Island 65.
5,000	− 5.0	+ 1.0	
10,500	− 4.0	....	Mrs. Offit's.
21,500	− 4.0	+ 1.5	
26,500	− 5.0	....	Opposite Islands 67 and 68 to Wood Cottage.
81,500	− 3.0	+ 1.5	End of Laconia Circle.

Tables of relative heights of high waters, levees, and ground, &c.—Continued.

MOUTH OF WHITE RIVER.

Distance in feet.	Elevation of ground.	Elevation of levee.	Remarks.	Distance in feet.	Elevation of ground.	Elevation of levee.	Remarks.
600	− 5.0	....	Napoleon crevasse of 1874.	2,000	− 2.0	+ 4.0	
				4,000	− 1.0	+ 4.0	
4,500	− 9.0	+ 1.0		1,000	0.0	+ 3.0	
4,000	− 5.0	....		2,000	− 3.0	+ 2.0	
3,000	− 6.0	....	Between Napoleon and Cypress Creek.	3,000	− 5.0	+ 2.0	
15,000	− 4.0	....		1,500	− 4.0	+ 2.0	
12,000	− 8.0	....		2,000	− 8.0	....	
8,000	− 5.0	....		1,500	− 6.0	....	Above Island 82.
2,700	− 6.0	+ 1.0		2,000	− 9.0	....	
400	−12.0	....	Great Cypress Bayou.	5,000	− 8.0	....	Above Island 82.
1,500	− 6.0	0.0		3,000	− 5.0	....	
1,000	− 5.0	....	Great Cypress Bayou.	3,000	+ 0.5	....	Above Island 82.
3,700	−11.0	0.0		7,000	− 2.0	....	Above Island 82.
1,500	− 7.5	− 4.0		7,000	− 1.0	....	
400	−12.0	....	Great Cypress Bayou.	3,000	− 3.0	+ 1.0	
2,500	− 6.5	+ 0.5		1,500	− 4.0	+ 2.0	
1,000	− 6.0	....	Between Chicot City and Cypress Creek.	1,500	− 2.0	+ 2.0	
1,500	−12.0	+ 1.0		2,000	− 3.0	+ 2.0	
400	− 8.0	− 1.0		3,000	− 4.0	+ 2.0	
800	− 6.0	− 1.5		10,000	− 3.0	....	
800	− 6.0	....	Between Chicot City and Cypress Creek.	7,000	− 3.5	....	Below Island 82.
1,600	− 7.0	− 1.0		3,000	− 1.5	+ 6.0	
2,500	− 8.0	0.0		600	− 8.0	....	1 mile above Luna.
1,500	− 8.5	− 0.5		2,000	− 1.0	+ 8.0	
1,000	−11.9	− 0.9		2,000	− 0.5	+ 7.5	
2,000	− 7.4	− 0.4		5,000	− 3.0	+ 4.5	
500	− 6.0	....	Between Chicot City and Cypress Creek.	4,000	− 4.0	+ 4.0	
2,000	− 8.0	0.0		3,000	− 3.5	+ 3.5	
1,000	− 9.5	0.0		4,000	− 3.5	....	Gap between bends, throwing out Pt. Chicot.
1,500	− 9.0	0.0		600	− 8.0	+ 4.0	
3,000	− 7.4	+ 0.6		1,500	− 4.0	+ 4.0	
500	− 6.0	....	Between Chicot City and Cypress Creek.	3,000	− 5.5	+ 4.5	
12,000	− 8.7	+ 0.3		1,500	− 7.0	+ 5.0	
800	− 5.0	+ 1.0		1,400	− 3.0	+ 3.0	
2,000	− 9.0	+ 0.5		2,000	− 2.0	+ 4.0	
1,000	− 6.5	+ 0.5		1,700	− 7.0	+ 5.0	
2,000	− 8.5	+ 0.5		2,800	− 1.0	+ 3.0	
1,000	− 5.5	+ 0.5		7,000	− 1.0	+ 5.0	
1,000	−10.0	0.0		3,000	−12.0	....	Oposite Island 84, Whiskey Chute Bayou.
1,500	− 3.3	+ 2.7		2,000	− 2.0	+ 4.0	
1,000	− 4.5	+ 1.0		7,000	− 2.0	....	Opposite Island 84.
500	− 5.0	....	At Chicot City.	5,000	− 2.0	+ 3.5	
500	− 7.0	+ 1.0		200	−16.0	+ 4.0	
1,000	− 8.0	+ 1.0		1,800	0.0	+ 4.5	
300	− 4.0	....	At Chicot City.	2,000	0.0	+ 4.5	
1,000	− 7.0	− 1.0		2,000	− 2.0	+ 4.5	
2,000	− 4.6	+ 0.4		2,000	− 1.5	+ 5.0	
2,000	− 4.1	+ 0.4		2,000	− 4.5	+ 5.5	
4,000	− 3.0	+ 1.0		2,200	− 4.0	+ 5.0	
2,000	− 4.0	+ 1.0		1,800	− 2.5	+ 5.0	
4,000	− 3.5	+ 1.0		1,500	− 1.5	....	
120	− 9.0	....	Opposite lower end of Island 79.	1,600	− 4.5	+ 7.5	
1,500	− 6.0	+ 1.0		2,500	− 7.0	....	American Bend.
2,500	− 4.0	+ 1.0		3,100	− 3.8	+ 3.2	
1,000	− 5.0	+ 1.0		3,000	− 2.0	+ 4.0	
2,500	− 6.5	+ 0.5		2,600	− 1.5	+ 5.5	
2,500	− 7.0	+ 1.0		2,700	− 8.0	+ 6.0	
1,000	− 6.0	+ 3.0		2,500	0.0	+ 6.0	
3,000	− 5.0	+ 2.0		200	− 6.0	+ 6.0	
4,000	− 8.0	0.0		1,000	− 2.5	+ 5.5	
2,000	− 7.0	+ 2.0		3,000	− 2.0	+ 5.0	
3,000	− 4.5	+ 1.5		2,200	0.0	+ 5.0	
2,000	− 4.0	+ 1.5		800	− 2.0	+ 4.0	
1,000	− 4.0	+ 1.0		3,600	− 2.0	+ 4.0	
500	− 3.0	+ 0.5		3,000	− 1.5	+ 4.0	
1,500	− 3.0	+ 1.0		2,400	− 0.5	+ 4.5	
3,000	− 4.3	+ 0.7		600	− 4.0	+ 3.0	
1,000	− 4.5	+ 0.5		3,000	− 1.0	+ 3.5	
180	− 6.0	....	Below Eunice.	2,000	− 2.0	+ 3.0	
2,000	− 6.5	+ 0.5		5,500	− 4.5	+ 2.5	
200	− 4.0	....	Below Eunice.	2,500	− 4.0	+ 3.0	
2,000	− 3.0	+ 1.0		2,800	− 7.0	+ 5.0	
220	− 9.0	+ 3.0		1,200	−13.0	+ 4.0	
3,500	− 2.0	+ 3.0		3,000	− 7.0	+ 5.0	
2,000	− 4.0	+ 3.0		1,000	− 9.0	....	

Tables of relative heights of high waters, levees, and ground, &c.—Continued.

Distance in feet.	Elevation of ground.	Elevation of levee.	Remarks.	Distance, in feet.	Elevation of ground.	Elevation of levee.	Remarks.
2, 000	− 1. 0	....	Just below Island 87.	3, 000	− 8. 0	+ 1. 0	
2, 000	− 8. 0	....		1, 000	−10. 0	+ 1. 0	
2, 000	− 7. 0	....		2, 000	− 8. 0	....	Opposite Rosemary Land-
3, 000	− 5. 0	....					ing.
6, 000	− 4. 5	....	Just below Island 87.	5, 000	− 4. 0	....	
4, 000	− 3. 0	....	Do.	4, 000	− 4. 0	+ 2. 0	
3, 000	− 1. 0	+3. 0	Do.	2, 500	− 4. 0	....	Across Rollin's Bend.
2, 300	− 2. 5	+2. 5		1, 000	− 5. 5	+ 1. 5	
600	−11. 5	+ 4. 5		3, 000	− 4. 0	+ 2. 0	
1, 100	− 1. 0	+ 3. 0		3, 000	− 5. 0	+ 2. 0	
1, 000	0. 0	+ 3. 0		6, 000	− 6. 0	+ 2. 0	
4, 000	− 4. 5	....		14, 000	− 2. 0	....	
8, 000	+ 2. 0	....	East of Willow Lake	6, 000	− 5. 0	....	Around Lake Jefferson.
600	− 7. 0	....	from Sterling north.	5, 000	− 4. 0	....	
8, 000	− 3. 0	....		3, 000	− 2. 0	+ 5. 0	
500	− 7. 0	+ 5. 0		1, 000	− 6. 0	0. 0	
1, 500	− 1. 2	+ 2. 8		2, 000	− 6. 0	+ 2. 0	
4, 550	− 0. 9	+ 2. 1		2, 000	− 5. 0	0. 0	
450	− 3. 5	+ 2. 5		3, 000	− 4. 0	+ 1. 0	
2, 000	− 8. 0	+ 4. 0		2, 000	− 5. 0	+ 2. 0	
400	− 5. 0	0. 0		2, 000	−10. 0	+ 3. 0	
1, 200	− 5. 5	+ 1. 5		2, 000	− 5. 0	+ 2. 0	
900	− 3. 0	+ 3. 0		2, 000	− 7. 0	+ 2. 0	
730	− 6. 0	....	Crevasse made by United	5, 000	− 5. 0	+ 2. 0	
1, 000	− 7. 0	+ 3. 0	States gunboats.	2, 000	− 4. 0	+ 2. 0	
500	− 6. 5	....	Do.	2, 000	− 5. 0	+ 2. 0	
3, 500	− 5. 3	+ 3. 7		2, 500	− 4. 0	+ 2. 0	
7, 000	− 4. 5	+ 1. 5		1, 100	− 4. 0	....	Near road to Napoleon
3, 000	− 7. 0	+ 2. 0		1, 500	− 5. 0	+ 1. 0	crevasse of 1867.
6, 000	− 4. 5	+ 1. 5		1, 000	− 6. 5	+ 0. 5	

Ending at Louisiana line.

ARKANSAS RIVER, BEGINNING THREE MILES ABOVE AUBURN.

Distance in feet.	Elevation of ground.	Elevation of levee.	Remarks.	Distance, in feet.	Elevation of ground.	Elevation of levee.	Remarks.
89, 760	− 5. 0	+ 2. 0	South Bend.	1, 700	− 5. 0	+ 1. 0	
52, 800	− 6. 0	+ 1. 0		700	− 6. 0	0. 0	
3, 000	− 6. 0	+ 1. 0		4, 000	− 6. 0	+ 1. 0	
1, 050	− 7. 0	....		5, 000	− 3. 0	+ 1. 0	
3, 000	− 5. 0	+ 1. 0		4, 000	− 5. 0	+ 1. 0	
260	− 5. 5	....	Bayou and crevasses at	5, 000	− 3. 0	+ 1. 5	
3, 000	− 5. 4	+ 0. 6	Red Fork.	3, 000	− 3. 0	+ 1. 0	
700	− 9. 0	....		3, 000	− 5. 0	+ 1. 0	
2, 900	− 5. 0	0. 0		3, 000	− 6. 5	+ 1. 5	
180	− 6. 0	....					

APPENDIX G.

PROCEEDINGS OF THE COMMISSION APPOINTED UNDER THE ACT OF CONGRESS APPROVED IN JUNE, 1874.

FIRST DAY.

NEWPORT, R. I., *July* 20, 1874.

The following named met together at 10 a. m., viz: Maj. G. K. Warren, Maj. H. L. Abbot, and Capt. W. H. H. Benyaurd.

The following dispatch was received from Messrs. Hébert and Sickels, the other commissioners:

Cannot possibly reach Newport before Tuesday. Wait for us.

The following is a copy of the order under which the commission assembled:

General Orders No. 73.] WAR DEPARTMENT, ADJUTANT-GENERAL'S OFFICE,
Washington, July 2, 1874.

By direction of the President, Maj. G. K. Warren, Maj. H. L. Abbot, and Capt. W. H. H. Benyaurd, Corps of Engineers, United States Army, are hereby assigned, and Jackson E. Sickels and Paul O. Hébert appointed, to serve as a board of commissioners under the act approved June, 1874, "to provide for the appointment of a commission of engineers to investigate and report a permanent plan for the reclamation of the alluvial basin of the Mississippi River subject to inundation."

Major Warren is designated as president of the board.

Captain Benyaurd is designated as disbursing-officer for the appropriation provided by section 3 of the act.

The board will assemble at Newport, R. I., on the 20th instant, or as soon thereafter as practicable, for the purpose of organizing and entering upon the performance of their duties.

The following is the act of Congress above referred to:

AN ACT to provide for the appointment of a commission of engineers to investigate and report a permanent plan for the reclamation of the alluvial basin of the Mississippi River subject to inundation.

Be it enacted by the Senate and House of Representatives of the United States of America in Congress assembled, That the President be, and is hereby, authorized and directed to assign three officers of the Corps of Engineers, United States Army, and to appoint two civil engineers, eminent in their profession, and who are acquainted with the alluvial basin of the Mississippi River, to serve as a board of commissioners, the president of said board to be designated by the President of the United States. It shall be the duty of said commission to make a full report to the President of the best system for the permanent reclamation and redemption of said alluvial basin from inundation, which report the President shall transmit to Congress at its next session, with such recommendations as he shall think proper.

SEC. 2. That the members of the commission who may be appointed from civil life shall receive compensation at the rate of five thousand dollars per annum. The commission may employ a secretary, at a rate of compensation not exceeding two hundred dollars per month for the time he is employed; and the necessary traveling-expenses of the members of said commission not officers of the Army, and of the secretary, shall be paid, upon the approval of bills for the same, by the Secretary of War.

SEC. 3. That the sum of twenty-five thousand dollars, or so much thereof as may be necessary to carry into effect the foregoing provisions, is hereby appropriated, and shall be subject to disbursement by the Secretary of War, in accordance with the provisions of this act.

Approved June, 1874.

By order of the Secretary of War:

(OFFICIAL.) THOMAS M. VINCENT,
Assistant Adjutant-General.

The members present occupied their time till 1 p. m. in general consideration of the preliminaries to the subject, and adjourned to meet at 9 a. m. on the 21st instant.

G. K. WARREN,
President of Commission.

SECOND DAY.

TUESDAY, *July* 21.

The commission met at 12 m.; all the members present. Various letters received by different members in regard to positions on the commission as commissioner, secretary, or engineer, &c., were presented and read, and an informal discussion of the cases were made. The following were the persons whose names were presented:

Applicants.	State.	For what.
Thomas Pearsall	Alabama	Commissioner.
J. W. Bissel		Do.
J. J. Williams	Tennessee	Do.
A. D. Banks	Mississippi	Secretary.
C. M. Fauntleroy	Louisiana	Do.
H. A. Peeler	do	Do.
A. F. Wrotnowski	do	Do.
C. G. Forshey	do	Do.
J. A. Porter	Mississippi	Assistant.
——— Meigs	Tennessee	Do.
Chas. Thrupp	Illinois	Do.

Without deciding anything in these respects, the members of the commission proceeded to exchange views generally on the subject committed to them, and continued in session till 4 p. m., when they adjourned to meet the next day at 10 a. m.

G. K. WARREN,
President of Commission.

THIRD DAY.

WEDNESDAY, *July* 22.

The members of the commission met at 10 a. m.

Informal discussion of the subject, considered on the preceding day without acting definitely, was continued, but approached the subject-matter of the work of the commission sufficiently near to outline the course of future proceedings.

Adjourned at 3½ p. m., to meet next day at 10 a. m.

G. K. WARREN,
Major of Engineers, President of Commission.

FOURTH DAY.

THURSDAY, *July* 23.

The commission met at 10 a. m. An approximate estimate was made of the expenses of the commission and the probable cost of securing necessary data, reserving a large sum for contingencies, as follows:

Disposition of fund.

Commission's report and business to conclude in January. Time July, August, September, October, November, December, and January—seven months.

Appropriation	$25,000 00
Pay of two commissioners seven months	5,833 33
Pay of secretary	1,400 00
Expenses of secretary	766 67
Expenses of two commissioners	2,000 00
Commissioner in Mississippi three months, at $500	1,500 00
Commissioner in Louisiana five months, at $500	2,500 00
Commissioner in Arkansas four months, at $500	2,000 00
Flood-question discussion	500 00
Flood data	1,000 00
Office-rent seven months, at $25	175 00
Office-messenger seven months, at $60	420 00
Office-clerk seven months, at $200	1,400 00
Stationery and office-furniture	505 00
Contingencies	5,000 00
	25,000 00

On motion it was

Resolved, Not to proceed at present to the appointment of a secretary.

On motion it was

Resolved, That A. D. Banks, of Mississippi, be appointed clerk to the commission, at a salary of $200 a month. This was done, and he immediately entered upon his duties.

General Abbot offered the following resolutions; which were read separately and adopted:

Resolved, That, although this commission fully recognizes the advantages sometimes to be derived from a judicious use of artificial reservoirs, in moderating the destructive floods of rivers, it considers this method of protection against overflow to be entirely inapplicable to the low lands of the Mississippi.

Resolved, That no reduction in the height of the floods of the Mississippi can be obtained by diverting any of its tributaries from their present channels.

Resolved, That the commission considers that the local benefit above their sites, which results from cut-offs, is more than counterbalanced by the injury sure to result below, in an increased flood-level and caving of the banks; and that, therefore, as a measure of protection against floods, they are pernicious and unjustifiable, and should never be allowed upon the Mississippi.

Whereas long-continued and accurate observation has established the fact that the Mississippi water, far from being charged to its maximum capacity with sedimentary matter, often carries a smaller percentage at high water than in its medium and low stages; and whereas all authentic records of actual soundings made above and below the sites of large crevasses justify the belief that no deposits have ever occurred in the channels below them in consequence of said crevasses:

Resolved, That outlets of limited capacity, merely sufficient to reduce the flood-level a few feet, would be advantageous, provided a free channel to the Gulf could be found for water so abstracted from the river.

Whereas actual measurements have shown that in the flood of 1851 water abstracted from the Mississippi River by crevasses, and subsequently returned through the Tensas bottom-lands and Black and Red Rivers, actually raised the high-water mark for the year at Red River Landing about 2 feet, without any corresponding increase in discharge over that previously noted:

Resolved, That the expedient of withdrawing water from one part of the river, to be subsequently returned below, is sufficiently dangerous to be adopted unwillingly and only as a choice of evils.

Resolved, That heretofore all cultivation of the Mississippi bottom-lands owes its success to the construction of levees, and that this commission has confidence that the system, properly applied, is adequate to the protection of the country against floods. Whether it should be exclusively trusted, or be combined with outlets, is a matter to be decided by economical considerations.

On motion it was

Resolved, That the president of the commission request the Chief of Engineers and the Chief Signal-Officer to forward to General Abbot, Willet's Point, New York Harbor, all data in their offices available for the discussion of the Mississippi flood of 1874, viz: copies of all gauge-records kept between December, 1873, and June, 1874, both inclusive; all precipitation-charts and rain-records kept in the Mississippi Valley during the same period; any notes collected by employés of the Government, or otherwise, respecting the condition of the different principal tributaries during and immediately preceding the flood; any similar notes respecting dates and heights of high-water marks on the Mississippi at points not occupied by regular observers; and, lastly, any authentic information respecting the dates of occurrence and size of crevasses, especially in the upper part of the alluvial region.

Resolved, That a similar application be made to the chief engineer of Louisiana, and to the boards of levee commissioners of the counties of the State of Mississippi, situated along the front of the Yazoo bottom-lands, and to the governor of Arkansas, and to the governor of Missouri.

Resolved, That Commissioner Abbot is hereby requested to study the notes and records respecting the flood of 1874, obtained from the officers named above, and to report to the commission the character of this flood as compared with those which have heretofore occurred on the river in regard to the respective difficulties of restraining the same, and that the sum of fifteen hundred dollars ($1,500) be set apart for the expenses incurred in this investigation and discussion.

On motion, it was—

Resolved, That Commissioner Paul O. Hébert, of this commission, is hereby authorized and requested to obtain and furnish this commission all necessary information in regard to the flood of 1874, within the limits of the State of Louisiana, the height of water at different points, the number and locality of crevasses, the probable quantity of water voided, the number of cubic yards necessary to close these crevasses, and the probable cost thereof, the quantity of cultivated land wholly or partially overflowed, and any statistics in regard to production obtainable from the census or otherwise; also any other information pertinent to the subject.

And that Commissioner Hébert may, at his discretion, visit the State of Louisiana to accomplish the objects of this resolution:

Resolved, That the sum of twenty-five hundred dollars ($2,500) be set apart for the expenses incurred in obtaining this information.

On motion, it was—

Resolved, That Commissioner Jackson E. Sickels, of this commission, is hereby authorized and requested to obtain and furnish this commission all necessary information in regard to the flood of 1874, within the limits of the States of Arkansas and Missouri, the height of water at different points, the number and locality of crevasses, the probable quantity of water voided, the number of cubic yards necessary to close these crevasses, and the probable cost thereof, the quantity of cultivated land wholly or partially overflowed, and any statistics in regard to the production obtainable from the census or otherwise; also any other information pertinent to the subject.

And that Commissioner Sickels may, at his discretion, visit the States of Arkansas and Missouri to accomplish the objects of this resolution.

Resolved, That the sum of two thousand dollars ($2,000) be set apart for the expenses incurred in obtaining this information.

Resolved, That Commissioner Benyaurd, of this commission, is hereby directed to obtain and furnish this commission all necessary information in regard to the flood of 1874 within the limits of the State of Mississippi; the height of water at different points; the number and locality of crevasses; the probable quantity of water voided; the number of cubic yards necessary to close these crevasses, and the probable cost thereof; the quantity of cultivated land wholly or partially overflowed, and any statistics in regard to the production obtainable from the census or otherwise; also any other information pertinent to this subject.

And that Commissioner Benyaurd may, at his discretion, visit the State of Mississippi to accomplish the objects of this resolution.

Resolved, That fifteen hundred dollars ($1,500) be set apart for the expenses incurred in obtaining this information.

Resolved, That the president of the commission be authorized and requested to write to the governors of Missouri, Arkansas, Mississippi, and Louisiana to supply all information available respecting the levees within the limits of their States, and to communicate the same to the commissioners assigned to duty in these States.

On motion, it was—

Resolved, That when this commission adjourns it shall meet again in New York on Tuesday, the 28th instant, at the Army Building.

The commission proceeded to elect a secretary. Ex-Governor Hébert withdrew the name of Maj. A. D. Banks, and C. M. Fauntleroy was unanimously elected secretary.

At 4 p. m. the commission adjourned.

G. K. WARREN,
Major Engineers, &c., President of Commission.

PROCEEDINGS OF THE COMMISSION APPOINTED UNDER THE ACT OF CONGRESS APPROVED IN JUNE, 1874.

TUESDAY, JULY 28.

NEW YORK, *July* 28.

Commission met at Army Building, New York, at 12 m.

On motion, it was—

Resolved, That the reading of the minutes of former proceedings be dispensed with.

Resolved, That Newport, R. I., be the permanent headquarters of the commission.

On motion of Ex-Governor Hébert, it was—

Resolved, That A. D. Banks, esq., be directed to collect and compile in the form of a report, for the uses of this commission, all accurate statistics obtainable of the productions of the alluvial region proposed to be reclaimed from overflow, both before and since 1861, and that at his discretion he may visit, if necessary, the State capitals of Missouri, Arkansas, Mississippi, and Louisiana to get such information as may be necessary to carry out the instructions of this resolution, his traveling expenses not to exceed $150.

Resolved, That it is the intention of the commission in their preliminary conclusions that its members shall obtain, or strive to obtain, all the information within their respective districts, or specialties necessary for a full consideration of the questions submitted to the commission, on or before December 5, 1874.

Resolved, That when the commission adjourns to-day it is to meet at Washington, D. C., on December 5, 1874; provided, however, that a previous meeting may be called by the president at any time or place judged by him to be expedient.

On motion, at 1.15 p. m. the commission adjourned.

G. K. WARREN,
Major Engineers.

FIRST DAY, SECOND SESSION.

MONDAY, *December* 7, 1874.

Proceedings of the commission, Washington, D. C., December 7, 1874.

Commission met at 10 a. m., at the office of the Chief of Engineers, U. S. A. Present, G. K. Warren, Maj. of Engineers, U. S. A., Henry L. Abbot, Maj. of Engineers, U. S. A., Capt. W. H. H. Benyaurd, U. S. Engineers, and Charles M. Fauntleroy, secretary.

A letter was received from P. O. Hébert, stating that, owing to personal illness and other matters, he would be unable to attend the meeting of the board on the 7th. All letters received since the last meeting of the commission were read and placed on the file of the commission.

The report and drawings of Mr. C. G. Forshey, relating to borings at Lake Borgne outlet, were laid before the commission by the president, Major Warren.

Major Abbot laid before the commission a report, embodying the information called for by the resolution of the commission, relating to a comparison of recent floods with that of 1858.

Captain Benyaurd submitted his report and maps upon the condition of the levees, &c., in the State of Mississippi, from the northern line of said State to Vicksburg.

The secretary also submitted his report upon the extent of the lakes and other low areas in the bottom-lands of Red River Valley that might be made available as reservoirs to restrain the floods, and also as to the subject of protection of the overflowed lands of this valley.

The board adjourned at 3 o'clock p. m., to meet at 9 a. m. to-morrow.

G. K. WARREN,
Major Engineers, &c., President of Commission.

SECOND DAY.

TUESDAY, *December* 8, 1874.

The commission met at 9 a. m. All the members of yesterday present.

It having been ascertained that Mr. Commissioner Sickles was in the city, upon the assembling of the commission, a communication was sent to him through his friend, Senator Clayton, who informed the messenger that Mr. Sickles would return to the city in a day or two, and that he would deliver the communication informing Mr. Sickles of the place and meeting of the board.

The board occupied the day in reading and discussing the matter before it, including the reading of the secretary's report.

At 4.15 p. m. the board adjourned to meet at 10 a. m. to-morrow.

G. K. WARREN,
Major Engineers, President of Commission.

THIRD DAY.

WEDNESDAY, *December* 9, 1874.

The commission met at 10 a. m. All the members of yesterday present.

The minutes of yesterday were read and approved. A telegram was received from P. O. Hébert, dated New Orleans, 7th December, stating that he would be on to-morrow.

It being ascertained that Mr. Sickles was in Washington yesterday, after adjournment that day, he was informed by a member of the commission that the board was in session. He stated that he intended to go to New York, on business, by the train that night, and would be back the following day.

During the meeting the report of Captain Benyaurd of the condition of the levees in Mississippi was read, and various matters connected with it and the general subject before the commission were debated.

A recess was taken between 1 and 2 p. m.

A letter was written to Mr. A. D. Banks, addressed Washington, D. C., requesting him to forward his report. The commission adjourned at 3.30 p. m. to meet to-morrow at 9 a. m.

G. K. WARREN,
Major Engineers, &c., President of Commission.

FOURTH DAY.

THURSDAY, *December* 10, 1874.

The commission met at 9 a. m. All the members of yesterday present.

The minutes of yesterday were read and approved.

Major Abbot read a portion of his report, making a comparison of the floods of 1874 with that of 1858.

During the meeting Mr. Sickles reported his presence about 12 m.

The report of C. G. Forshey upon borings, surveys, and estimates for the proposed outlets into Lake Borgne was read.

At 3.15 p. m. the board adjourned to meet at 10 a. m. to-morrow.

G. K. WARREN,
Major Engineers, &c., President of Commission.

FIFTH DAY.

FRIDAY, *December* 11, 1874.

The commission met at 10 a. m. All the members of yesterday present.

The minutes of yesterday were read and approved. A telegram was received from P. O. Hébert, at Greensborough, N. C., dated 10th December, stating his detention there by accident to the engine, and that he would be on by the train to-morrow.

The commission directed the notes of borings at Lake Borgne outlet, made by C. G. Forshey, to be plotted.

At 1 p. m. the board adjourned, to allow individual members to investigate special matters appertaining to the business before the commission, to meet at 10 a. m. to-morrow.

G. K. WARREN,
Major Engineers, &c., President of Commission.

SIXTH DAY.

SATURDAY, *December* 12, 1874.

The commission met at 10 a. m. All the members of yesterday present.

At 10.20, all the members of the commission present, P. O. Hébert having reported his presence. A letter was received from C. G. Forshey, of date New Orleans, December 8, and placed upon the files of the commission.

P. O. Hébert presented to the board several maps of crevasses on the

Lower Mississippi, with verbal explanations of the same to the board; also, several tabular documents in regard to levees and crevasses, past and present.

Mr. Doughty appeared before the commission and exhibited his model for making a continuous water-tight fence or wall of wood for the interior of levees, with explanation as to its use.

At 1.20 the board adjourned to meet on Monday next at 10 a. m.

G. K. WARREN,
Major Engineers, President of Commission.

SEVENTH DAY.

MONDAY, *December* 14, 1874.

The commission met at 10 a. m. All the members of Saturday present, except P. O. Hébert, who reported his presence at 10.40 a. m.

A letter was received from C. G. Forshey, together with six boxes of samples of borings taken from between the Mississippi River and Lake Borgne, twelve miles below New Orleans; the letter was placed upon the files of the commission.

P. O. Hébert presented and read his report on the alluvial basin of the Mississippi River; with this report he presented maps.

At 11 the board took a recess of thirty minutes, and paid a visit of ceremony to the Secretary of War, accompanied by the Chief of Engineers, General Humphreys.

At 12, the board resumed the business of the session. Commissioner Hébert moved the following resolution:

Resolved, That this board do now proceed to adopt a system for the permanent reclamation and protection of the alluvial basin of the Mississippi River, and resume the consideration of the subject as it was left at Newport, July 21.

This resolution was seconded by Mr. Sickles.

Pending the consideration of the motion, Major Abbot asked that the resolutions introduced by him, and which were adopted at the Newport session of the commission, be read; which was accordingly done.

The question was then called for, and, after debate, was adopted.

Major Abbot offered the following resolution, which was seconded:

That in the opinion of this commission, the examination of Red River, made by the Secretary, has failed to discover any fit location for reservoirs, suited to restrain the floods of that river from injuring the alluvial region of Louisiana, below its mouth, and in the opinion of this commission no such localities exist.

Pending the consideration of the foregoing, a member requested time to examine the report before voting upon the resolution.

At 2 p. m. the board adjourned to meet at 11 a. m. to-morrow.

G. K. WARREN,
Major Engineers, &c., President of Commission.

EIGHTH DAY.

TUESDAY, *December* 15, 1874.

The commission met at 11 a. m. All the members present.

The minutes of yesterday were read and approved.

At 11.20 the board took a recess until 1 p. m., and paid a visit of ceremony to the President, accompanied by the Secretary of War.

At 1 p. m. the board resumed the business of the session.

P. O. Hébert moved that the resolution of Major Abbot in regard to the location of reservoirs to restrain the floods of Red River, be adopted.

The resolution, being seconded, was adopted by the board.

Major Abbot moved, and the motion was seconded, that the board do now proceed to the consideration of the question of outlets.

Pending the consideration of the resolution, at 3 p. m. the board adjourned, to meet at 10 a. m. to-morrow.

G. K. WARREN,
Major Engineers, President of Commission.

NINTH DAY.

WEDNESDAY, *December* 16, 1874.

The commission met at 10 a. m. All the members present.

The minutes of yesterday were read and approved.

The board proceeded to the consideration of the question of outlets.

The following resolution was moved by P. O. Hébert, and was seconded:

Resolved, That in the opinion of this commission, all natural outlets below the mouth of the Red River, including the Atchafalaya, should be left open, and while guarding against any enlarging of the outlet from the Mississippi, every means should be employed to facilitate the escape of extravasated water in such manner as will be most advantageous to the lands along the outlet, and that one of these outlets, the Bayou Plaquemine, having been closed, the commission are of the opin- that it should be re-opened, provided thorough examinations, including borings, shall show that the same can be done without danger of its disastrous enlargement; and provided also, that before it be opened, due provision be made for the protection of its banks by an efficient system of levees.

The foregoing resolution, having been considered, was adopted by the board. The board took a recess of half an hour. At 12.30 they resumed the business of the session.

Capt. W. H. Powell, Fourth United States Infantry, placed before the commission, on behalf of the patentee, Mr. A. G. Brawner, his plan for improved levees. The plan was placed on the files of the commission.

P. O. Hébert read extracts of his reports as chief engineer of the State of Louisiana to the legislature, in the years 1846 and 1847, upon the subject of outlets and cut-offs upon the Mississippi.

Major Abbot read extracts from Humphreys' and Abbot's work on the Physics of the Mississippi River, discussing the question of an outlet at Lake Providence.

Major Abbot moved the following, which was seconded:

Resolved, That the only sites for artificial outlets which are open to consideration are those of Bonnet Carre and Lake Borgne, and that there are so many objections to them that the subject should be postponed until the commission has further considered the difficulties of the levee system.

At 3 p. m. the board adjourned to meet at 10 a. m. to-morrow.

G. K. WARREN,
Major Engineers and President of Commission.

TENTH DAY.

THURSDAY, *December* 17, 1874.

The commission met at 10 a. m. All the members present, except Mr. Sickles, who was excused from the day's session to prepare his report.

The proceedings of yesterday were read and approved.

On motion of P. O. Hébert it was—

Resolved, That the president of the commission be requested to obtain the report of the borings at a proposed site of the Fort Saint Philip Canal.

The motion was seconded and adopted.

Captain Benyaurd moved, and the motion was seconded and adopted, that the board adjourn now, 12 m., to await the report of Mr. Sickles; to meet again to-morrow at 11 a. m.

G. K. WARREN,
Major Engineers, President of Commission.

ELEVENTH DAY.

FRIDAY, *December* 18, 1874.

The commission met at 11 a. m. All the members of the commission present.

The minutes of yesterday were read and approved.

In reply to the motion of P. O. Hébert, in yesterday's proceedings, the president stated that upon inquiry he had ascertained that the report of the borings at a proposed site of the Fort Saint Philip canal was at present in the hands of the commission at New Orleans, and would be shortly attainable by the return of that body to Washington.

Mr. Sickles presented and read his report, so far as giving the results of his examinations and surveys, from Commerce, Mo., to the Arkansas River.

Mr. A. D. Banks presented and read his report and statistics of the productions of the alluvial region proposed to be reclaimed by overflow.

Judge E. Jeffords and Mr. W. A. Haycraft, members of the board of levee commissioners, of the second district of Mississippi, appeared before the commission, on behalf of their board, with a tender of service.

At 2 p. m. the board adjourned to meet to-morrow at 11 a. m.

G. K. WARREN,
Major Engineers, President of Commission.

TWELFTH DAY.

SATURDAY, *December* 19, 1874.

The commission met at 11 a. m. All the members present except Mr. Sickles. A message was received from him stating that he would be present at 1 p. m.

The minutes of yesterday were read and approved.

At 1 p. m. Mr. Sickles presented his report, showing the condition of the levees in Missouri and Arkansas as they are, accompanied with tabular statements; also, an estimate showing the number of cubic yards necessary to close the crevasses, and make a continuous levee.

At 3 p. m. the board adjourned to meet on Monday next at 11 a. m.

G. K. WARREN,
Major Engineers, &c., President of Commission.

THIRTEENTH DAY.

MONDAY, *December* 21, 1874.

The commission met at 11 a. m. All the members present.

The minutes of Saturday were read and approved.

Mr. Sickels submitted additional data in connection with his report.

Major Abbot moved the following:

Resolved, That the president of the commission be authorized to provide for the engraving of the plate of gauge-curves, illustrating the recent floods of the Mississippi.

The motion being seconded, was adopted.

At 2.30 p. m., on motion, it was resolved that in order to allow the several members time and opportunity to prepare themselves for the discussion of particular points, that the board do now adjourn. The motion being seconded,

The board adjourned until Wednesday next, at 11 a. m.

G. K. WARREN,
Major Engineers, President of Commission.

FOURTEENTH DAY.

WEDNESDAY, *December* 23, 1874.

The commission met at 11 a. m. All the members present.

The minutes of Monday were read and approved.

P. O. Hébert presented a tabular statement of levees caved into the Mississippi River, from caving banks alone, in Louisiana, from October, 1866, to October, 1874, compiled from office-notes of board of State engineers of Louisiana.

The president of the commission offered the following:

Resolved, That inasmuch as all the special reports and investigations heretofore instituted by this commission are now received, and inasmuch as most of the general features of the subject have been discussed between the members of the commission in meetings when all were present:—

Resolved, That we adjourn to allow the members to mature their final conclusions on the subject, to meet again on Monday, January 4, 1875, at 11 a. m.

Resolved, also, That the Army engineer officers of the commission be hereby authorized to return in the interim to their stations, to transact necessary official business requiring their attention.

The motion being seconded, at 1.30 p. m. the board adjourned, to meet again on Monday, January 4, 1875, at 11 a. m.

G. K. WARREN,
Major Engineers, President of Commission.

FIFTEENTH DAY.

MONDAY, *January* 4, 1875.

The commission met at 11 a. m. All the members present except Captain Benyaurd and Mr. J. E. Sickels.

The minutes of Wednesday, December 23, 1874, were read and approved.

A communication was received from Mr. Sickels, reporting his absence as occasioned by malarial fever. At 1 p. m. Captain Benyaurd reported his presence.

Major Abbot presented a draught of a general report, which was read and considered.

Pending the consideration of the above, at 3 p. m. the board adjourned, to meet to-morrow at 12 m.

G. K. WARREN,
Major Engineers, President of Commission.

SIXTEENTH DAY.

TUESDAY, *January* 5, 1875.

The commission met at 12 m. All the members present except P. O. Hébert and Jackson E. Sickels.

The minutes of yesterday were read and approved.

The board proceeded with the consideration of the draught of a general report submitted by Major Abbot on yesterday.

At 2 p. m. Mr. Sickels reported his presence, and submitted a map showing levels and breaks from Louisiana line to Auburn, Arkansas River; also, extent of overflowed region.

At 3 p. m. the board adjourned, to meet to-morrow at 11 a. m.

G. K. WARREN,
Major Engineers, President of Commission.

SEVENTEENTH DAY.

WEDNESDAY, *January* 6, 1875.

The commission met at 11 a. m. All the members present.

The minutes of yesterday were read and approved.

The commission proceeded with the consideration of the draught for a general report.

Pending this consideration, at 3 p. m. the board adjourned, to meet to-morrow at 11 a. m.

G. K. WARREN,
Major Engineers, President of Commission.

EIGHTEENTH DAY.

THURSDAY, *January* 7, 1875.

The commission met at 11 a. m. All the members present except J. E. Sickels and P. O. Hébert.

The commission proceeded with the consideration of the draught for a general report.

At 1 p. m. Commissioner Sickels reported his presence. P. O. Hébert absent by reason of sickness.

Pending the consideration of the draught, at 3 p. m. the board adjourned, to meet to-morrow at 11 a. m.

G. K. WARREN,
Major Engineers, President of Commission.

NINETEENTH DAY.

FRIDAY, *January* 8, 1875.

The commission met at 11 a. m. All the members present.

The minutes of yesterday were read and approved.

The commission proceeded to consider the form and matter of a general report.

Pending the consideration of the above, at 3 p. m. the board adjourned, to meet to-morrow at 11 a. m.

G. K. WARREN,
Major Engineers, President of Commission.

TWENTIETH DAY.

SATURDAY, *January* 9, 1875.

The commission met at 11 a. m. All the members present except Commissioner P. O. Hébert.

The minutes of yesterday were read and approved.

The commission proceeded to consider the form and substance of a general report.

At 2 p. m., P. O. Hébert reported his presence.

Pending the consideration of the general report, at 3 p. m. the board adjourned, to meet Monday at 11 a. m.

G. K. WARREN,
Major Engineers, President of Commission.

TWENTY-FIRST DAY.

MONDAY, *January* 11, 1875.

The commission met at 11 a. m. All the members present except Commissioners Hébert and Sickels.

The commission proceeded to the consideration of the estimates to accompany the general report.

At 1 p. m. all the members of the commission present.

At 4 p. m., pending the consideration of the estimates, the board adjourned to meet to-morrow at 11 a. m.

G. K. WARREN,
Major Engineers and President of Commission.

TWENTY-SECOND DAY.

TUESDAY, *January* 12, 1875.

The commission met at 11 a. m. All the members present.

The minutes of yesterday were read and approved.

D. F. Kenner, vice-president of the Louisiana Levee Company, was introduced to the commission and expressed his views in regard to the levees in Louisiana.

The commission proceeded to consider the question of estimates. At 1.30 p. m. the board adjourned—to allow the details of the estimates to be worked out—to meet to-morrow at 11 a. m.

G. K. WARREN,
Major Engineers, President of Commission.

TWENTY-THIRD DAY.

WEDNESDAY, *January* 13, 1875.

The commission met at 11 a. m. All the members present except Commissioners Sickels and Hébert.

The minutes of yesterdey were read and approved.

The commission proceeded with the question of estimates, pending which at 4.15 p. m. the board adjourned to meet to-morrow at 11 a. m.

G. K. WARREN,
Major Engineers, President of Commission.

TWENTY-FOURTH DAY.

THURSDAY, *January* 14, 1875.

The commission met at 11 a. m. All the members present except Commissioner Hébert, absent by reason of indisposition.

The minutes of yesterday were read and approved.

The commission proceeded to complete the estimates and revise the report; pending which, at 5 p. m., the commission adjourned to meet to-morrow at 11 a. m.

G. K. WARREN,
Major Engineers, President of Commission.

TWENTY-FIFTH DAY.

FRIDAY, *January* 15, 1875.

The commission met at 11 a. m. All the members present except Commissioner Hébert.

The minutes of yesterday were read and approved.

The following motion was seconded and adopted:

Resolved, That the president of the commission be authorized to transmit the specimens obtained from the borings made under direction of the commission, at the site of the proposed outlet to Lake Borgne, to Prof. E. W. Hilgard, at Ann Arbor, Mich., for investigation and report; and that an amount, not exceeding $400, be set apart from the appropriation for the expenses of the commission, to pay for the work.

Resolved, also, That Professor Hilgard's report, when completed, be sent to the Chief of Engineers, United States Army, and the final disposition of the specimens be left with that officer.

At 12 m., Commissioner Hébert reported his presence.

In order to allow emendations to be made in the general report, at 2.20 p. m. the board adjourned to meet to-morrow at 11 a. m.

G. K. WARREN,
Major Engineers, President of Commission.

TWENTY-SIXTH DAY.

SATURDAY, *January* 16, 1875.

The commission met at 11 a. m. All the members present.

The minutes of yesterday were read and approved.

The general report having been read, was unanimously adopted, and at 4.30 p. m. the board adjourned to meet on Monday next at 11 a. m.

G. K. WARREN,
Major Engineers, President of Commission.

TWENTY-SEVENTH DAY.

MONDAY, *January* 18, 1875.

The commission met at 11 a. m. All the members present.

The minutes of yesterday were read and approved.

The commission received and read the completed report of Commissioner Sickels.

On motion, it was resolved that the president of this commission be directed to transmit through the proper official channel the report of this commission to the President of the United States.

On motion, it was resolved that the thanks of this commission be tendered to General Gouverneur Kemble Warren for his uniform courtesy, as presiding officer, to the individual members of this commission during its deliberations.

Resolved, That the thanks of this commission be tendered to Col.

Charles M. Fauntleroy for the efficient manner in which he has performed his duties as secretary of the commission.

On motion, it was resolved that this commission do now adjourn *sine die.*

G. K. WARREN,
Major of Engineers and President of Commission.
CHS. M. FAUNTLEROY,
Secretary to Commission.

DIAGRAMS AND CHARTS.

A.—DIAGRAM SHOWING COMPARATIVE HEIGHTS OF RECENT FLOODS IN THE MISSISSIPPI RIVER.

B, C, D, E.—PRECIPITATION CHARTS OF SIGNAL-SERVICE, UNITED STATES ARMY FOR FEBRUARY, MARCH, APRIL, AND MAY, 1874.

○

www.ingramcontent.com/pod-product-compliance
Lightning Source LLC
LaVergne TN
LVHW021403110826
845150LV00007B/1771